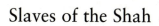

Slaves of the Shah

SLAVES OF THE SHAH

New Elites of Safavid Iran

Sussan Babaie
Kathryn Babayan
Ina Baghdiantz-McCabe
Massumeh Farhad

I.B. TAURIS

LONDON · NEW YORK

Published in 2004 by I.B.Tauris & Co Ltd
6 Salem Road, London W2 4BU
175 Fifth Avenue, New York NY 10010
www.ibtauris.com

In the United States and Canada distributed by Palgrave Macmillan,
a division of St. Martin's Press, 175 Fifth Avenue, New York NY 10010

ISBN 1 86064 721 9
EAN 978 1 86064 721 5

A full CIP record for this book is available from the British Library
A full CIP record for this book is available from the Library of Congress
Library of Congress catalog card: available

Typeset in Sabon by Dexter Haven Associates Ltd, London
Printed and bound in Great Britain by TJ International Ltd, Padstow, Cornwall

Contents

Illustrations

Acknowledgements

The publication of this book was generously funded by the Soudavar Foundation in Geneva, and by the Office of the Vice President for Research and the Department of the History of Art, the University of Michigan, Ann Arbor. We are most grateful for their support and encouragement.

From the outset, Robert McChesney enthusiastically backed this joint enterprise. His initial comments after the first presentation of the ideas for this book at the Second Biennial Conference of the Society for Iranian Studies in 1998 confirmed the importance of our inter-disciplinary approach to the subject of slave studies. We are also most grateful to him for reading the final draft. Iradj Bagherzade, the Publisher and Managing Editor of I.B. Tauris, shared our excitement for the project at that very conference, offering us without hesitation a publication contract. Though he recognized that joint authorship could jeopardize projects and friendships, he never wavered in his trust in the 'sisters' and their determination to see this book to com-pletion. His good humour and patience made the process of publishing with I.B. Tauris a pleasurable experience. We owe the anonymous readers much gratitude for their insightful critiques that have clarified and strengthened our arguments. We gratefully acknowledge Tom Lentz and Gülru Necipoğlu for reading and commenting on a draft of the manuscript and Abolala Soudavar for his encouragement and support. We thank Mr Ali Reza Anisi, the former Director of the Gulistan Palace Library in Tehran, for facilitating access to that estimable collection. Without Margaret Lourie's meticulous editorial touch, our text would have been a bumpier read. Several Tufts students helped judge the readability of parts of the manuscript, and we are grateful for their efforts. We would also like to thank Helen Snively and Mary Ann Kazanjian for their editorial comments, Vika Gardner and Aline Bataseh for their help with the bibliography, and

Robert Haug for assisting us with the maps. Finally, Carol Huh deserves a special thanks for assembling the final draft of the manuscript and for securing permissions for the publication of the images. Thanks to Janet Yarker for creating the index.

To our families, we owe more than words can adequately express.

Note on Transliteration and Usage

We have followed the transliteration system of the *International Journal of Middle Eastern Studies* (IJMES), with a few modifications. For the purpose of a general readership we have omitted diacritical marks and have adopted common usage of terms for major provinces, cities etc. Terms such as *Shahnama* are spelled without the final 'h'. All dates are given in the common era.

1

Slaves of the Shah

*The epitome of the world is Iran, the epitome of
Iran is Isfahan, and the epitome of Isfahan is the
qaysariyya (royal bazaar), and there I am.*

Mulah Salih Qazvini (d. 1705)[1]

Our collaboration dates back to the symposium 'The Marketplace of
Identities: Cross-Cultural Themes in Seventeenth-century Isfahan',
held at the Getty Center for the History of Art and the Humanities in
January 1996. There we discovered our shared interest in the visual
and literary expressions of Safavid culture (1501–1722). Each of us
had taken a separate disciplinary path to arrive at similar readings of
the post-Shah Abbas I era (1629–66). Contrary to common assumption
among Safavid historians, we considered it not a period of decline
but one of vitality and innovation. The foundation for this book was
finally laid in 1998, when we organized a joint panel on the Safavid
slave household at the Second Biennial Conference of the Society for
Iranian Studies.[2] Beyond the prospect of presenting Safavid historiography with the first in-depth study of the slave system, this publication
has given us a unique opportunity of learning and sharing and a
sense of the exciting leaps scholars can take when collaborating on
a project.

The institution of the *ghulam-i khassa-yi sharifa* (royal household
slave) – the subject of this book – is the thread that ties our research

together. It is one of the systems of rule the Safavids capitalized on in the early seventeenth century to consolidate authority. Slaves from the Caucasus dominated Safavid politics in this era, yet the subject still remains to be studied thoroughly. Emanating from new readings of art, architecture, economy, religion and politics, this book initiates an inquiry into different dimensions of Safavid slave society. Although not a comprehensive study, together our research forms a mosaic that conjures a picture richer than any of us had individually imagined. Because of our multicentric approach to Safavid slave society we decided to write a joint introduction to explain our conception of the book. Individually each chapter explores a particular aspect of the institution of slavery, but collectively the book underlines the social networks of slaves and their engagement in the political and cultural life of Safavid Iran.

It is indeed possible to write a history of the organization of slavery in the seventeenth century, but instead we have highlighted cases that typify the agency of the slaves of the royal household and encapsulate the potentialities and vulnerabilities of their status. Furthermore, we deliberately focus on the first half of the seventeenth century as a way to gauge the impact of the centralizing policies of Abbas I (1587–1629). The reigns of the two subsequent monarchs Shah Safi I (1629–42) and Shah Abbas II (1642–66) offer an abundance of primary Persian sources in contrast to the dearth of chronicles for the closing decades of the Safavids. While European travelogues testify to the continued prominence of slaves in politics until the fall of the Safavid dynasty, these representations need to be explored alongside Persian religious, epistolary and literary sources. We hope that our book will provide a threshold for such future Safavid studies.

In modern Western history, the term 'slavery' is usually associated with images of plantation slaves and as such the term itself fits poorly into the Islamicate understanding and practice of slavery. Although agricultural slavery did exist in the Islamic world, the most common form of slavery was domestic and military. Western slavery is tied to constructions of race and ethnicity that in theory exclude the possibility of manumission and empowerment. In the Islamic world, slavery is a process that begins with enslavement of non-Muslims, converts them and recommends their subsequent manumission. It is religion rather than ethnic affiliation that justifies enslavement in Muslim legal discourse. The potential for becoming a free Muslim differentiates the Islamic system of slavery from the Judeo-Christian model. While the particularities of Islamic slavery may lead to romantic readings, the fact remains that former slaves attained positions of power, such as generals, governors, viziers and sultans (*mamluks*).

The Islamic practice of slavery is modelled on the example of the Prophet Muhammad, who broke with the ancient tradition by freeing his household slave, Zayd, adopting him as a Muslim son and marrying him off to his cousin. As with many other customs, the believer emulates Muhammad in the path of piety and submission. Religiously sanctioned, slavery in Islam is believed to reward the pious with a place in heaven. Just as the master attains salvation, the slave's conversion transforms his identity from the abject other to that of a member of the Muslim community (*umma*) with all of its attendant social stratifications. Slaves are thus incorporated as concubines and adopted sons into the household. Sheltered, fed and educated, they enter a relationship that presumes unconditional loyalty and service to their master. Although Muhammad urged kindness toward the enslaved, they remained at the mercy of their master, who possessed them both physically and legally. Notwithstanding the abuse they frequently suffered, slaves did develop intimate ties with the master's family as one of its members – bonds that endured beyond their legal ownership.

In general, only the elite owned slaves, whether as adopted sons (pages), eunuchs or concubines. All slaves were uprooted, but eunuchs were desexualized as well. Their castration gave them access to the most private sphere of the household, the harem, where they were entrusted with the special task of protecting and serving the women and educating the children. Trained in a variety of arts and sciences, from reading and writing to horsemanship and the crafts, eunuchs were also assimilated into cultural and social codes that governed their private and public lives. In turn, eunuchs transmitted their knowledge and skills to a new generation of the household, both biological offspring of their master and adopted slave-sons. As mentors, they forged strong bonds with their wards, and these relationships, nurtured through trust, loyalty and mutual dependence, endured over time and space. Loyalty, however, was not unconditional, nor did it guarantee protection from the shifting power dynamics of the household.

Eunuchs also enjoyed proximity to women of the household, in particular to concubine-mothers. Once the concubine gave birth to a son and became the mother of a free and legitimate male heir, her status within the household changed. Like the eunuch, the concubine-mother (*umm walad*) entered the homosocial world of domestic politics. Eunuchs, adopted sons and concubines now functioned as channels through which the patriarch directed power to his advantage. This triumvirate could neutralize potential challenges from sons to patriarchal authority. They could also serve the interests of other elements of the household, creating competing configurations of power around sons of the master living in the harem. Moreover, eunuchs, concubines and military slaves created networks of alliances that extended beyond the household into the realms of the court, the marketplace and the battlefield.

In the Islamic world, the outlines of the institution of domestic slavery are manifest on a grander and more complex scale in the context of a royal household. In this larger domain, military slaves were introduced to protect, expand and administer the realm. Once educated at court, the most talented and loyal among them were privileged as adopted sons and sent out to the barracks or the provinces as representatives of the royal household. They served in key positions as viziers, governors and generals and helped to uphold dynastic sovereignty by countering internal opposition from tribes or prominent local notables.

Historically, military slavery allowed Muslim rulers to contain the decentralizing tendencies of tribal forces. With the spread of Islam's visionary ideals through conquest, Arab tribes came to settle in and around urban centres between the lands of the Nile and the Oxus. Already during the reign of the first Islamic dynasty, the Umayyads (661–750), Arab tribal solidarities along with messianic uprisings threatened the hegemony of the empire. Out of this faltering system an empire arose in Baghdad that was backed by a new configuration of forces composed of Persians and Arab tribes loyal to the Abbasids (750–1258), a family whose legitimacy hinged on their descent from the Prophet's uncle, Abbas. The realignment of tribal connections and local interests once again exposed the vulnerability of the Abbasids, prompting them to turn to Turkic forces residing outside the abode of Islam (*dar al-Islam*) on its eastern periphery. Once uprooted from their tribal groupings, these Turkic warriors were considered well-suited for military slavery. As local antagonism toward the new military elite was endemic, the Abbasids moved away from Baghdad and created a new centre of authority in nearby Samarra. The open spaces on the banks of the Tigris allowed the Abbasids to build an altered socio-military structure.

Although short-lived, Samarra was a palace conceived on the scale of a city by and for the Abbasid household and their military slaves.[3] There eunuchs played a pivotal role, training a newly converted military elite, who would protect the Abbasid boundaries, now expanding from North Africa to Central Asia. The structural ties that bound slaves to their tutors, the eunuchs, served as the backbone of imperial sovereignty. This new socio-military slave system was meant to function in unison with the caliph, yet it formed its separate alliances threatening the hegemony of the Abbasids. The influx of already-converted Turkic tribes continued to undermine Abbasid sovereignty as regional dynasties in the eastern provinces, such as the Samanids (819–997), the Buyids (932–1062), the Ghaznavids (997–1186) and the Saljuqs (1038–1194) established themselves also by drawing on military slavery. The fabric of Abbasid control began to unravel with such challenges from the East and the establishment of rival caliphates like the Fatimids (909–1171) on the western frontiers. Intermittent incursions of Turkic tribes into sedentarized eastern domains culminated in the Mongol invasions and the conquest of Baghdad in 1258.

The murder of the caliph marked the end of Abbasid rule and opened the Islamic world to new formations of Turco-Mongol supremacy. Ironically, it was the Mamluks of Egypt, a military slave sultanate (1250–1517), who halted the western expansion of the Mongols. This clash was symbolic of a recurring tension between slave armies and tribal forces that shaped the dynamics of regional politics in the following centuries. It has been argued by the eminent Mamluk scholar David Ayalon that were it not for military slavery, the western Islamic frontiers would have collapsed under foreign incursions, whether the Mongols or the Crusaders.[4] The Turks and Mongols did settle in the East, in Asia Minor and the Iranian plateau, where a symbiosis of nomadic steppe and Irano-Muslim traditions gave birth to a variety of legitimizing discourses articulated by the Ilkhanids, Timurids, Ottomans, Safavids, Uzbeks and Mughals. Each derived their universalist legitimacy from either the Chingiz Khanids or the Oghuz Turks, as well as Irano-Islamic ideals of kingship and statecraft. And each chose a particular military strategy of rule.

Islamic historiography has focused mainly on the subject of slavery in the Abbasid, Mamluk and Ottoman realms.[5] Whereas all post-Mongol polities were brought to power by tribal armies, only the Ottomans and the Safavids appropriated military and domestic slavery as an imperial institution. The Safavid case fills a major gap in the historiography of slave studies and further underlines the distinctive nature of this Muslim institution. It also provides a basis for future comparative studies.[6]

The founder of the Safavid dynasty, Shah Ismail (r. 1501–24) was a mystic who claimed to be the Messiah and aimed to establish a divine Shi'i kingdom on earth championed by an army of Turkman devotees. These disciples, referred to as Red Heads (Qizilbash), became the governors and generals who administered and protected the Safavid realms. Following the death of the mystic-king Ismail in 1524, Iran was plagued by two civil wars (1524–36 and 1576–90) between rival tribal factions that nearly eclipsed Safavid rule. Already during the reign of Ismail's son, Shah Tahmasb (r. 1524–76), a slave military solution was introduced as Christian Georgian slaves captured in battle were forcibly brought to the court in Qazvin. It was Shah Abbas I (r. 1587–1629) who fully institutionalized military and domestic slavery and broke with the Safavid tribal and messianic past. Here began the slave chapter of Safavid history – newly converted slaves were appointed to occupy key military and administrative posts, supplanting the Qizilbash elite.

The introduction of the slave system created a new basis of rule that allowed Shah Abbas I to defuse the threat of tribal solidarities by adopting a master–slave paradigm. The designation *ghulam* (slave) in Safavid political discourse signifies loyalty to the patriarch, be it

the master of the household, the governor or the Shah. The master–
slave schema in the Safavid context manifests itself in three dominant
forms – tribal, *shahsevan* (lovers of the Shah) and converted slaves.
The Safavid rise to and precarious hold on power depended on their
relationship with Turkman tribal chiefs (khans), originally from
Anatolia and Syria. These new tribes were reconfigured around a
mystical devotion to the Safavid shahs. As representatives of individual tribes, the khans were rewarded with positions of power in
return for military support and loyalty. Power bestowed could mean
power seized; indeed, the khans created their own alliances, challenging the authority of the shahs.

The new master–slave paradigm, already opted for by Shah
Tahmasb and consolidated by Abbas I, served as a counter-measure
to the tribal mode of rule. To create fissures in the tribal structure,
Abbas I patronized individual tribal members, such as Ganj Ali Khan,
demanding in return their unconditional loyalty and love to the
person of the Shah, hence the term '*shahsevan*' or lovers of the Shah.[7]
This development introduced a new conception of authority where
devotion was no longer based on either spiritual belief or the interest
of tribal collectives, but on individual relationships and gains.[8]

The slave system completed this break away from the past and
proved to be the most effective means to preserve the vitality of the
Safavid household with the Shah at its apex. Uprooted from their
indigenous socio-political networks, the slaves were transplanted into
a reconfigured imperial court. Once enslaved, the Shah invested them,
through conversion, with a new Muslim identity predicated upon
Shi'i loyalty to the 'Shadow of God on Earth', the Safavid Shah. The
shift from master–disciple to master–slave system of rule entailed
similar expectations of loyalty and devotion. The slaves' social and
religious transformation, however, rendered them structurally more
linked to and dependent on the household. Safavid historiography
tends to limit *ghulam*hood to converted Christians. Yet, Safavid
practice and discourse suggests greater elasticity in the functional
definition of loyalty and devotion to the royal household. This broader
conception of *ghulam*hood encompassed not only the converted
Christian slaves or the lovers of the Shah, the *shahsevan*, but also
allowed a castrated commoner such as Saru Taqi to enter the arena

of politics. That no civil wars threatened the Safavid throne in the seventeenth century is testimony to the less precarious nature of the master–slave model.

Shah Abbas I's decision to move the capital from Qazvin to Isfahan encapsulates the antagonism wrought by a new socio-military system, one that could not survive within a Qizilbash-dominated order. Conceived at a similar historic juncture as Samarra, Abbas I's Isfahan served as a new physical and cultural environment from which the ruler and his slave household extended their power throughout the empire.

The creation of Isfahan as a capital city coincides with a major shift in Safavid administrative practice. Whereas in the past Safavid princes had been entrusted to Qizilbash provincial governors, now they were kept at court in Isfahan under the close supervision of eunuchs, who had replaced Qizilbash tutors as loyal servants of the household. This development eclipsed the independent power of Qizilbash governors, which had allowed them to manipulate princes and use them as pawns against the ruling king. The physical presence of princes at court also strengthened their ties to their mothers and in turn enhanced the sphere of female influence. Together with the eunuchs, who had access to both the domestic sphere of the harem and the public world, this triumvirate centred itself in the orbit of Safavid politics by relying on princes as the catalyst for actualizing their political and economic interests. When concubines replaced princesses as mothers of future heirs after the death of Abbas I, the power of eunuchs, slave-mothers and military slaves penetrated from the harem to the palace in Isfahan and beyond into the provinces.

Part of Shah Abbas I's vision for centring the capital in Isfahan entailed the consolidation of the clergy and the introduction of the Armenian merchant community as two auxiliary pillars in addition to that of the slaves. A Shi'i clerical establishment (*ulama*) had been patronized by the first Safavid shahs (Ismail and Tahmasb) as representatives of the new religion of the Iranian realms in which Sunnism had been hegemonic. These Shi'i clerics interpreted Divine Law (*shari'a*), providing religio-legal legitimacy for the political aspirations and the centralizing tendencies of the Safavid Empire. The third pillar was represented by a community of Armenian merchants who were deported from Julfa on the Aras River by Abbas I in 1604 and settled in New Julfa of Isfahan. The brutality of the resettlement notwithstanding, the protected status of the Armenians in Isfahan signified direct integration into the royal household, and their mercantile skills were effectively used to facilitate the exchange of Persian silk for foreign silver. As members of the royal household, the *ghulams* and the Armenians were partners in the production, sale and export of silk. This collaboration ensured the flow of silver back into the royal treasury to pay the salaries of court functionaries and finance imperial building projects.

The transformation of the household was accompanied by the conversion of state lands (*mamalik*) into crown lands (*khassa*) (Fig. 1). As was the practice in the first century of Safavid rule, Qizilbash governors of state lands wielded considerable control over the financial and military administration of their province. Unlike the *ghulams*, the Qizilbash did not depend on the royal treasury for their salaries. Rather, they were awarded land grants (*tiyul*), the source of their independence. Their principal contribution, in turn, consisted of providing the shahs with troops and provisions during campaigns. When Shah Abbas I replaced Qizilbash governors with slaves, he facilitated the conversion of such state lands into his personal dominion. The Shah's vision of a centralized empire could only be realized, however, once he was able to quell the Qizilbash uprisings and put an end to the second civil war in 1590. Consolidating the western (Ottoman) and eastern (Uzbek) frontiers, Abbas I began to incorporate revenue from the provinces directly into the private treasury of his court, a process that fully matured under the reigns of his successors, Safi I (1629–42) and Abbas II (1642–66). Now, the royal treasury, enriched by new revenues generated from crown lands as well as silk exports, could finance the salaries of military and domestic slaves of the household, support the construction of a new capital city and sustain the process of centralization.

The year 1590 marks a turning point in Safavid history. It not only coincided with the end of the second civil war and the decision to keep princes at court (cage system), but it also inaugurated a new millennium of Islamic history. One thousand years had elapsed since the Hijra – the advent of Islam. Muslim apocalyptic discourse envisioned the arrival of a Messiah who would establish a divine kingdom on earth in the year 1000 (1590–91). Abbas I would have to contend with one such millennial expectation. From amongst the mystical order of the Nuqtavis arose a dervish who claimed to be this Messiah. His charisma had attracted a wide following, ranging from Qizilbash courtiers to denizens of Safavid Iran, thereby threatening the sovereignty of Abbas I. The monarch eventually eliminated the Nuqtavi challenge, appropriating the symbols embedded in such apocalyptic expectations to represent himself as the legitimate ruler who would assume this new universal mandate.

The conception of Isfahan in 1590–91 represents Abbas I's vision of a divine kingdom on earth (Fig. 2). The new Isfahan was built outside the boundaries of the medieval city, but unlike Samarra it was intentionally connected to the old city. The expanded commercial network of the bazaar served as an artery linking the old urban centre to a vast public square (Maydan-i Naqsh-i Jahan), the site of a new focal point around which the economic, political and religious facets of Safavid reform gravitated. Architecturally, the square and its surrounding structures represented the main pillars of Safavid centralization. The royal bazaar, epitomizing the financial spine of the empire, was complemented on the opposite side of the square by the congregational mosque – the royal icon of Shi'i identity. On the perpendicular axis of the square, the palace and residence of the reconfigured household faced a private mosque that encapsulated the personal piety on which Abbas I based his divine vision.

In 1601, Abbas I embarked on another symbolic act, a pilgrimage on foot from Isfahan to Mashhad, as a public performance of pious devotion to Imam Riza, the son of the eponymous Imam Musa Kazim of the Safavid House. He rendered this act of piety with reverence for Imam Riza as part of a vow (*nazr*) he had made asserting his public commitment to the Shi'i faith.[9] The Shah's subsequent gift of the entire *maydan* as a benefaction to the 'Fourteen Immaculate Ones' (Muhammad, his daughter Fatima, and the 12 Shi'i imams), may have been linked to this very vow he had promised to fulfil in the name of the Family of the Prophet.[10]

After Shah Abbas I, the Safavid sedentarized court lived in and governed from the capital city. To accommodate this arrangement, the palace precinct, flanked by the square and a public promenade, became the centre of power. The ceremonial and residential spaces of the palace, segregated into public (*birun*) and private (*andarun*) spheres, complemented each other in the political dynamics of the household and the implementation of adopted policies. Concubines, royal children, pages and eunuchs – the reconfigured household – lived in the sanctity of the harem. Representing different branches of government, courtiers convened in the public arenas of the palace, from where they executed imperial decrees issued from the harem. Daily audiences and frequent banquets in the outer court provided the setting for the ceremonial enactment of politics. For the feeding, clothing and furnishing of the enormous household and its entourage, the palace required many different workshops that were responsible for activities ranging from cooking to tailoring to candle-making. The court also played a central role in cultural production by supporting palace workshops specializing in luxury items such as jewellery, precious objects, textiles and manuscripts. Additionally, its patronage extended beyond the court, where carpets and a variety of other portable objects were produced. The style and taste of the Safavid household played a central role in shaping a distinct visual language that permeated both the capital and the provinces.

As slaves began to consolidate their power, they seized the post of superintendent of the royal workshops (*nazir-i buyutat*) during the reigns of Safi I and Abbas II. *Ghulams* procured materials for the workshops and managed the production and distribution of luxury goods. The *nazir* (superintendent) finalized each workshop's budget and submitted it to the grand vizier for approval. Only then would the treasury provide the cash and goods to the workshops for court consumption. The real power of the *nazir* rested in his control over the expenditure of the entire royal household (*khassa*). At the height of *ghulam* hegemony, the post of grand vizier was held by the eunuch Saru Taqi (1634–45) and all key positions in the military and financial structure were occupied by slaves.

The places of leisure of the palace precinct lay alongside the public promenade of the Chahar Bagh (Four Gardens). Here an entire out-door culture of pleasure featured a tree-lined promenade that included water-channels, ornamental pools and a series of gateway structures available for public use. The promenade stretched beyond the Zayanda River over a bridge constructed by Allah Virdi Khan, the first *ghulam* to become governor and commander-in-chief of the army of Abbas I. Court functionaries were rewarded with the grant of large plots of land along the Chahar Bagh, in which they were mandated to build mansions in garden settings modelled after the palace (Fig. 5). These mansions lined the sides of the promenade south of the river all the way to Shah Abbas I's suburban palace of Hizar Jarib.

In addition to the residential quarters for the slave courtiers, an important component of the new Isfahan entailed the planned settlement of the Armenians and the merchant community deported from Tabriz. Under the supervision of the slave household, new residential quarters for Armenian and Tabrizi merchants were constructed on the western side of the Chahar Bagh. Interestingly, the Shi'i religious establishment resided primarily in the vicinity of the new square and seems to have been excluded from Shah Abbas I's planned suburbs.

Although the Armenian merchants of New Julfa preserved their identity as Christians, they, like the newly converted slaves, were acculturated into the Safavid household as well. This integration is manifest in the architecture and decoration of their private and public structures. Particularities of spatial organization and decorative strategies notwithstanding, Armenian churches are architectonically indistinguishable from contemporary mosques in Isfahan. The mechanisms of integration may be exemplified by the simultaneous involvement of Muhibb Ali Beg, the tutor of the *ghulams* and the supervisor of the royal buildings of Isfahan, in both the Maydan project and the New Julfa Cathedral, which ensured the uniformity of architectural language and building technology.

Mansions, whether belonging to converted slaves, Armenian merchants or the high-ranking clergy, share distinct characteristics that define their social status as elites. The royal example was appropriated in the architectural and decorative features of these mansions through inspired details like pillared porches, centrally planned reception halls, monumental figural wall paintings and processional garden settings. Such idiomatic quotations manifest the politico-cultural assimilation of the new elites. In this era of centralization, even provincial governors came to maintain a residence in Isfahan.

The conceptual and physical centring of the pillars of the empire in Isfahan marks a break with the Turco-Mongol nomadic heritage of the Safavids, inaugurating an age of absolutism.

In addition to building for the Shah in the capital, the royal household slaves were responsible for creating an infrastructure that would link the court to the provinces. In key revenue-producing centres, such as Fars, Kirman and Mazandaran, provincial slave governors contributed to the empire's economic vitality by facilitating Safavid reforms. Three slave-governors, Allah Virdi Khan in Fars, Ganj Ali Khan in Kirman and Saru Taqi in Mazandaran, built roads, bridges, bazaars and caravanserais, assuring the flow of craftsmen, goods, revenues and ideas. By appointing his slaves – a *ghulam*, a *shahsevan* and a eunuch – to provinces throughout his private domains (*khassa*), the reconfigured household in Isfahan extended itself to the peripheries of the empire. Together the extended Safavid family facilitated and safeguarded regional and international trade through both maritime and land routes.

On the eastern frontier of the empire, Shah Abbas I placed Qarachaqay Khan, a *ghulam* of Armenian origin, as governor of the economically and politically strategic province of Khurasan. Its capital, Mashhad, benefited from these developments and was revived as a centre of pilgrimage and Shi'i piety. During the period of Qizilbash dominance, the shrine of the founder of the Safavid order (Shaykh Safi, d. 1334) at Ardabil in the northwest was a locus of ancestral veneration. With the consolidation of Shi'ism after the accession of Shah Abbas I, Mashhad, the site of the tomb of the eighth Imam Riza, emerged as the new imperial religious icon. Supplanting the dynastic significance of Shaykh Safi's tomb with that of Imam Riza signalled a move away from a mystic past to a normative present. While the Qizilbash generals were devotees of this Safavid mystical order and solidified their ties through royal marriages, the *ghulams* were poised to uphold the new Shi'i identity of the Shah and entered the household as adopted brothers and sons. Abbas I's decision to transfer Qarachaqay Khan from Azerbaijan in the northwest to Khurasan also served simultaneously to preempt potential ethnic solidarities with the large Armenian community in Azerbaijan and safeguard the religious site of Mashhad from continuous Uzbek incursions.

For three generations this slave family governed and dominated the political and cultural life in Mashhad. Their interest in the arts of the book and other luxury goods, paralleled by Ganj Ali Khan's patronage of architecture in Kirman, placed them within the nexus of a Safavid elite who helped shape a hegemonic visual culture, permeating the centre and periphery. Painters, calligraphers and architects circulated between Isfahan and the provinces, crystallizing a distinctive Safavid artistic canon.

Groomed at court, slaves were educated and converted to a new identity that would define their privileged status. Their patronage of classical Persian literature, religious institutions and commerce demonstrates the degree of their participation in this altered Safavid system. While the assimilation of the Armenian residents of the capital did not entail a religious conversion, they too shared in the articulation of the Safavid imperial discourse that coloured their surroundings.

Slavery in the Safavid household reveals the power of emotional bonds that transcend the pragmatics of rule. In the sixteenth century, Shah Abbas I grew up in the eastern provincial capital of Herat under the tutelage of a Qizilbash governor. Iran was in the midst of the second civil war (1576–90), and Abbas I was a victim of Qizilbash politics, which jockeyed princes to promote their own interests. He shared these childhood experiences with royal pages in the harem; with them, rather than with his kin and Qizilbash tutors, he developed ties of brotherhood. Once he was placed on the throne, Shah Abbas I killed his Qizilbash guardian and then dismantled the practice of sending out his sons to Qizilbash-dominated provinces. Instead, the *ghulams* undertook the tutoring of the princes and pages in Isfahan, inculcating similar fraternal bonds that had marked his youth. To gain a sense of these bonds one need only note that, whereas paranoia led Abbas I to kill or blind all his sons, he granted the accoutrements of rule to his adopted brothers. The reciprocal loyalty of pages like Qarachaqay Khan and Ganj Ali Khan led to their appointment by Abbas I as governors of his key provinces. Relying on the personal devotion of his companions over the fickle Qizilbash elite, the Shah entrusted them with the implementation of his reformist vision.

As a protégé of the Shah, the *shahsevan* Ganj Ali Khan ruled the province of Kirman as an appanage, commanded troops and had the licence to build on a royal scale. The commercial centre and public square of Kirman exude his confidence as a trusted brother. Abbas I confided the command of his united armed forces to another slave, Allah Virdi Khan. In this era of Isfahani absolutism the Qizilbash could no longer control the military backbone of the empire. To confirm this break with the past, Abbas I appointed Allah Virdi Khan to the governorship of Fars. Indeed, he was a valiant warrior in the battlefield, for he earned the position of commander-in-chief once he secured the eastern province of Khurasan from the Uzbeks and the island of Bahrain in 1602, which paved the way for his son's recapture of the island of Hormuz from the Portuguese.

Abbas I's relationship with his slaves was not confined to frat-ernal ties. Allah Virdi Khan was in fact older than the Shah, and as contemporary sources portray him, he served as a father-figure. Muhibb Ali Beg, the tutor of the slaves, played a similar paternal role in Abbas I's household in Isfahan. Just as Allah Virdi Khan commanded the army, Muhibb Ali Beg trained a generation of slaves who managed the imperial enterprise in the first half of the sev-enteenth century. Two of the most important public structures in Isfahan bear the names of these father-figures – the Allah Virdi Khan Bridge and the Royal Mosque. Slave-members of this surrogate family articulated the Safavid language of power through the imple-mentation of military, administrative and economic reforms. This discourse of absolutism was visually represented in a multitude of forms, whether in illustrated Persian classics, in a bridge that connected the suburban settlements of slave courtiers and Armenian and Tabrizi merchants to the heart of the city, or in the congre-gational mosque that symbolized Shi'i piety.

According to Chardin's estimate, a thousand *ghulams* served the Shah and three thousand eunuchs resided at the court in Isfahan by the middle of the seventeenth century.[11] Little is known about the physical dwellings of the eunuchs and concubines, but we can assume that, as in the Ottoman case, they resided along with their female slave-owners within the threshold of the harem. Thus, they shared their habitat with the princes and future shahs of the household. The communication between the sanctified harem and the outer world was facilitated through a sequence of progressively restricted gateways that were collectively known as the Harem Gate and were located south of the Ali Qapu palace on the *maydan*. Black eunuchs guarded entry into the heart of the court, while both black and white eunuchs functioned as a conduit between the boundaries of the inner and outer domestic worlds. In the semi-public zone of the court (*birun*), eunuchs and *ghulams*, as well as Tajik and Turkman functionaries engaged in the daily administration of the palace and the realms, working in the chancellery, the guardhouse, the kitchens, the workshops, the gardens, the stables and the audience halls. A ready supply of pages, reserved for household service, is reported by Chardin to have resided in the so-called Khana-yi Gav (Cow House) in the Abbasabad district, where wealthy merchants lived.[12]

The most loyal and capable of the *ghulams*, like Qarachaqay Khan, rose to the highest echelons and enjoyed access to the Shah. They not only lived in the vicinity of the court in Isfahan, but also accompanied the Shah on campaigns, hunting expeditions, imperial receptions and audiences. This camaraderie between the Shah and his slave is captured in a number of official Safavid and Mughal paintings, representing them either alone or in the presence of the Shah (Fig. 3). Prominent slaves like Allah Virdi Khan, Qarachaqay Khan and his son were honoured with burial at the sanctuary of Imam Riza in Mashhad, a privileged space reserved for the internment of the Safavid bloodline.

Just as Shi'ism gained ascendancy in Abbas I's *shari'a*-based empire, the *ghulam* converts adopted the Shah's identification with and propagation of the faith through the patronage of religious institutions. Saru Taqi, for instance, utilized architecture to both inscribe himself as an individual member of the royal household and link his own name with servitude to the Shah. The collective identity of the household does not preclude the sense of individuality of prominent slave-members. Notwithstanding their privileged status, the *ghulams* were still bound by the discourse and dynamics of the court and were vulnerable to its competing interests. Muhibb Ali Beg, who held the prestigious post of the tutor of the *ghulams*, or the grand vizier Saru Taqi, did not escape the vicissitudes of court politics. Prominent as they were, one was disgraced and banished from the court, the other was murdered. Even Allah Virdi Khan's descendants, who inherited his position as governors of Fars and continued to serve the Safavid household, were not spared. Succession struggles after the death of Abbas I witnessed a competition between slave factions over the candidacy of Safavid princes. Allah Virdi Khan's grandson took advantage of the political vacuum by minting a coin in his own name, a claim to sovereignty that cost him his head.

Ethnic and social solidarities among the slaves could enhance collaboration and create fissures in the competition for access to the Shah, his concubine-mother and chief eunuchs – major actors in household politics. For instance, Georgian *ghulams* vied for influence amongst each other as well as against their Circassian counterparts.[13] Traces of resentment by the denizens of Isfahan reveal the irony in the status of the converted and politically entrenched *ghulams*. Muslim antipathy toward converted Armenians and Georgians took different forms. Turkmans resented them for they had usurped the reigns of power, replacing the Qizilbash emirs; clerics never got over their disdain for the 'unclean' (*najis*) Christians, even after conversion. Race, too, played a role in the way Isfahanis perceived the *ghulams*. The late-seventeenth-century testimony of an anonymous widow voices contempt for Aqa Kamal, the black eunuch treasurer of Shah Sultan Husayn (1694–1722).[14] On her pilgrimage to Mecca, she remarks playfully on a caravanserai constructed by Aqa Kamal in the vicinity of Isfahan, comparing its abject blackness to a brick oven (*kura*). In its darkness, she says, it resembled a palace in hell just as its ignoble builder resembled a pest. Black eunuchs were generally perceived as ruthless, coarse and ugly. Chardin, in his reference to another black eunuch, Aqa Kafur, who held the same position during the reigns of Shah Abbas II and Shah Sulayman (1666–94), adds rudeness towards foreigners and local dignitaries to these vile characteristics.[15]

Although the trajectory of *ghulam* dominance in Safavid household politics during the last half of the seventeenth century remains to be explored, the examples of Aqa Kamal and Aqa Kafur speak to the continued power they wielded. Both Persian and European sources attest to the supremacy of the *ghulams* at the accession of Shah Sultan Husayn in 1694. According to the *Dastur-i shahriyaran*, a rare Persian chronicle from late Safavid period, Aqa Kamal, the chief eunuch of the harem, chose the prince who would succeed, and publicly announced his name while the cleric Majlisi Jr placed the crown on the Shah's head and girded him with his sword. The Shah in return took an oath vowing to enforce the *shari'a*. The two pillars, the *ghulams* and the *ulama*, that Abbas I placed in Isfahan, were most active at the court of the last Safavid shah. Despite their cultural tensions, they remained rooted in the structures of power implemented a century earlier.

This book attempts to highlight the particularities of the Safavid slave system. Despite many shared characteristics, slavery in the Islamic world was not homogenous. A cursory comparison with the contemporary Ottomans reveals different constructs of family and inheritance informing Safavid practice. Ottoman slaves in theory did not inherit their fathers' posts, so as to preempt kinship-based rivalries. Slave families, however, were common in the Safavid world, even inheriting from fathers the same posts, whether courtly or provincial. Moreover, Safavid princesses were not married off to *ghulam* dignitaries, as was the case in the Ottoman household. Instead, princesses were either married to their royal cousins or given to notables such as the Tajik and the *ulama* as a way of maintaining a balance among a cross-section of interest groups at the court. The practice of blinding Safavid princesses, along with the princes, at accessions during the seventeenth century, as Chardin notes, confirms the notion that women born into Safavid family carried a charisma passed down through blood; theirs could never merge with that of slaves. As for the male lineage, taking slaves as concubines rather than legal wives preserved the patrimony intact. Concubinage was the main mode of reproduction for Ottomans as well. As Muslim rulers, both the Ottomans and the Safavids had to abide with Islamic law (*shari'a*) that allowed women to inherit. Land and resources were the possession of the family represented by the patriarch, shah or sultan, who ruled through his slaves. The concept of family and the set of relations with the patriarch vary in the case of the Safavids, for as we shall see, slaves participated in 'surrogate' patronage, sharing with the Shah an inscribed space, while Ottoman slaves exercised more independent agency, excluding the names of their sultans and rarely partaking in joint endowments.[16] Such varied means of cementing imperial bonds hinge on different perceptions of the household in this age of absolutism.

2

The Safavid Household Reconfigured: Concubines, Eunuchs and Military Slaves

The Safavid household was dominated by slaves in the urban setting of Isfahan – the first capital city (1590–1722) to become the permanent residence of the Shah, his harem and his courtiers. From the most private quarters of the harem, where black eunuchs, Caucasian concubines, wives and mothers lived with the Shah, to the outer courts where they participated in imperial assemblies, slaves served the Safavid family with a particular loyalty. It was the social and sexual status of male and female slaves who were uprooted or castrated that allowed them such intimacy. Submission was to be absolute, for these slaves were fed, clothed, educated and given a new identity as Muslims by their master or mistress, the source of slave power. Slaves entering the abode of Islam (*dar al-Islam*) had been 'deadened' to society, and then through a process of conversion they metamorphosed into the *ghulaman-i khassa-yi sharifa*, or the 'slaves of the royal household' as a distinct category in Safavid discourse.[1]

Once acculturated into their novel roles as members of the royal family, eunuchs, along with male and female slaves, exercised tremendous power. Within the gender-segregated culture of the palace in Isfahan, eunuchs were the channel through which women participated in the public homosocial world of men.[2] And those eunuchs who were designated as teachers of unemasculated slaves trained their adopted sons for military and administrative careers. Such a mentoring relationship with military slaves allowed eunuchs to extend their reach beyond the court in Isfahan into the battlefield of politics.

This triangular configuration of slave-concubines, eunuchs and military slaves forged social networks of imperial alliances that were woven at its very core in Isfahan.[3]

Irony surrounds the conception of slavery in Islamic contexts, for in practice the least respected individuals came to be entrusted with the most strategic posts of the empire. Eunuchs were sexually and socially abject. As male slaves they were legally possessed (*malaka*) by free Muslims, and their castration rendered them neither male nor female in a male-dominated culture defined by gender hierarchies and spatial differentiation.[4] Eunuchs represented a third gender.[5] Bereft of their ability to procreate, they could not form a biological family and hence had no organic support group.[6] Because of their desexualized status, eunuchs were selected to serve in the vicinity of the most sacred possession of the patriarch, the Shah's female kin. And black eunuchs, who were considered even more repulsive, were retained specifically for harem service. They not only served women of the Safavid Shah's harem in large numbers; their chief was at times a black eunuch himself (*rish safid-i haram*). If he were not also head of the royal treasury, another black eunuch was entrusted with that office.[7] Furthermore, since no Muslim could be enslaved legally, it was Slavs, Turks, Caucasians, Indians and Africans who became subject to slavery in Islam. The Safavids possessed mainly Georgian, Armenian and Circassian slaves, who had been captured as booty in battle, received as gifts and tribute or bought in markets.[8] In the seventeenth century the Safavids came to employ sexually and ethnically marginal groups made to exercise control. In return, loyalty earned these slaves access to the Shah's most prized possessions – his women, his sons and his treasury.

Slavery entailed a process in Islamic contexts; masters were religiously authorized to manumit their slaves in time. If the master engaged in this pious act of conversion, he would be awarded a space in paradise. Such piety coloured the conception of slavery in Islam and is one of its particularities. Qualities of trust and loyalty were central to the institution of household and military slavery in Islam as well. The master was encouraged to act with kindness, compassion and caring toward the slave. Thus, the medieval philosopher Nasir al-din Tusi (d. 1274) emphasized a mutual relationship between master and slave that is so dependent on love, good faith and trust. Master and slave each had a moral obligation toward the other. The path of submission to Islam prescribed good deeds and a showering of grace in return. According to Tusi,

> The master must have firmly established in his servants' hearts [the conviction] that there is no manner or means for them to leave him, in any way or for any cause whatsoever. Such a course is not only closer to courtesy and appropriate to loyalty and generosity, but it leads the servant to observe the requirement of compassion and affection, conformity and carefulness; for such behaviour proceeds from the latter [only] when he recognizes himself as a partner and a participant in the grace and wealth of the one he serves, and when he is secure from dismissal or transfer.[9]

There was a practical side to this religious act, for as the Saljuq Vizier Nizam al-Mulk (d. 1092), presumed author of *The Book of Government,* writes in his chapter concerning the necessity of training slaves:

> One obedient slave is better
> than three hundred sons;
> for the latter desire their father's death
> and the former long life for his master.[10]

Since tension between father and son concerning authority is one of the themes most narrated in Persian epics and advice literature, the loyalty of the slave is represented as an asset for patriarchal rule.[11] Unlike his biological son, the slave is assumed not to rebel, and the king is to treat him justly. History, however, provides a variety of roles for slaves that differ from this idealized portrayal in philosophical discourse, though the predicament of father–son rivalry remains an impetus for the patriarch to draw on slavery.

TURNING TO THE INSTITUTION OF SLAVERY

Particular historical contexts in which household and military slavery was adopted as a mechanism of imperial rule reveal two predominant features: concubinage and military slavery. As a dynasty attempted to consolidate power within a patriarchy, concubinage became the favoured mode of reproduction.[12] Challenges from within the agnatic family (cousins), from notables and tributary dynasts, were hence undermined. With concubinage the patrimony too was kept intact, for Islamic law grants wives the right to inherit from their husbands. The crystallization of a dynastic theory of succession, often fixed within the male line, was accompanied by military slavery. David Ayalon has pointed out that concubinage and military slavery are two aspects of the same socio-political system practised by the Abbasids, the Mamluks, the Ottomans and also, as we shall see, the Safavids. And in the case of both the Abbasids and Safavids, two sites of power, Samarra and Isfahan, became associated with this turn to slavery. As both empires broke away from their reliance on the tribal armies that had secured them initial supremacy, they came to distance themselves from the apocalyptic tenor of their revolutionary rhetoric. At this historical moment they turned both to the institution of slavery and to divine (*shari'a*) legitimacy as interpreted by the religious establishment (*ulama*).

Military slavery in Islam has been the subject of considerable debate, with some scholars contending that slavery is intrinsic to Islam as a religion because it deters Muslims from playing an active role in public affairs, whether civil or military.[13] Jürgen Paul's study of military slavery during Samanid rule (819–1005) in Transoxiana suggests a more useful interpretive framework, privileging aspects of political pragmatism and cultural constructs of loyalty to explore the particular historical contexts in which military slavery was embraced in Islamicate polities.[14] The Safavids (1501–1722) exemplify how slavery was introduced to neutralize the decentralizing tendencies of tribal solidarities, breaking away from a mystical structure of authority based on a master–disciple schema. In the case of the Safavids, slave armies did not replace tribal ones; they merely supplemented them. But slaves were guaranteed a firmer ground with their control of firearms as the Shah's musketeers and armed cavalry. The Safavids appointed a eunuch to head the imperial arsenal (*jabbadar bashi*), whereas in the first century of rule this post had been held by a Qizilbash. The two previous Turco-Mongol states (Timurids and Aqquyunlu) from which the Safavids emerged had been backed by Turkic tribal armies. Both had failed to maintain their power. The Safavids adopted a solution that the Saljuqs in Iran before them had practised and the Ottomans had perfected. The redefinition of Safavid authority came a century after they had barely survived two civil wars against blocks of Qizilbash. In Isfahan they finally centred their power within a fixed male line protected by eunuchs and military slaves, moving away from their Turco-Mongol nomadic heritage.

With the advent of the Mongols in 1258, the ideal of a universal Sunni caliphate lapsed, giving birth to an era of experimentation with various nomadic steppe traditions, which derived their legitimacy from either the Chingiz Khanids or the Oghuz Turks, as well as from Irano-Islamic ideals of kingship and statecraft. The Timurid, Turkman, Safavid, Ottoman, Timurid-Mughal and Uzbek idioms can be viewed as distinct products of such syntheses of traditions. Marshall Hodgson terms these empires 'military-patronage states', for Turco-Mongol political practice was embedded in a conception of shared power distributed in the form of appanages among the entire dynastic house. In practice, land belonged to the paramount ruling clan and, by extension, to those favoured for their court service (military, financial, religious or artistic): a practice that bifurcated Islamicate society into the famous military–subject (*askeri–reaya*) administrative division.

Turkman converts to the Safavid cause had organized themselves militarily into *oymaq*, a Mongol term loosely translated as 'tribe'. Safavid historians have viewed the *oymaq* as a tribal unit bound by kinship, neglecting the religious and political forces that initially cemented these ties.[15] My research (Kathryn Babayan) has focused on the spiritual landscape of the Qizilbash, on the nature of loyalty that created such intense bonds between the Qizilbash and the Safavid family. The origins of the Qizilbash *oymaq*, their internal organization and early association with the Safavid house (*dudman*), still await study. Martin Dickson's dissertation, however, sheds light on the political nature of the post-revolutionary Qizilbash.[16] Dickson examines the tribal system at the moment when the Safavids had conquered Iran – an era in which the process of transformation from a revolutionary movement to an empire was in its infancy. He focuses on the political role of the major *oymaqs* during the first 16 years of Shah Tahmasb's reign (r. 1524–76), when the Safavid domains were experiencing their first civil war (1524–36). He sees each Qizilbash tribe functioning as a 'closed class group with special privileges'.[17] Whatever their origins may have been, by the reign of the first Safavid shah, Ismail (r. 1501–24), Dickson observes, 'An individual no longer became a Qizilbash by simply becoming a convert to the cause of the Safavid House. An individual became a Qizilbash only by being born into one of the *oymaqs* associated with the Safavid House.'[18] A tribe that had originally coalesced through the espousal of a messianic ideology was now cementing its blood ties. Membership in the Safavid imperial order was becoming hereditary in the classical age (1501–90), and Qizilbash devotees became members of the extended family in their capacity as spiritual sons of Safavid masters.

In accordance with steppe tradition, Ismail parcelled out his domains to his sons, sending them as governors to their appanages. Tahmasb, Ismail's eldest son and successor, was thus sent out at age four (in 1516) to Khurasan, the farthest province from the hearth. Three more Safavid princes (Ismail II, Khudabanda and Abbas I) would emerge as shahs from Khurasan, the seat of the heir apparent in the classical age, until Abbas I broke away from the appanage system and introduced the cage (restricting the princes to the harem) and slave systems. In keeping with steppe tradition these Safavid princes were also assigned a Qizilbash guardian (*lala/atabek*), directly linking the fate of a princeling with a single tribe. Through such a practice of land distribution the Qizilbash became partners in the Safavid corporation, each receiving an appanage referred to as *tiyul* for their tribe, as well as a member of the dynasty (female or male) with whom to participate politically in the system.

Some Qizilbash were categorically incorporated into the Safavid household through marriage (*musahira*). Tahmasb's tutor, Durmish Khan Shamlu, for example, was his paternal cousin.[19] The Shamlu tribe was linked to the Safavids through matrilineal lines. Women born into the Safavid household were used to construct collateral blood ties with those Qizilbash with whom they shared temporal power. Safavid princesses were also assigned a Qizilbash guardian (*dede*), and were awarded land either in the form of entire villages or as endowment revenues (*waqf*). Moreover, in the seventeenth century, because Safavid females were seen as especially charismatic, they were blinded along with their brothers, for fear that either they or their future offspring might lay claim to the throne.

Tahmasb continued to appoint Safavid princes as titular governors, first sending out his royal brothers Sam (d. 1567), Bahram (d. 1549) and Alqas Mirza (d. 1550). But he was forced to rethink the notion of corporate sovereignty for the Qizilbash, who were in open revolt during the first 12 years of his reign (1524–36), jockeying him around and using his brother Sam Mirza as a contender during the Grand Sedition of 1534.[20] The provincial appointment of Ibrahim Mirza, the grandson of Ismail and nephew of Tahmasb, signals an initial reform Tahmasb instituted to deal with this inherent weakness of steppe political tradition. What concerns us prior to Ibrahim Mirza's first major appointment to Mashhad in 1556–57 is his matrilineal lineage. His mother, Zaynab Sultan Khanum, was a member of the old line of Shirvanshahs, one of several local Persian (Tajik) dynasties claiming pre-Islamic antecedents, which were not yet fully integrated into the Safavid system, but played a growing role in the political struggle between the Safavids and the Qizilbash. Blood ties with Persian notables reveal Safavid attempts to gain local legitimacy and power. By this time all of Tahmasb's brothers had rebelled against him, and had either been killed or imprisoned. Now Tahmasb was sending his sons and nephews, third-generation collateral members of the Safavid House, to provincial appanages.

Ibrahim Mirza's appointment as governor of Mashhad coincided with the appointments of his brothers to Sistan and Qandahar and the reappointment of his cousin, the future Khudabanda, to Herat. The date (1556–57) is significant in any periodization of the early Safavid period, for it represents the culmination of a Safavid-dominated balance that was manifest in such phenomena as royal appointments to major provinces and the shift of the political and religious capital from Qizilbash-inspired Tabriz and Ardabil to a shari'a-dominated Qazvin. Tahmasb's religious renunciation (tawba) of the pleasures and arts denied by the shari'a was emblematic of this new Safavid mood. Qazvin was a foretaste of Isfahan.

The appointment of Ibrahim Mirza to Mashhad differed in one significant detail from the usual Safavid household appointments to the provinces. Instead of the usual Qizilbash guardian representing a single tribe's stake in the designated province and acting as the military security for that province, Ibrahim Mirza was provided with a mixed group of five hundred ranking officers culled from all the tribes.[21] This by no means meant the abolition of the lala system

elsewhere; rather, it is to be seen as a further sign of Safavid supremacy, tempered by concern over the Qizilbash will to participate
equally within the system. The Safavids would also reform the tribal
armies, creating the corps of Qurchis from mixed tribes as a way of
breaking tribal solidarities.[22] The provincial administration appointed
with Ibrahim Mirza was typical in that its upper echelons were centrally appointed Persian bureaucrats (Tajiks). What was atypical,
but nonetheless significant, is the administrative influence given to
the appointees of the religious institutions. This is in keeping with
the special nature of Mashhad as the gradually evolving cult centre of
Imami Shi'ism and the Safavid reliance on the clerical establishment
in the process of centralization. It is in seventeenth-century Mashhad
that we shall encounter a family of Armenian slave-converts to Islam,
Qarachaqay Khan and his son Manuchihr Khan, who played a
central role in the military safeguarding of the Safavid realms and in
patronage of the arts (see Chapter 5).

One event during Ibrahim Mirza's tenure as governor in the east
serves to illustrate the evolution of Safavid political practice: his
leading role in suppressing the major tribal revolt of the Takkalu *lala*
of Herat, Qazaq Khan, in 1564–65. This revolt was not completely
typical either. It was normal enough in the sixteenth century for
Takkalu guardians to use weak or minor Safavid figures (in this case
the future Khudabanda) to enhance their relations with the Safavids.[23]
It was also normal for the rival tribe to join with the Safavid House
in suppressing the ambitions of any single tribe at the expense of the
others. Much more interesting is the atypical aspect of this revolt,
since the Takkalu had neither the prestige nor the power to rally
other dissidents, ambitious Turkman tribes or Tajiks to their cause.
They turned instead to an institution extraneous to the Qizilbash-
inspired Safavid imperium: the slave (*ghulam*) system that had been
used by the Ottomans and was in turn to enable the Safavids to gain
hegemony in the seventeenth century.[24] In the particular event being
described here, it was, however, the Turkman commander rather than
the Safavids who had recourse to slaves. We are told that Qazaq
Khan bought ten thousand slaves, whom he armed and trained for
both military and bureaucratic functions.[25] This was clearly a new
type of threat to the Safavid–Qizilbash balance so precariously

established by Tahmasb, and its suppression required the armed intervention in which Ibrahim Mirza figured so prominently.

Slave armies first appear in Safavid annals (1564–65) as troops
recruited by a Turkman Takkalu tribe that had lost its appanage and
the accompanying Safavid princeling – key means of political access.
To assert their hegemony over rival Qizilbash tribes and their Safavid
masters, they imported an element external to the Qizilbash–Safavid
equation. But by the reign of Abbas I, the grandson of Tahmasb, the
Safavids would come to appropriate military slavery as an imperial
institution. Abbas I ended the second civil war (1576–90) that had
erupted at his grandfather's death, removing the rebellious Afshar
and Zu'lqadar tribes from their appanages in Fars and Kirman. He
named a Georgian slave, Allah Virdi Khan, as governor of Fars in
1595, along with an administration of three hundred slaves. In consolidating power, Abbas I made use of the household slaves Tahmasb
had begun to train as palace pages. Abbas I, however, increased their
number and thoroughly initiated them into the administration of the
court and the provinces. According to Shah Abbas I's court chronicler,
Iskandar Bek Munshi, three hundred and thirty thousand slaves were
captured by the Shah on his Georgian campaign (1614–15).[26] This
date, then, marked the first significant influx of slaves into the
Safavid system for the personal use of the royal family. The Qizilbash
lost their privilege of receiving appanages, along with their role as
tutors of princes, key elements in their bid for equal participation in
Safavid politics.

Shah Abbas I appointed a Kurd, Ganjali Khan Zik, as governor
of Kirman in 1603. Although Kurds had been included in the
Qizilbash system, Ganjali Khan was recruited from within an altered
order in which individual tribesmen were invited to break away from
their tribal hierarchy and pledge allegiance to the person of the Shah,
becoming *shahsevan*. Like royal household slaves, some of these were
brought up at court, and together they came to share the military and
administrative responsibilities of the empire. The sons of notable
Kurds, Arabs, Georgians and Lurs were thus brought up at Shah
Tahmasb's court as part of a tributary relationship they shared with
the Safavids. Half a century earlier, in 1554, Shah Tahmasb had captured prisoners of war as a religious tax (*khums*) during his campaign

into Georgia, incorporating forty thousand slaves into his court. Alongside these enslaved Georgians he had established the practice (*'adat)* of educating sons of illustrious families together with Safavid princes in palace schools. Here is where bonds of loyalty would be developed to shape an extended household. Sharaf Khan Bidlisi, a Kurdish chief who was schooled at Tahmasb's court, wrote in 1596: 'When I turned nine [in 1551] I entered the private harem (*haram-i khass)*...for three years [1551–54] I served the family (*silsila)* of that refined (*pakiza atvar)* shah as a page at the inner palace'.[27] Bidlisi speaks of his education entailing instruction in the Quran, readings on the principles (*ahkam)* of the *shari'a*, piety and purity (*taqva va taharat)*. Due to Shah Tahmasb's religious disposition, Bidlisi was introduced to religious scholars (*ulama va fuzala)*, who warned against associating with evil people and instead encouraged friendship with the virtuous. And once Bidlisi attained maturity, he was taught the martial arts (*sipahigari)* – archery, polo, racing, swordsmanship and the precepts of chivalry – humaneness and generosity (*qava'id-i insaniyat va adamgari)*.[28] Such was presumably the curriculum of Safavid princes and court pages, whether slaves or notables – crafting the culture of a new Safavid elite.

Domestic slavery was a common practice among notable families throughout the Islamic world. Early references in the chronicles to slaves belonging to the Safavid family (*ghulaman-i khandan-i Safaviyya)* point to the use of household slavery by Shahs Ismail and Tahmasb.[29] There is certainly an awareness of its military cognate in Safavid circles, when the Qizilbash historian Hasan Bek Rumlu, writing in the middle of the sixteenth century, refers to the Ottoman slave system (*ghulaman-i khwandigar)* and to the Mamluks of Egypt (*ghulaman-i misri)*.[30] The practice of training palace pages for service at court and in the battlefield is discussed by Nizam al-Mulk in his manual on statecraft, which taught Persianate monarchs how to rule. Nizam al-Mulk situates the practice in medieval Islam with the Persian dynasty of the Samanids ruling in Transoxiana.

> This is the system which was still in force in the time of the Samanids. Pages were given gradual advancement in rank according to their length of service, their skill and their general merit. Thus after a page was bought, for one year he was commanded to serve on foot as [a rider's] stirrup...and

this page was not allowed during the first year to ride a horse in private or in public...When he had done one year's service, then they gave him a small Turkish horse, with a saddle covered in untanned leather, and plain bridle...After serving for a year with a horse and whip, in his third year he was given a belt to gird on his waist. In the fourth year they gave him a quiver and bow case, which he fastened on when he mounted.[31]

The advancement of the slave entailed increasing access to the accoutrements of power, from the horse to the quiver and bow, to a tent and slaves.

Every year they increased his rank and responsibility until he became a troop-leader, and so on until he became a chamberlain. When his suitability, skill and bravery became generally recognized and when he had performed some outstanding action and been found to be considerate to his fellows and loyal to his master, then and only then, when he was thirty-five years of age, did they make him a general [emir] and appoint him to a province.[32]

Service, both military and domestic, to the royal household would be the test of loyalty. In return the master would bestow the gift of power to his adopted son and former slave.

The famous medieval philosopher Nasir al-din Tusi speaks of the slave as integral to the ideal household. The term 'household', according to Tusi, 'does not refer to a house made out of brick and mortar, stone and wood. Rather does it refer to a particular combination between wife and husband, begetter and begotten, servant and one served, and the possessor of property and property itself.'[33] In Tusi's conception of the household the slave's subservient status was shared with women and children of the family; obedience to the patriarch was to be absolute. Although Tusi is defining an abstract family, in practice royal women of the Safavid household did yield power through their roles as mothers, wives and slave-owners, precisely because they occupied these social functions.

THE HEGEMONY OF CONCUBINES, EUNUCHS AND MILITARY SLAVES (1629–66)

With the death of Shah Abbas I in 1629, a bloody massacre marked the end of Safavid classical rule at the court in Isfahan.[34] Forty women were killed in the harem. All of Abbas I's grandsons born to his daughters were either blinded or murdered. A faction of royal slaves that Abbas I had introduced to consolidate his dominion eliminated a branch of the Safavid family. Qizilbash (Shaykhavand), Persian notables (Mar'ashi) and sons-in-law (*damad*) of Abbas I were removed from their posts. Although Shah Abbas I had killed all of his sons and had instituted the cage system for his grandsons, maternal and paternal cousins fought for the crown at his death. The dramatic massacre of 1632 would end the succession struggles, securing the throne for Abbas I's grandson, Shah Safi, born to a Georgian concubine. To eradicate matrilineal and collateral lines, Safavid princesses – sisters, cousins and aunts of the new Shah – were killed along with male children of royal blood. The Safavid household was being redefined around patrilineal descendents of Shah Ismail, who gained legitimacy through a sacred Shi'i genealogy sanctioned by the clerical establishment and protected by slave-elites. The composition of the harem was to be altered drastically as Safavid royalty, both female and male, was liquidated. The massacre of all competing cousins delayed opposition to a new generation of the descendants of Shah Safi, creating a clean slate that propelled mothers into the orbit of politics.[35]

In this Isfahani era of Safavid rule, during which princes began to reside in the capital rather than in the provinces, the harem became a central locus of power. Gradually, as the tribal structure of the Qizilbash was deconstructed, slaves were appointed as provincial governors, whose authority included control over tribes (*mir-i il va oymaq*). Shah Abbas I's reforms had far-reaching social implications, particularly for the Qizilbash, who were accustomed to special honour and respect. For many Qizilbash it meant not only that they no longer enjoyed special political and economic privileges but also that many of the tribes were now governed by the slaves who had been named governors of provinces in which they lived. The court historian Iskandar Bek Munshi explains that

> since some of the tribes (*oymaq*) did not possess qualified candidates to take on high posts once their Qizilbash generals (*emirs*) and governors had died, a slave (*ghulam*) was appointed, due to his justice, skill, bravery and self-sacrifice, to the rank of general of that clan (*il*), army (*qushun va lashkar*) and to the governorship (*hukumat*) of that region (*hukumat*).[36]

The whole tribal structure of the Qizilbash had been affected by Abbas I's centralizing reforms. The Qizilbash general who guaranteed the political and economic interests of the tribe was rendered impotent once a slave to whom he had to be subservient replaced him. The local power of the Qizilbash general was thus undermined, creating fissures in the intricate web of tribal allegiances and loyalties that had enhanced solidarity.

Mulla Salih Qazvini, writing about Isfahan toward the end of Safavid rule, reveals through an anecdote a sense of resentment against non-Muslims in power. He relates that a crazy man (*majnun*) from Isfahan complained to a general (*emir*) that in this town only the religiously impure (*najis*) had authority, rather than human beings. The general responded: 'Indeed, the impure are the ones riding horses and donkeys, and me I am walking on foot'.[37] The reference here to the impure is to non-Muslims, most probably Armenians and Georgians, who prevailed publicly in Isfahan, distinguishing themselves through their status that allowed them access to horses. Was the 'crazy' man talking to a Turkman general whose power had been eclipsed by recent slave converts to Islam? Tajik notables (*ulama* and bureaucrats) must have also felt resentment towards slaves who were culturally alien to Persianate landscapes. Another anecdote, recorded by Abd al-Hayy Razavi Kashani, illustrates this tension. Majlisi Sr. (d. 1660), a popular religious scholar and preacher in Isfahan, is said to have asked Rustam Khan, the slave commander-in-chief of Shah Safi's military: 'While you are busy establishing order amid the troops or when the trumpet and drums are sounded, announcing the launching of the battle, do you feel grandeur and authority to such an extent that you may exit from obedience to God?' Rustam Khan is said to have replied cunningly, 'It is strange for you to think that these types of grand illusions overcome one at such times and not while one is praying or reciting the call to prayer'.[38] Slave patronage of the arts, roads, bridges, bazaars, caravanserais and religious shrines should thus be understood as attempts to forge a positive image to assuage such public sentiments.

With the breaking of Qizilbash power, Safavid princes, like their mothers, came to be secluded physically in the harem.[39] To wield power, it was no longer sufficient to dominate the military and provincial scene. Although provincial control and military prowess were necessary to maintain peace in the provinces and to ward off foreign incursions, the heart of political power lay in Isfahan, the royal residence of the Safavid household. In this newly reconfigured household in Isfahan, slave-concubine-mothers would become more powerful as representatives of the family. Although Abbas I had married all but one of his daughters to Persian religious notables with strong local ties, his sons had been given concubines.[40] Together with their agents the eunuchs and military slaves, concubine-mothers of the Shah became more politically viable. Just as in the Ottoman case, the cage system instituted by Abbas I in 1590 had already begun to alter the relationship between mothers and sons. This newly established practice was part of the impetus for a shift from the active political participation of aunts, sisters and daughters of Safavid monarchs to the predominance of the role of the queen-mother. Since Abbas I had personally experienced the insecurities of the crown, he had abandoned the appointment of princes to the provinces.[41] Confining the princes to the harem precincts further tightened the umbilical cord between a prince and his mother, strengthening her role and that of the eunuchs responsible for educating royal sons, and maintaining order and security in the harem. The cage system, while restricting the role of the Qizilbash guardian, enhanced the role of the Shah's mother, and by extension that of the harem, in politics. In the seventeenth century, queen-mothers emanated from slave backgrounds and sustained their status as concubines. Concubinage rather than marriage was a preferred form of reproduction adopted by both Ottomans and Safavids so as to preserve the patrimony. The social and political role of concubines was invariably linked to their sons; mothers of princes could legitimize their agency as guardians and representatives of future Safavid monarchs. The chief eunuch's function as tutor of princes and military slaves now allowed him, instead of the Qizilbash guardian, to enter imperial politics.

The collaboration among military slaves, eunuchs and concubines manifests itself in court politics throughout the reign of Shah Safi and into the early years of Shah Abbas II.[42] This triangular configuration challenged traditional pressure groups at court and undermined the Turco-Mongol system that had involved female members of the

Safavid line in politics. In the sixteenth century, when a Safavid monarch died, different factions of Qizilbash rallied around Safavid princes, with their sisters or aunts participating in succession struggles. Twice in that century such rivalries had led to civil wars that lasted more than a decade each. At the death of Shah Abbas I there was no civil war; instead struggles among courtiers prompted the assassination of harem women, their children and their court allies. Military slaves that Abbas I had appointed as governors in the provinces had served their purpose of controlling the Turkman tribes in each of their provincial jurisdictions. Even though the realm was rife with both internal uprisings in Gilan and Georgia (Kakhet and Kartil) and external incursions from the Ottomans and the Uzbeks, Safavid forces were united in their defence of the empire.[43]

In this Isfahani era of Safavid rule, to employ the name 'Qizilbash' in reference to the Turkman tribes may be misleading. The chronicles from the reigns of Shah Safi and Abbas II do continue to use the term, but they do so anachronistically, it would appear, to refer to the military forces of the Turkman as 'qizilbash' and 'sufi' (junud-i qizilbash va jaysh-i sufi). In fact, the Qizilbash were no longer a co-hesive group of devotees bound by their privileged status in the Safavid system; rather it was the ghulams who were honoured with such distinctions. Seventeenth-century chronicles use the term 'qizilbash' habitually, and perhaps sentimentally. One can see the term itself evolving in meaning, as it began to be used as an adjective, denoting bravery and military prowess, keeping only the warrior aspect of the legendary Qizilbash.[44]

The chapter of ghulam hegemony unfolds when the new Shah, Safi, along with his harem, set up their winter quarters (qishlaq) not far from Hamadan, in expectation of the Ottoman armies. The court astrologer, Mulla Muhammad Tahir, had advised the harem to leave Hamadan for fear of an Ottoman attack. Zaynab Begum, the influential aunt of Shah Abbas I and matriarch of the harem, was separated from Shah Safi and his retinue (urdu). The harem was sent to Gulpayigan in the vicinity of Isfahan, and the Shah headed west-ward to Shahr-i Zor to join a rising courtier, the Georgian slave Rustam Bek (divan begi).[45] It is during this period that the Qizilbash commander-in-chief (sipahsalar) of the Safavid armies, Zaynal Khan

Shamlu, was assassinated by a slave named Bahram, an old eunuch of the harem.[46] Zaynal Khan Shamlu's association with Zaynab Begum had developed through customary networks of loyalty and authority that tied Qizilbash disciples in veneration to the Safavid family. At the death of Abbas I the two collaborated in Mazandaran, gathering signatures from the grandees of the empire, who endorsed Safi's candidacy. Moreover, Zaynab Begum's tutor was a Shamlu (Shah Ali Bek), and, although her marriage was never consummated, she had been betrothed to a member of that tribe (Ali Quli Khan) as well.[47] Two days after Zaynal Khan Shamlu's assassination, Rustam Bek was received by Shah Safi.

According to Rustam Bek's biography (*Tarikh-i Safavi Khan*), he had been brought to court at age ten or eleven (in 1598–99), had entered the harem and been educated in the palace school system.[48] He gradually rose in rank, first as aide-de-camp (*yasavul suhbat*) and then as chief military judge (*divan begi*).[49] After thirty years of service at court he was now awarded the important task of safe-guarding the Safavid realms from Ottoman incursions. Rustam Bek's success in defending Baghdad against the Ottomans (8 November 1630) and in capturing Hilla (9 March 1631) ensured victory for his faction of slaves. As a result of his impressive performance on the battlefield, both the titles commander-in-chief (*sipahsalar*) and head of the infantry (*tufangchi aqasi*) were bestowed upon him.[50]

The commander-in-chief of the reformed Safavid armies was in charge of all military units, both tribal and slave (*qizilbash, qurchi, ghulam* and *tufangchi*). A decade earlier Abbas I had named the first slave, Qarachaqay Khan, to this post.[51] An Armenian from Erevan who had been captured as a prisoner of war, Qarachaqay Khan was enrolled among the slaves of the royal household and had been man-umitted (*hurriyat*) due to his loyal service.[52] 'Since he was inherently capable, he was favoured (*tarbiyat*) with royal service and daily advanced in rank.'[53] The gradual progression in the status of court pages delineated by Nizam al-Mulk corresponds to Qarachaqay Khan's career. From the rank of tailor, *qaychigari*, he entered the artillery department (*mir-i tupkhana*), then led (*sardar*) the musketeers until he was given his own troops (*sardar-i sipah*). The honorific Turco-Mongol title 'Khan' was bestowed upon him once he was appointed governor of Azerbaijan and Mashhad. Ultimately he came to lead a unified Safavid military, commanding over all units of slaves and tribes. As we shall see (in Chapter 5), although Qarachaqay Khan and his descendants would revivify Mashhad as a cultural centre, initially he met much resistance. Qarachaqay Khan was killed in 1625 four years prior to the death of Abbas I, while fighting some Turkmans who had revolted against the rising hegemony of slaves like him.

Rustam Bek was one of the successful products of the slave system who had adopted the military functions of the Qizilbash, replacing the 'exaggerated' (*ghuluww*) form of devotion to their mystic-king with a personal allegiance to a shah who ruled over the Safavid domains. At Abbas I's death his appointment symbolized a new era in Safavid history in which slaves would now head the military branch – traditionally the domain of the Qizilbash. In the first century of Safavid rule one general, the *amir al-umara*, was designated as the supreme representative of all the troops provided by each tribe.[54] The honourary title of *sipahsalar* was (re)introduced and institutionalized by Abbas I as part of his reforms. The Persianate etymology of the term is symbolic of Abbas I's attempt to create a centralized patrimonial Iranian Empire based on loyalty to the Shah, free of tribal solidarities and messianic expectations.

Rustam Bek would replace the Qizilbash military commander in collaboration with a network of slaves now embedded in the household. For the duration of Shah Safi's reign these slaves dominated the court, vying among themselves for power.[55] With the bestowal of key military positions (*sipahsalar* and *tufangchi aqasi*) upon Rustam Bek, coupled with his partner Khusraw Mirza heading the corps of slaves (*qullar aqasi*), the main military and administrative backbone of the Safavid Empire had been transferred from the Qizilbash to a new elite of slaves. Khusraw Mirza was a Georgian slave of royal blood, the son of King David XI of Kartil, who was trained at court by eunuchs alongside young slave recruits. As already mentioned, the Safavids had adopted the practice of holding as hostages young princes of regional ruling families with whom they had a tributary relationship. At Abbas's death, Khusraw Mirza held the position of governor (*darugha*) of Isfahan, reserved since the days of that monarch exclusively for the royal Georgian princes raised at court.[56] Royal

Georgian slaves of the household now ensured order in Isfahan, which carried judicial authority. Upon Safi's succession to the throne, the valiant name of Rustam Khan was bestowed upon Khusraw Mirza, along with the position of *qullar aqasi*, which placed him at the head of all the slaves.[57] The granting of pre-Islamic Persian names from the *Shahnama* to the personal slaves of the Safavid household is consistent with the Safavid intent to bolster their legitimacy as patrimonial monarchs evoking ancient Iranian glory.

The post of chief of all slaves (*qullar aqasi*) was formerly held by another Georgian convert, Imam Quli Khan, but he was not of Georgian royalty. Imam Quli's father, Allah Virdi Khan, was the first slave appointed by Abbas I to a gubernatorial seat in the southern province of Fars, in 1595. Safavid slaves, unlike Ottoman slaves, were able to inherit their father's assignments, thus the Safavid particularity of factions centred on slave families. Allah Virdi Khan's Georgian family (Undilajes) was being eclipsed by a Georgian nobility of slaves, who would continue to play an important role in Safavid politics until the demise of this dynasty in 1722.[58] Slaves at the Safavid court did not sustain ethnic solidarities; in fact this example reveals social hierarchies of slaves that marked one Georgian of royal lineage from another Georgian of common background. According to the chroniclers, Imam Quli Khan's son (Davud Khan) was involved in a separatist movement in Georgia (with Tahmuras Khan, the *vali* of Georgia), and the whole family was executed a few months after the Bloody Mab'as Massacre of 1632.[59] It is at this junction that Rustam Khan attained the governorship (*vali*) of Georgia (Kartil).[60] Slaves were most vulnerable during succession struggles when the court was split between competing princes and their clients in the household. The slaves of the household were not a united group: rivalry between slaves born of royal Georgian blood and regular slave recruits are evident. Moreover, Georgian dynastic politics now manifested itself at court in Isfahan. Georgian history needs to be studied in the context of Isfahan.

At the court in Isfahan the tutor of the slaves, Muhibb Ali Bek, forged links between Shah Safi's concubine-mother and the outer world of the barracks and battlefield.[61] Muhibb Ali Bek had personally carried the famous letter from Mazandaran to Isfahan announcing

Shah Abbas I's death. We can assume that, when Zaynab Begum (Shah Abbas I's aunt) and her protégé Zaynal Khan Shamlu sent the letter ordering the officials at court in Isfahan to keep a close eye on all princes and to await their arrival, they had trusted Muhibb Ali Bek as an ally. But instead he had made arrangements for Safi's coronation to be carried out, despite these orders from Mazandaran. As the teacher and trainer of slaves he had nurtured patron–client relations with his students. He had probably called on his former students like Rustam Bek and the Georgian prince Khusraw Mirza to secure their position at court around a fixed patrilineal (Haydari) line of Safavid shahs in the name of Shi'ism.

At the Safavid court the function of tutor to the slaves (*lala-yi ghulaman*) was entrusted to a senior *ghulam*, such as Muhibb Ali Bek. The tutor trained slaves for court service until they reached puberty. Once the pages grew a beard, a sign of masculinity in Islamic gendered discourse, they would enter the service of the chief of the slaves (*qullar aqasi*).[62] As slaves, depending on their performance and network of patronage, they could attain the loftiest military and or administrative positions of the realm. Slaves continued to maintain relationships with the eunuchs who had trained and protected them during their tenure at court. And eunuchs were presumed to serve the Safavid masters, who castrated them, with unequalled loyalty.[63] This is why in official administrative manuals eunuchs are awarded the title 'Intimates of the Shah', or *muqarrab al-khaqan*.

Initially, only black eunuchs had been employed for Safavid service. Chardin comments that even in the age of Shah Sulayman (r. 1666–94) only the Safavid Shah could own black eunuchs.[64] By this time, however, white eunuchs had been introduced at court. Abbas I maintained one hundred castrated Georgian slaves in Isfahan.[65] He created two new centurion (*yuzbashi*) posts – one to act as preceptor to black eunuchs and the other to white unemasculated slaves.[66] The evolution of the posts held by eunuchs, as portrayed in the two extant administrative manuals, reflects the growing prominence of eunuchs at the court in Isfahan. The official chronicles from the reigns of Shahs Safi, Abbas II, Sulayman and Sultan Husayn attest as well to the ascendancy of black eunuchs in collaboration with concubines of the harem in Safavid politics. As in the Ottoman case, perhaps the chief black eunuch (in the post-1574 era) acted as the personal tool of the queen-mother while the chief white eunuch served the sultan.[67]

These 'Intimates of the Shah', the *muqarraban al-khaqan*, represent a third category (*bab*) of functionaries enumerated in the Safavid administrative manuals. They appear after the men of religion (*ahl-i shar'i*) and the men of the sword (*emir*) who are referred to as the 'pillars of government' (*arkan-i dawlat*). Eunuchs are singled out for their worthiness to enjoy physical proximity to the Shah.[68] White and black eunuchs had access to five crucial harem posts – all of whose duties concerned the most private affairs of the Shah. Two of the most prominent were that of chief eunuch (*rish safid*) of the harem and keeper of the royal treasury (*sahib-i jam'i khazana-yi 'amirah*). These two seasoned eunuchs were the guardians of the Shah's household and of his treasury.

As for the chief eunuch of the harem, at first this post was monopolized by black eunuchs. Once Abbas I introduced white eunuchs, the post could be held by a trustworthy eunuch, either black or white.[69] Chardin speaks of the power of the chief eunuch, Aqa Shahpur, under Shah Sulayman, 'His position awarded him such respect that everyone feared him in the city [Isfahan]. A recommendation from him was worth as much as a decree from the grand vizier.'[70] In fact, Chardin reveals that one of his main sources on court affairs was a eunuch, a confidant of Shah Sulayman's aunt.[71] What Chardin reports on court cabals is corroborated by contemporary Safavid chronicles demonstrating the degree to which these eunuchs were entrenched in politics.

The harem communicated with the outer court (*birun*) through the *ishik aqasi bashi* of the harem, who was strategically stationed at the threshold. Not being a eunuch, he did not enjoy access to the harem but was linked to it by the chief eunuch (*rish safid*), who resided in and regulated the affairs of the harem. In the absence of the Shah, theoretically, the chief eunuch filled the monarch's role.[72]

The reports which the frontier amirs sent to the *Ishik Aqasi Bashi* [of the divan] or those sent by the amirs resident at the court (*mustawfi*, vizier) to the harem were first handed to the *Ishik Aqasi* of the honourable harem who has a guardhouse (*kishik-khana*) of his own. This official passed them on to the chief of the harem eunuchs, and the latter presented them inside the harem to the king, and brought back the reply. [Then] the *Ishik Aqasi Bashi* summoned the amirs to the *kishik-khana* and personally declared to them how the king had decided in reply to the reports.[73]

According to the prescribed chain of communication, the harem was linked to the outer court by the *ishik aqasi* of the harem, who was physically located between interior (*andarun*) and exterior (*birun*) royal spaces, acting as an intermediary. Any faction at court that wished to gain political control placed its members in these key posts. As power was being consolidated within the Safavid household (princes, princesses, concubines, eunuchs, military slaves) the chief eunuch of the harem had to strike an alliance with the *ishik aqasi bashi* of the harem and divan. The grand vizier Saru Taqi is an exception, for as a eunuch he embodied both roles, entering in and out of the harem without threatening, at least sexually, Safavid male honour.

Beyond being guardians of the Shah's harem and treasury, senior eunuchs were also in charge of the Shah's arsenal (*jabbadar bashi*), his wardrobe and private accessories (*mihtar-i rikab-khana*), and his pages (*lala-yi ghulaman*). All the accoutrements of sovereignty were protected by these eunuchs; they regulated its public display. The eventual monopoly under Shahs Sulayman and Sultan Husayn (r. 1694–1722) of eunuchs over the Shah's arsenal, treasury, harem and slaves attests to their hegemony in the administration of the household.[74]

The *Dastur al-muluk* speaks of two tutors in the age of Shah Sultan Husayn, one for the royal household slaves (*ghulaman-i khassa*) and the other for potential slaves (*ghulaman-i anbari*).[75] The former were those personal pages and soldiers who were actively employed by the Shah, while the latter, as suggested by their names (*anbari*), may have been a reserve of trained *ghulams* not yet employed for court service.[76] Chardin estimates that about three thousand eunuchs resided at court. He claims that very few were black, coming from India, mostly Malabar and the Gulf of Bengal. Each female member of the harem had at least two eunuchs in her service. Grandees too would employ between six and eight eunuchs in their homes. There they played a similar role to that of their courtly counterparts, acting as tutors of elite children instead of palace pages and princes, teaching them to read and write and providing

them with a rudimentary knowledge of religious precepts and of ele-
mentary sciences.[77]

An extensive staff of slaves administered the necessities of courtly
life in Isfahan.[78] In the case of Shah Abbas I, the slaves' tutor Muhibb
Ali Bek, along with a wide network of his trainees, exercised power
beyond the court, crafting Isfahan into a capital city. His name
(Muhibb Ali Bek b. Muhammad Quli Khan) appears on an inscription
at the main entrance to the Royal Mosque that served as a Safavid
icon of Shi'i identity in Isfahan. We will discuss in Chapter 4 how
he had supervised (*mushrif*) the construction of this congregational
mosque built by Abbas I in his new capital. Once the mosque complex had been completed, Muhibb Ali Bek became its superintendent
(*tawliyat*). He must have been independently wealthy since, after the
Shah, Muhibb Ali Bek was the major donor to the endowment (*waqf*)
of the Mosque.[79] He bequeathed his inheritance for religious purposes,
as a sign of devotion to his patron Shah Abbas I's faith. This gesture
was a public act of affirmation of Muhibb Ali Bek's Muslim identity
as well. His alliance with the chief merchant of Isfahan, *malik al-
tujjar* (Mulayim Bek), points to another force that bound this slave
faction together: financial interests.[80] Not only were the slaves infil-
trating the military and harem administrations, as we shall see in the
next chapter, they had also entered the commercial sector as well and
would become important participants in the economy of Safavid
Iran. Slave ties to the Armenian community of merchants that
Abbas I had resettled in Isfahan as his personal silk merchants and
diplomats would permit the displacement of an Isfahani commercial
elite entrenched in the old city quarters – the financial and political
arena that was eclipsed by the new building project of the Maydan
Naqsh-i Jahan, in which these slaves played such a prominent role.

With the Bloody Massacre of 1632, Sultan al-Ulama (Mar'ashi),
the grand vizier, would not only lose his office and have his sons
blinded, but his family's economic interests in Isfahan would be
threatened as well. One of his relatives (Mir Qutb al-din) had been
vocal in his objections to Shah Abbas I's initial plan to redevelop the
old market district of Isfahan, since this Mar'ashi family of religious
notables had substantial investments in both land and commercial
property in this district.[81] The Mar'ashis of Isfahan had probably

been linked to Alid confraternities based in the old bazaar.[82] Such local religious, political and commercial networks were being undermined by the hegemony of the slaves at court, who would supervise and invest in the new urban development of Isfahan.

Nearly three years after the accession of Shah Safi, Rustam Bek's faction of slaves, with control over the military and harem administration, were able to bolster the Shah's candidacy, and now they were strong enough to do away with their opponents at court.[83] A former elite of Persian religious notables and Qizilbash was dislodged.[84] The sons of Sultan al-Ulama, along with the sons of the minister of religion, education and justice (*sadr*) and the superintendent (*mutavalli*) of the Mashhad shrine, were blinded in retaliation. These three members of the clerical establishment shared another important characteristic that gave meaning to the blinding of their sons: all three were sons-in-law (*damad*) of Abbas I.[85] Zaynab Begum, the aunt of Shah Abbas I, was evicted from the harem, for now the Georgian concubine-mother of Shah Safi became the matriarch. Shah Abbas I's daughter, Zubayda Begum, who had fought for her son's right to the throne, was killed. The classical age in which the harem was controlled by Safavid women of royal blood had lapsed. Now nameless slave concubine-mothers would dominate.[86]

The triumvirate of concubines, eunuchs and military slaves continued to colour political participation in Isfahan for the next decade of Safi's rule and into that of Abbas II. The Safavid case parallels the Mamluk one in that systems based on military slavery shared the feature of collaboration among soldiers, eunuchs who served as guards in the harem and concubines who resided in it. It was a courtier-turned-eunuch, Saru Taqi, who would dominate the scene with the help of another concubine, the queen-mother of Shah Abbas II.[87] Although Saru Taqi was a Muslim from Tabriz, he should be classified as a eunuch, having been castrated under Abbas I as punishment for engaging in sodomy (Fig. 3).[88] Safavid sources, except for the *Afzal al-tavarikh* of Fazli Bek Khuzani, are silent about the castration of Saru Taqi, perhaps due to a court culture that celebrated male same-sex desire – Shah Abbas I himself setting an example.[89] According to Fazli Bek, a young furrier named Mu'min had accused Saru Taqi along with five companions, claiming that they had sodomized and dishonoured him. As a punishment Saru Taqi was castrated in 1616 and his possessions were confiscated, but, as Charles Melville suggests, his status had not been damaged by this disgrace, for a year later Shah Abbas I granted him the vizierate of Mazandaran. At Safi's accession, Saru Taqi was governor in the provinces of both Gilan and Mazandaran.[90] As we shall see in the following chapters, he had supervised Shah Abbas I's creation of two new towns in Mazandaran, a development project that involved the building of trade routes and the resettlement of fifteen thousand families from the Caucasus (Qarabagh, Shirvan and Georgia). With the help of his patron at court, a slave who oversaw the accounts (*darugha-yi hisab*), Saru Taqi was able to enter political life in Isfahan, where in fact his castration allowed him to play the role of a eunuch, in that he could enter the harem.

But first Saru Taqi had to eliminate the grand vizier, whose position he coveted. He instigated an investigation into court finances to discredit the ruling grand vizier, Mirza Talib Khan Urdubadi, and the tutor of the slaves, Muhibb Ali Bek. Saru Taqi's biography reveals a personal animosity for Mirza Talib Khan's notable Persian (Urdubadi) family of bureaucrats, which traced their lineage back to the medieval philosopher Nasir al-Din Tusi.[91] Once Saru Taqi's uncle had died, the whole family had fallen into disgrace. Later, under Abbas I's rule, when Mirza Talib Khan's father, Hatim Bek Urdubadi, became grand vizier in 1591, Saru Taqi's father had asked him for a post but had been denied.[92] Saru Taqi eventually entered an altered court system in which slaves had already begun to curb the power of Persian notables and the Qizilbash. Unable to make use of his uncle's connections at court, he joined the military and had been forced to climb the administrative ladder by working his way through the provincial echelons. He ultimately took his revenge, first by blemishing Mirza Talib Khan's honour and subsequently by instigating his assassination in 1633.[93] Saru Taqi was to take over both his post of grand vizier and the sumptuous house that Mirza Talib Khan's father had built in Isfahan.[94] Mirza Talib Khan's party represented those who had united politically behind Shah Safi and had reaped financial benefits from their alliance. They had increased the monies due to Muhibb Ali Bek (tutor of the *ghulams*) and Mulayim Bek (*malik al-tujjar* and *zarrabibashi*) and were accused of tampering with the accounts (*nuskha*).[95] Such were the intricate webs of alliances and patron–client relations that gave shape to the Rustam Bek slave faction.

Saru Taqi had not acted alone to overthrow Mirza Talib Khan. The assassination was a harem coup with an alliance that began to blossom at the birth of Safi's successor, Abbas II, on 31 December 1632, nearly two years before the assassination of Mirza Talib Khan.[96] Only after the birth of Abbas II did his mother, having provided Safi's first male heir, gain standing within the ranks of harem women. The channels through which Saru Taqi was able first to discredit Mirza Talib Khan, and then to attain the lofty position of grand vizier, clearly specifies the harem as a means of patronage.[97] The contemporary chronicler of Abbas II, Muhammad Yusuf Valih, states that Saru Taqi's key to success lay in his close relation to the slave Ughurlu Bek, who served in the financial administration (*darugha-yi hisab*).[98] This slave gained access to Shah Safi through his daughter, who was influential in the harem in the year of Abbas II's birth. Within harem politics of the post-cage system the first concubine to bear a male heir to the Shah conventionally acquired political status.[99] And we must not forget that Saru Taqi was a eunuch who had direct access to the harem, an advantage previous grand viziers lacked.

Saru Taqi dominated Safavid household politics for the next decade (1634–45), breaking the autonomy of landed notables and amassing territory and revenue into the *khassa*. As we shall see in Chapter 4, he actively engaged in building projects throughout the realms. Once Safi died in 1642, his son Abbas II succeeded him in a smooth transition. Saru Taqi maintained his position as grand vizier, eliminating such slaves as Rustam Bek (whose ally in the harem was probably Safi's Georgian slave-mother) to consolidate power within his reconfigured faction.[100] Foreign travellers like Chardin speak of the close relationship between Saru Taqi and Abbas II's mother, Anna Khanum:[101]

> The power of mothers of Persian kings looms large when they [shahs] are at a young age. Abbas II's mother had much influence, which was absolute. They [queen-mothers] were in close contact with the prime minister and would help each other mutually...Saru Taqi was the agent and confidant of the queen-mother; he would gather immense fortunes for her. She governed Persia at her will through her minister.[102]

His connection with the harem was key to Saru Taqi's success in attaining the lofty position of grand vizier – testimony to the importance of the harem in politics at this juncture in Safavid history. Once again, Chardin's observations, written between 1665 and 1677, corroborate this thesis:

> What pains the ministers of Persia most is the harem, which is the women's palace where he [the Shah] holds a form of private council that generally prevails over everything else, dictating law. The council is held between the queen-mother, the grand eunuchs and the most cunning and favoured concubines. If the ministers do not tailor their advice to the passions and interests of these cherished persons who as a matter of speaking possessed the king for longer hours, while they [ministers] would see him just momentarily, they ran the risk of having their advice rejected, and this often led to their own ruin.[103]

Although as grand vizier Saru Taqi possessed ultimate power in the outer court, without support from the harem his faction remained ineffective. In addition, since the heart of the pro-Safi *ghulam* faction lay in the harem, in the person of Safi's mother, that power could only be matched from within. Ironically, Saru Taqi's castration turned out to be a political blessing. Along with the altered role of the harem, the position of the military slaves and eunuchs had improved. The slave connection with the harem was strong, whether through female relations living in the harem or through other eunuchs in the harem who had studied with their peers in the palace school.

Saru Taqi's hold on power, however, was bound to the vicissitudes of shifting political dynamics of the household. He was assassinated by another courtier, the Turkman Jani Khan, probably with the consent of the reigning monarch, Abbas II, who was attempting to gain his independence from his mother and her slave allies.[104] For the next two decades of Abbas II's reign (1645–66), Persian notables (*ulama* and bureaucrats), along with individual Turkmans, would dominate the political scene, sharing power with the *ghulams*, yet maintaining a balance so as to prevent slave hegemony.[105] With Saru Taqi's assassination the first chapter of *ghulam* supremacy came to a close.[106] According to Chardin, Anna Khanum, furious at the assassination of her partner Saru Taqi, sent one of the principal eunuchs (probably the chief eunuch of the harem) to the assassin, Jani Khan, asking him to explain his actions. Jani Khan responded rudely, calling Saru Taqi a dog and a thief, and then proceeded to insult the queen-mother personally:

> Saru Taqi was a dog and a thief who should have been killed long ago. Tell this to the grand duchess and tell her that he was a true scoundrel of Julfa...and I shall prove within five months that this cursed dog has extorted two hundred thousand pounds. He [Jani Khan] was saying this to irritate the queen-mother because the revenue of this suburb is the appanage of the king's mother and not one dime can be levied without her orders.[107]

Chardin represents the queen-mother as receiving tax revenues from the Armenian community of Julfa. He calls this income her 'taxe de la Chaussure' (footwear tax), stating that this is an old Persian custom practised since Achaemenid times once Egypt fell to the Persians. Abbas I had established the Armenians of Julfa as his diplomats and financiers, who traded Persian silk for European silver.[108] As we shall see in the next chapters, they were the major source of revenue enabling Abbas I, Safi and his successor Abbas II to construct Isfahan as the apocalyptic 'City of Paradise'. Saru Taqi was one of the most important builders for this reconfigured Safavid household. He supervised the construction of one of the holiest Shi'i sites of pilgrimage, the tomb of Ali in Najaf, which Rustam Bek, the Georgian slave-general, had recaptured from the Ottomans in Iraq in 1631.[109] Saru Taqi spent his own wealth to erect commercial and religious buildings – a mosque and a bazaar in Isfahan. The Safavid household slaves were agents through whom a new imperial idiom was crafted in Isfahan, inscribed visually through buildings and articulated discursively in the Shi'i rhetoric of kingship.

Saru Taqi supervised the addition of the roofed structure (*talar*) onto the Ali Qapu Palace, the threshold from which the hidden Messiah was to manifest himself. With the dramatic suppression of rival Nuqtavi disciples who declared that the advent of the new Muslim millennium (1590–91) would witness the end of the Islam, thus inaugurating an age of Persian (Ajami) rule under the auspices of one of their devotees, Shah Abbas I reserved the right to messiahship for a descendant of Ali, more particularly for his own Safavid patriline.[110] In Shi'i eschatology Isfahan enjoyed a symbolic association with such holy manifestations.[111] The vast stage of the *talar* was superimposed onto the Lofty Gate that commanded a panoramic view of the entire square, from which Abbas II could display power (Fig. 2). Saru Taqi was the administrator who built spaces for Safi and Abbas II in which they could direct the yearly Karbala dramas, imposing their control through urbanized ceremonial structures that allowed them to partake in the creation of Shi'i collective memory. These vast *talar* were intended for the performance of lavish audiences, commemorations and feasts that allowed Safavid monarchs to manage social and religious expression within their orbit of authority.

In the Isfahani era the court chronicler Iskandar Bek Munshi expounded a new theory of sovereignty that reserved and limited legitimacy to the neo-eponymous Ismaili patrilineal Safavid line – to direct male descendents of Ismail and Tahmasb. 'Sovereignty and kingship are the right of Shah Ismail and Tahmasb's family, who having sent their dust-and-wind-borne opponents to hell with the fire of their well-tempered swords, revealed and manifested Imamism and spread it throughout the world.'[112] Here Iskandar Bek Munshi is introducing a new language of authority that was in the process of replacing the classical Safavid synthesis between Turco-Mongol and Iranian practices. According to this chronicler, what separated Ismail and his male descendents from other members of the Safavid extended family was their revival and defence of Imamism in Iran. As propagators of this faith, Ismail's descendants were sole heirs to its dominion. With the first Safavid coronation in Isfahan (of Shah Safi, in 1629) Turco-Mongol steppe political heritage was overshadowed by a new synthesis of patrimonial Iranian monarchy and Shi'i (Imami) temporal concepts of rule. Officially, Safi's candidacy was sanctioned over that of his rival cousin (Sayyid Muhammad Khan Shaykhavand) because he embraced Shi'ism. Shah Safi was the first Safavid monarch to be enthroned by a cleric, Mir-i Damad (d. 1631), who in turn was one of the first native Iranians (Astarabadi) to have achieved the rank of grand jurisconsult (*mujtahid*) in the history of the Safavid Empire.[113] Mir-i Damad was the one who called out to the denizens of Isfahan Shah Safi's name during the sermon (*khutba*) portion of the Friday prayer he recited at the magnificent Mosque Shah Abbas I had built as a symbol of his affirmation and adherence to Shi'ism.[114]

The metamorphosis of Caucasian slaves into elite members of the Safavid household coincided with an official Shi'i language of authority that altered hierarchies of loyalty and consolidated a patriarchal family. As legalisms and an emphasis on the Word overshadowed the mystical heritage of the Safavids, master–disciple paradigms of rule were not abandoned. Shorn of their spiritual content, they found a different incarnation in the royal household. There within the domestic sphere they merged with familial vocabularies, crystal-lizing a particular set of relationships that tied slaves around the person of the Shah. As mothers, tutors, soldiers, generals and treasures of the Shah they exercised power on his behalf in Isfahan and in the provinces. Slaves were the Shah's adopted sons, brothers and fathers, who gradually accumulated political and economic power from the domestic to the local and regional. And when, as in the case of Imam Quli Khan's slave-family, they acted against the welfare of the household, they were executed. The reconfigured Safavid household extended beyond earthly domains, for as descendents of the Family of the Prophet the shahs too were slaves who served the Twelve Imams. The Safavid family venerated God as master-patriarch followed by Ali, the imams and the shahs in descending order. As we shall see in the following chapters, the Shah and his slaves engaged in pious gifting, reserving their inheritance in perpetuity for the building and upkeep of mosques – centres for the propagation of Shi'ism.

Let us turn to the ways in which slaves entered the commercial and financial sectors, as they came to enunciate their new identities through building, collecting and patronizing the arts and sciences.

3

Armenian Merchants and Slaves:
Financing the Safavid Treasury

Shah Abbas's transfer of the axis of Safavid power to Isfahan was motivated by economic as well as political considerations. His mercantile initiatives helped to finance his political reforms within Iran and to provide for his war efforts against the Ottomans. He deliberately relocated the capital in order to consolidate the political and religious power of the Safavids, develop state capitalism and establish Iran as a world power.[1] Several decades later, in his 1673 description of Isfahan, the traveller Jean Chardin enumerates 1802 caravanserais within the capital.[2] This figure alone, although probably exaggerated, shows that Isfahan had become a vibrant commercial centre. Yet, no episode of Iran's long history matches the early seventeenth century in evoking the image of a commercial efflorescence under Shah Abbas I.[3] Abbas's planned policies were evident in the construction of a vast infrastructure in order to facilitate long-distance trade through Iran.

Among the most salient of the measures taken by the monarch to encourage trade were the construction of caravanserais, the building of new roads and the appointment of officials such as the *rahdars*, the royal guards well-known to European commercial travellers. These steps served to control and protect merchants and their goods on Safavid territory. He also took measures for several merchant communities to settle in Isfahan. Merchants displaced from Tabriz, in northwest Iran, and Indian merchants were very active in the economy of Isfahan.[4] The Julfan Armenians, deported to Iran in

1604, constituted the most prominent among the new trading groups brought to his capital by Abbas.

Settling the Julfans to Isfahan was central to the political reforms undertaken by the Shah. There is a clear consensus among scholars that the lion's share of Iran's international silk trade in this period was in the hands of the Julfan Armenians. Less well-known is the fact that this group of Christian merchants financed another group deported from the Caucasus, the *ghulams*, the royal slaves of the *khassa*. The financing of some of Abbas's new administration of *ghulams* by the silver imports of the Armenians gave the Julfan Armenians a central role in Iran's political economy.[5] Once resettled in Iran, the Armenian merchants of Julfa encouraged the organization of silk production and accelerated the export of raw silk to Europe, not for their profit alone, but for the benefit of the royal household, the *khassa*, where the profits in silver and gold were deposited by the Armenian provost. This financing mechanism will be demonstrated in detail in this chapter.

Europeans consumed about 200,000 to 250,000 kilos of mostly raw silk per year, 86 percent of which came from Iran.[6] Silk was thus a commodity that attracted the interest of the European trading companies. What some historians have called the 'rise of the West' was also a time of the rise of the bourgeoisie and the demand for silk in Europe.[7] According to Halil Inalcik, profits accrued from the European demand for Iranian silk formed the structural basis for the development of both the Safavid and Ottoman economies.[8] Even during imposed blockades and Safavid–Ottoman wars, Iranian silk continued to be traded across the Ottoman world, reaching Europe through the main markets of Aleppo, Bursa and Izmir. The Julfan Armenians were prominent on these markets, where they traded Iranian silk against silver and cloth.

The Julfans were visible as international exporters of Iranian silk to Europe; less noticed is the crucial commercial role played by the *ghulams*. As previously discussed, Armenians and Georgians, as converted *ghulams*, were integrated into the army and the administration, many among them attaining the highest administrative and military ranks within the empire. The same prominent *ghulams,* who held administrative posts, also played a major role in the silk trade within the borders of Iran. For example the tutor of the *ghulams*, Muhibb Ali Bek Lala, was Abbas's main silk factor in Isfahan. The English East India Company (EIC) and the Dutch East India Company (VOC) negotiated their trade with Lalah Bek, as Muhibb Ali Bek Lala is called in European company archives.[9] He was the head merchant of Isfahan, but also held the highest post in the mints. Therefore he supervised the flow of both silk and silver within the Safavid realm. Administrators played a major role in commerce, just as the Julfan merchants played a political role as members of the *khassa* and as Safavid ambassadors in Europe.

Social order in Safavid Iran is described as a tribal and military one.[10] It is argued here that, unlike in Europe, in Safavid Iran there was no clear division between a tribal and military class and a merchant one. The *ghulams* in the military and the bureaucracy, as well as the Armenian merchants exporting silk, participated both in the practice of politics and commerce. This becomes amply clear through a study of the silk trade, where both groups play multifaceted roles. The organization of the silk trade, which is the subject of this chapter, demonstrates the interdependence of the wealthy Julfan Armenian merchants with the *ghulams* in the military and the bureaucracy. The silk trade should therefore be studied not only through the well-known exporters of silk, the Christian Armenians of New Julfa, but in conjunction with the converted *ghulams*, who played a major commercial role within Iran.

THE JULFANS AND *GHULAMS* ALLIED AS MEMBERS OF THE *KHASSA*

Abbas I's reign witnessed the transformation of the royal household, the *khassa*, which achieved unprecedented economic control as this monarch and his successors converted state lands (*mamalik*) into the private domain of the Safavids. *Ghulam* administrators and Armenian merchants were part of this reconfigured household. Together they were agents of economic and political change. Several prominent *ghulams* known only for their political participation played just as significant a role in the economic realm. Silk, the most prized Safavid commodity, was managed and traded by these two key groups of the household.[11]

The Julfans rose to prominence on the Ottoman silk markets after their deportation to Iran in 1604. Their commerce profited from their political status in Iran, membership within the *khassa*, the royal household. It was instituted by edict under Abbas I and reconfirmed by Shah Safi (1629–42). The second royal edict, dated 1631–32, spelled out the Armenians' attachment to (*muti'aliq*) and alliance with (*mansub*) the royal household (*bi sarkar-i khassa-yi sharifa*) as well as the Shah's great compassion and affection for the New Julfans.[12] The decree was addressed to their provost. It ensured the protected status of this Armenian community by prohibiting transgressions against their goods and property throughout the realm. These edicts allow for a radically different reading of the role of the Armenians, who have previously been characterized as a bourgeoisie, an economically active group of outsiders without any political role.

The Julfans were part of one of the branches of the palace government sharing the status of the converted Caucasian *ghulams,* and the suburb of New Julfa was also institutionally linked to the court.[13] As previously discussed the Armenian suburb depended directly on the Shah's mother, the most important member of the royal household, who collected the annual taxation owed by the New Julfans. The Christian Armenian merchants, their protector the queen-mother, the *ghulams*, all reaped the benefits of the silk trade.[14] This was the new elite that supported Safavid power in Isfahan. Silk became an economic weapon of political control, both against the Ottomans and within Iran by enriching the political clients of the Safavid court and consolidating Safavid power.

It will be demonstrated below that the Armenian silk trade brought in silver that became cash pay for Abbas's new army of *ghulams*, ending his dependence on the feudal lords who had troubled him during his accession. Paying a dependable army for fighting the Ottomans was not the only purpose this imported silver served. A study of the mints show that imported silver also brought pay to bureaucrats, and facilitated Abbas's internal reforms by providing pay for the *ghulams* in his administration. The controllers of the assay, mint masters, superintendents of buildings and grand viziers reaped salaries or profits, and at times both, from the silk trade.[15]

The Safavid court developed a political economy planned around the accelerated production and export of silk and the import of silver. Different groups of deported Christian Armenians and converted slaves from the Caucasus formed the pillars of this planned policy. The success of the silk trade depended on the close collaboration of the Armenian merchants and the *ghulams*. Due to Abbas' reforms and victories, *ghulams* now replaced Qizilbash governors in the main silk-producing and transporting provinces of Safavid Iran. The *ghulams* safeguarded and controlled the sale of silk within Iran, while the Armenians exported silk through Ottoman domains into Europe. The Armenian silk merchants allied to the slaves of the royal household helped to implement Abbas I's economic policies by increasing silk production, accelerating export and financing the royal treasury. The pivotal role played by the relocated populations of the Caucasus during the first fifty years of the seventeenth century is just beginning to be noticed.[16] Until recently, it was believed that the minorities in Iran were insignificant compared to the important role played by the *millets* religious authorities in the Ottoman Empire.[17] The role of the Caucasian population in Iran has parallels in the political use made of the populations of the Balkans by the Ottomans.

JULFA ON THE ARAS

Before they arrived in Isfahan the Julfan Armenians were silk traders, but their importance on the main Ottoman silk markets dates to Abbas I's reign. Florentine, Genoese and Jewish merchants kept records of Safavid silk exported to Europe by Iranian merchants between 1487 and 1500.[18] Throughout the fifteenth and sixteenth centuries, the merchants who came from Iran to Bursa to sell silk were overwhelmingly Muslim, called Azemi in the Italian records. Some Iranian merchants settled in Bursa and acted as partners for their agents in Iran.[19] Although Muslim merchants continue to trade in the seventeenth century, no study of their trade has ever been undertaken, making them invisible to scholarship. The Iranians either sold directly to the Italians in Bursa or sent their own agents to the Balkans and to Italy. The Julfan Armenians, rarely mentioned in the Bursa records before, came to replace Muslim merchants from the reign of Shah Abbas.[20] In Aleppo, on the other hand, a main market for the sale of raw silk to Europe, the Julfans were active much earlier, in the sixteenth century.[21]

Safavid designs on old Julfa were inspired by the economic vitality of the Julfan Armenians, whose global market share was substantial. Old Julfa on the Aras was located in Nakhichevan, present-day Azerbaijan. This town of silk traders was important enough to be marked on one of the first world maps by Ortelius. Edmund Herzig advances some explanations for its unusual prosperity. Several royal edicts dating back to Shah Tahmasb's reign demonstrate previous ties between the Safavids and Julfa, even while Julfa was under Ottoman rule. A few travellers testified that tribute was paid to both the Ottomans and the Safavids. Old Julfa's wealth might have been due to its location at the crossing of several trade routes, which made it a centre of East–West trade. It may have been spared by the Ottoman–Safavid wars of the 1570s and 1580s in part because it was not a Safavid administrative outpost, and perceived as neutral.[22] Yet Edmund Herzig concludes that these factors do not fully account for the Julfans' success. Julfa survived as an isolated enclave of wealth in the midst of a theatre of war. One possible explanation is Safavid protection. Previous relations with Shah Tahmasb extend Safavid ties with Julfa to earlier times. When Abbas I visited Khoja Khachig Shafraz, the ruler of old Julfa in 1603, he stayed for three days. This was after a long-established relationship initiated by the Armenian Church in 1590. Gold coins were showered at the Shah's feet, and he was given the keys of the town of Julfa by the provost. Shah Abbas I deported the entire population to Isfahan and burned old Julfa a few months after his visit.[23]

Unlike the *ghulams* the New Julfans were not prisoners of war, captured and then converted to Islam as slaves. As portrayed by another royal edict, the Armenians were

> A population who for our [Safavid] sake has left their fatherland of two or three thousand years, Jula, has left behind loads and loads of gold and silk and come to your home; is it worth waging war on these people for a few

melons and a few manns of grapes and cotton? In Jula there were houses on which two thousand Tumans were spent; they destroyed them and took their ilk and came here.[24]

Despite the false impression created by such official language, the Armenians were deported by force. The Julfans' move of 1604 took the form of a mutually beneficial agreement between one Julfan family and the Shah, albeit one that imposed much suffering and sacrifice on the part of the Julfans.[25]

THE SUBURB OF NEW JULFA

A year and a half after their departure, after spending a winter in Tabriz, the Julfan Armenians were settled on the banks of the river that ran through the centre of Isfahan. While a new suburb was being built, they were lodged, by royal order, in houses evacuated by their Muslim inhabitants. In 1605 the deported Julfans were settled in a new suburb of Isfahan, south of the Zayanda River. New Julfa was built as an entirely Christian Armenian suburb of the capital, with several churches, markets and other public institutions. It was sheltered not only from Muslim trespassers but also from competing Catholic missionaries operating out of Isfahan. Its elite status and protection remained intact at least until the middle of the seventeenth century.

The first church in New Julfa was completed in 1607, the Church of Surb Hakob. In the same year, before the suburb was entirely constructed, an Armenian from New Julfa had already gone to Venice as an ambassador for the Safavids. The inscription on this first church reminds the visitor to pray for those who undertook the perilous journey to Europe: 'You who pass by this place say a "God have mercy" for the deceased who have perished in the open sea. This is the tomb of their Sarkis 1056/1607'.[26] The cliché that Armenian cooperation with the Safavids was coerced persists.[27] From the beginning of their stay, the Armenians travelled all over the world freely, and, save for a short period in 1652, when old Julfa was destroyed again by Abbas II and travel was briefly forbidden, there were no efforts made to coerce them to stay. The appearance

of the first embassy in 1607 – Venetian – was far from an isolated
case of political representation. Even after 1661, during a period of
relative decline, they represented the shahs as Persian ambassadors
in Europe.

Shah Abbas I wanted the centre of Armenian faith to be in Iran,
in New Julfa. He planned to dismantle their main church, stone by
stone, and have it carried to Isfahan. The Julfans did not let the Shah
dismantle their mother church, Edjmiazin, in historic Armenia. Only
a few stones were brought from there. A cathedral built by Abbas
in 1615 for the Armenians was seen as a new spiritual beginning. It
was marked with a new calendar: the year 1615 was used as year 1
in Julfan account books across the world. A 1619 royal land grant
was the material reality of a new spiritual centre as envisioned by
Abbas I. The New Julfan year was to move synchronically with the
Persian solar calendar. Celebrating Nowruz rather than marking
the Armenian era in their secular account books demonstrates their
willingness to be integrated into the Safavid Empire.[28]

Carmelites residing in Iran relate that in 1608, 'the Armenians of
the New Julfa [sic] constantly asserted that 400,000 of their families
had been transplanted by Abbas I during the course of the war'.[29]
Population estimates for New Julfa vary. If one accepts, however,
that the population of Isfahan was approximately 500,000 and
that the Safavid realm had between six and eight million subjects
under Abbas I, then the figure of 400,000 Armenians given by the
Carmelites could be a real overstatement.[30] This figure may include
those resettled in silk-producing regions and enslaved Armenian children. Once again according to the Carmelites, the privileged Christian
Julfans, who had the means to save some Armenian prisoners from
forced conversion, complained that

> in the first overrunning...10,000 children and girls had been carried off
> into Muslim households and the practices of Islam: although the shah had
> ordered that the Armenian patriarch and bishops as well as the parents
> should be permitted to buy back and ransom those Armenian slaves, he did
> not do much to facilitate such a measure.[31]

All population figures for Safavid Iran are from the travel accounts
of foreign observers, such as Chardin or Carmelite missionaries, and
should be accepted with caution.

The provosts or *kalantars* (aldermen) of New Julfa were responsible for its autonomous municipal government while subject to the Safavid court. Under their provost, the Julfans were organized in a tight system of 22 leaders, heads of their neighbourhoods, all subject to the provost. In turn they had other merchants who answered to them. The Armenians comprised several ranks of merchants; most prominent among them were the Khojas, a sedentary group of financiers and urban investors in the silk trade. Four families constituted the patricians; one of these, the Shafraz, served as the provost of New Julfa until 1656. The Safavid edicts were addressed to the provost Khoja Nazar (r. 1618–36). That Khoja Nazar Shafraz was the second to greet Shah Safi at his accession in 1629, by throwing 150 tumâns (coins) at his feet, speaks of the high rank the provost held in the hierarchy even among the elite.[32] A small political elite had access to the shahs in Safavid Iran. Closeness to the Shah signalled political power, and order of precedence was of the utmost importance.[33]

New Julfa was exclusively inhabited by wealthy merchants until 1647. Before the murder of Saru Taqi and the demise of the patron of New Julfa, the queen-mother, for a new political faction, no Armenian artisan or labourer had a right to live there. The construction of the suburb was a gradual process and, as discussed in the next chapter, the *ghulams* and royal builders were involved in the building of its main cathedral. The bridge between New Julfa and the new quarters of Isfahan was named for Allah Virdi Khan, the famous *ghulam* general of Abbas I, who helped conquer the Caucasus. The bridge linked the best Armenian houses located on the river bank to the new quarters of Isfahan inhabited by the notables of the court. New Julfa became the municipally autonomous seat of an internationally entrenched network of wealthy merchants who resided in magnificent houses and neighbourhoods.[34]

New Julfa's merchant and municipal organizations were linked. The centrality of New Julfa in the international network of Armenian merchants, as far away as Tibet or Amsterdam, can be gauged by the judicial authority of the provost over all worldwide litigation.[35] The commercial administration of New Julfa may have been autonomous, but its success had much to do with the Shah's favour.

Another 1634 royal edict by Shah Safi also spells out protection against officials of the city of Isfahan and exemption from its expenditure, as well as New Julfa's independence from the fees for the administrators of the capital.[36]

ARMENIAN SILVER IMPORTS TO IRAN

In the words of a prominent French traveller, Jean Baptiste Tavernier, who visited Isfahan several times after 1638:

> So all the gold and silver of Persia comes from foreign lands, and particularly from Europe, as I have said in the chapter on moneys. From the reign of Shah Abbas I to the reign of Shah Abbas II, one saw more silver in Persia than presently; and the Armenian merchants brought it from Europe to Persia, where it was reduced to local money.[37]

The Armenians were therefore the key players, both within Iran, for silver imports, and in the long-distance export of silk. The fact that the profits from the silk exports came back to Iran was a major incentive for the Safavid Shah to favour the Julfans and keep out the European companies.[38]

Despite the Eurasian scope of the Julfan trade, it was Safavid Iran that profited most directly from Armenian commerce until the middle of the century, as the uses of silver in Iran demonstrate. Obtaining bullion and forbidding its escape, as well as monopolizing the production and sale of such a key commodity as silk, was seen by many early modern polities as the surest way to consolidate a state, and as a means of political control. Abbas I took both measures. Mercantilist views were not confined to European courts. Shah Abbas I forbade the export of gold and silver in 1618, paralleling some seventeenth-century European monarchs who aimed to keep gold and silver within their borders.[39] Iran had little cash flow except for what was imported.

In Iran, as elsewhere, prohibitions were not effective; much of the silver reaped from the export of silk was in turn exported to India, playing a major role in Iran's trade balance with its most important trading partner. The *abbasi* silver coin, the best-known Safavid currency, was in very high demand on the Indian market. In return for selling silk in Europe, the Julfans brought back silver and European cloth, glasses, mirrors, telescopes, paintings, books and clocks. None of these were as vital to the Iranian and Indian markets as silver. All the gold and silver entering Safavid realms came through the Ottoman and Russian markets, brought in by the Armenians. Safavid and European sources show that despite the involvement of the European East India Companies in the silk trade, the Armenians acted as the conduit through which much of this silver cash flowed. While English factors in Iran and India were always short of cash, often writing home in vain to obtain some, the more successful Dutch faced prohibitions and had to take Iranian silk for their trade in goods; nevertheless, they managed to export silver from Iran into India.[40]

Throughout this period India remained the most important trading partner in Iran's Eurasian trade. It was the recipient of the silver reaped by the Armenian exports of silk. In exchange India was a major exporter of cotton, gems and many other goods to Safavid Iran. It has been argued by Sanjay Subrahmanyam that, as the Armenians became prominent, some notable Iranian merchants left and redirected their activities from India, the land of commercial opportunity.[41] The large settlement of Iranian merchants in Surat and Golconda created important trade connections. These royal favours gave the Julfans significant advantages over the other merchants of the realm. There was an advantage for the Shah in these privileges, as neither the *ghulams* nor the Armenians had any social ties except with the palace. They were therefore subordinate to the Shah's aims.

On the other hand the Armenians had many trading ties, not only with Europe, but also with several groups of Indian merchants, as well as with Iranians in exile.[42] Julfan connections with India were also very strong, as many families also left New Julfa when they failed to achieve the highest ranks within the merchant oligarchy ruling the Armenian suburb. The Diocese of New Julfa had jurisdiction over all the Armenian churches of India. The Armenians of India were part of the same administrative unit as New Julfa.[43] The connections the Julfans had in India gave them great advantages for the success of their network across Eurasia. Within this Eurasian trade the New World silver imported via Europe by the Julfans played a major political role within Iran by helping to finance Abbas's new administration and army.[44] The Safavid enterprise of empire-building through war was tied to the cash reaped from the commerce of silk. As a first step Abbas had to control the silk-producing Caspian region and accelerate production.

THE CASPIAN REGION AND THE CULTIVATION OF SILK

Long before he displaced the Julfans, Abbas I had first consolidated his power in the Caspian Sea area, where Gilan and Mazandaran were the two most important silk-producing regions. After Abbas I concluded the second civil war in 1590, Gilan and Mazandaran were turned into crown lands, to which *ghulam* governors were appointed. *Ghulam* viziers sent one-third of the revenues from these provinces to the royal household's treasury. This conversion into crown lands (1598 and 1599) and the ascendancy of *ghulams* as governors eclipsed the autonomy of local notables.[45] Shirvan was conquered in 1607 but never became crown land, even though its governors subsequently were *ghulams*, as in the rest of the silk-producing provinces.[46] These reforms mark the beginning of the important role played by the *ghulams* in the silk trade.[47] The silk trade also involved the relocation of Armenians and Georgians from the Caucasus to the Caspian shore in order to produce silk and grow mulberry trees.

Several European travellers, among them Jean Chardin and Pietro Della Valle, indicate that the Caspian region was resettled with populations from different towns of the Caucasus, but their testimonies do not concur. According to Della Valle, the Armenians who resettled there never worked with silkworms or mulberries but were asked specifically to grow grapes for wine.[48] Georgians were given the task of taking care of the silkworms. Jean Chardin, on the other hand, names both groups:

> That prince the mighty conqueror transported thither a prodigious number of People from Armenia and Georgia...seeing among other things that the Silk-Worms bred very kindly, and came to Perfection in those Parts. His mother who was of Mazendaran, which might of consequence be called his

native Country...solicited him on the other hand to repeople the Country... Abas caus'd towns to be built, and magnificent palaces to be erected, in several places of that Country, and all this to encourage the increase of the colony, but the malignancy of the air was so cross to his designs and projects, though laid and carried out with the utmost care and diligence and that when I was in Mazendaran with the court about forty years ago, the number of Christians was reduced to about four hundred families, from the thirty thousand that were there at first.[49]

Paul Ricault also speaks of the Armenians in the culture of the silk-worm in Armenia.[50] The Armenians of Julfa would come to the Caspian shore every year to take their share of silk for sale on the Ottoman markets. Most of the silk spun in Europe in early modern times was produced on the Caspian shore and in regions that are now part of northwestern Iran. In 1612, Abbas I built the town of Farahabad, a summer resort best described in a letter written from there by Pietro Della Valle, who visited Shah Abbas in January 1617.[51] He could oversee the region from this palace. Several important roads were constructed to facilitate the transport of silk. One ran the entire length of the Caspian shore, and the other ran from Farahabad all the way to the south of present-day Tehran.[52] To control the transport of silk, the Shah appointed many road guards (*rahdar*). A guarantee of safety on the road, the *rahdar* system was also an effective means of royal political control.

The New Julfans travelled to the Caspian shore and to the Ottoman markets annually. Abbas I deployed these seasoned Armenian merchants to fulfil his vision of a reconfigured empire at a moment in the seventeenth century when European demand for raw silk had accelerated. Julfan networks in the Ottoman and European markets facilitated their trade in gold and silver; their prominence and skills in exporting the silk produced in Iran proved to be critical to Abbas I.

THE SILK AUCTION OF 1619

The royal silk auction of 17 September 1619, presided over by the *ghulam* Muhibb Ali Bek, was pivotal in crystallizing the economic bonds between the Safavid household and the Armenian silk merchants. Pietro Della Valle and four English factors in Iran describe this event.

The EIC had already arrived on the Safavid scene as a new customer for raw silk but was outbid at this auction by the Armenians.

The English refusal to match the price left them with no silk that year. Della Valle wrote that the high price of 50 tumâns per load paid by the Armenians undercut the newcomers, who offered no more than 43.2 tumâns. A letter dated 16 October 1619, from the four company factors at Isfahan, confirms these numbers and the Armenians' cornering of the entire silk market.[53] The protests of the disappointed English target the relationship between the Shah and the Armenians. They also saw a bond with the *ghulams*, complaining that the 'officials of the Shah' refused to sell them carpets unless they conceded to the price for silk set by the Armenians. Suspecting that the Armenian price for silk was fixed in advance, the English expressed disbelief. They claimed it was the price of silk that the Shah required of the Armenians at their return from the Aleppo markets.[54] What they did not know was that the Armenians had an advantage, that royal silk was in fact consigned to them. A 1619 edict, discussed below, clarifies how the Shah allowed Armenians to purchase silk on credit, delaying their outflow of cash until their return from Aleppo and Bursa with European silver.[55]

Through the silk monopoly the Shah became the chief merchant in the country, thus disrupting the existing economic power of local notables in Iran. The Safavids had used other means to gain economic prominence. Documents studied by Jean Aubin show a mixture of land-ownership and mercantile activity among notables, even money-changing (*sarraf*) by wealthy Tabrizi families. The Safavids, who originated in Ardabil, had bought many of the land holdings of these local lords in order to consolidate their power.[56] This purchasing policy could not be employed throughout Iran. Shah Abbas now competed for economic preeminence by relying on Armenians and *ghulams*. As the 1619 silk auction brought the Shah what he had hoped for, a royal land grant was bestowed upon the Armenian merchants of New Julfa.[57] The land grant, dated Shawwal 1028 (September–October 1619),[58] turned New Julfa into a franchise, the dominion of the merchants.

A LOST PERSIAN SOURCE AND THE ROYAL MONOPOLY OF SILK

Discovered by Charles Melville, a lost Persian source, the *Afzal al-tavarikh*, preserves yet another contemporary edict that delineates the new silk monopoly imposed by the Shah in 1619.[59] This edict, which preceded the silk auction, further clarifies the relationship among the *ghulams*, the Shah and the Armenian silk merchants. It confirms English suspicions about the auction. It mandates that 'Whatever silk there was in every district be sold to the superintendent of the royal household (*sarkar-i khassa-yi sharifa*)'.[60] Merchants attempting to buy even a single *mann* should be restrained and punished.[61] The royal decree is addressed to the *ghulam* viziers and administrators of the provinces of Gilan, Shirvan, Ganja and Qarabagh, and cities such as Tabriz and Ardabil.[62] These provincial centres, where the silk was produced and transported, were important allies for maintaining the royal monopoly. The document specifies the Shah's prices for next season's production: a *kharvar* of silk (290 kilos) would be purchased from the producers for 30 Tabrizi tumâns. It further stipulates that Anatolian merchants could purchase directly if they paid 46 tumâns, 16 tumâns above the production price, suggesting the importance of the customary purchases of merchants from the Ottoman Empire. Most importantly, wealthy Georgian and Armenian merchants were consigned the region's main production of silk.

The silk of Gilan was consigned by decree to a Georgian Jew, Khoja Lalazar Yahud, who originally came from Kakheti but was deported to Farahabad along with a thousand households from his home town. The silk of Shirvan and Qarabagh, on the other hand, was consigned to Khoja Safar and Khoja Nazar of New Julfa, both members of the ruling Shafraz family. Most interestingly, this 1619 royal decree establishes a clear link between the provost and ruler of New Julfa, Khoja Nazar, and the Shah's silk factor, Muhibb Ali Bek. As the head of a highly organized network of Armenian merchants, Khoja Nazar employed many factors to travel and sell the silk in Europe and the Ottoman Empire for a 4 percent commission.[63]

The decree specifies that the silk reserved for the Armenians should be sold in the Ottoman Empire (*dar al-saltanah-yi Istanbul*), with

Khoja Nazar acting as the Shah's treasurer for the cash procured. Once he had bought the equivalent in scarlet, gold and Turkish textiles, he was required to send the proceeds to Muhibb Ali Bek in Isfahan,[64] whose position as tutor of the *ghulams*, discussed in the previous chapter, extended his political influence well beyond the harem. He controlled the royal silk trade and was depicted by Pietro Della Valle as the Shah's treasurer and silk factor. The Italian traveller also wrote that Muhibb Ali Bek had grown rich and that the Shah allowed him to run the silk trade as he pleased.[65] Of the silver revenues given to him by Khohja Nazar, one-sixteenth belonged to him legitimately.[66] Yet, according to Visnich, the Dutch factor in Iran, the royal monopoly of the silk trade was incomplete, and he alludes to silk being hidden by producers and sold abroad in secret. It would be unusual not to find any cheating in the sale of such an expensive commodity as silk, but it has led to the argument that the silk monopoly was not implemented.[67]

THE *GHULAMS* AND THE 1622 CONQUEST OF HORMUZ

The wish to secure Hormuz against the Portuguese, and the need for naval forces, explains the interest Shah Abbas took in the EIC despite his formal commercial deal with the Armenians. The 1622 victory over the Portuguese gave the control of Hormuz and Fars to the family of the *ghulam* Allah Virdi Khan, general of Abbas's armies. His son, Imam Quli Khan, a general like his father, wrested Hormuz, a main trading post, from the Portuguese. Bandar Abbas became the main commercial port for silk and for trade with India.[68] Imam Quli Khan played an important role in Abbas I's silk trade in two capacities. As governor of Fars and Jarun (Hormuz), he facilitated Armenian trade through the maritime transport of silk and silver. He was an intermediary between the English traders and the Shah.

As governor-general, Imam Quli Khan would expedite transport of the silk bought by the English in Isfahan to Bandar Abbas, personally granting the English exemptions from paying the road tax, or *rahdari*. He also served as a go-between in the negotiations among the English, the Shah and Mulayim Bek, the head merchant of Isfahan (*malik al-tujjar*).[69] Right after the fall of Hormuz, the Shah himself consented to the first trading privileges granted by Imam Quli Khan to the VOC. Thus, this slave governor of Fars imposed his own duties with the Shah's consent.[70] Bandar Abbas was all-important until under Abbas II it was overshadowed by Basra for silver imports to India. After 1640, the English ceased to export silk and, while the VOC export began only after 1623, it became a far more important trade.[71]

THE *GHULAMS* AND THE ARMENIANS END THE ROYAL MONOPOLY ON SILK

Whether or not it was ever totally implemented, the royal monopoly ended within a decade, upon Abbas I's death. The Armenians supported this break with trade restrictions by offering the Shah a substantial sum in gold at the monarch's enthronement ceremony. That the second person to greet the new Shah on the throne and to throw coins at his feet was none other than Khoja Nazar, the provost of New Julfa, does not preclude the pivotal role played by the Armenians in breaking the royal monopoly on silk, despite Safi's will.[72] The silk monopoly unravelled due to the efforts of some *ghulams* who had backed Safi's candidacy. This faction of *ghulams* was allied with rebellious forces in Gilan. Khoja Nazar and the Armenians he ruled were also allies of the notables in Gilan who revolted against the monopoly.

Upon the accession of Shah Safi in 1629, the famous eunuch Saru Taqi was the governor of two main silk-growing regions, Gilan and Mazandaran. Muhibb Ali Bek, the Shah's silk factor and the recipient of Julfan money, was disgraced. Saru Taqi attributed some fraudulent accounting and the embezzlement of half a million tumâns to Muhibb Ali Bek and Mulayim Bek, respectively the head merchant (*malik al-tujjar*) of Isfahan and the mint master (*zarrabibashi*). The latter was called 'the king's fiscal' by Thomas Herbert, who visited this *ghulam*'s palace in 1628. The Shah's silk trade was centralized in the hands of these two *ghulams* and Khoja Nazar of New Julfa under Abbas I; together they were the financial pillars of the silk trade.[73]

The disgrace of Muhibb Ali Bek and Mulayim Bek was the first major episode in a chain of events that would give power to a new alliance of slaves, among which Saru Taqi would rise to the rank of grand vizier.[74] A political shift, which gave more power to both these *ghulams* and to the Armenians, removed the restrictions on the sale of silk imposed by Shah Abbas I. In a related event, the silk depots of Gilan were looted during a revolt in 1629. According to the English, the Armenians were allied with the majority of Gilani notables.[75] The *Tarikh-i Gilan*, a history of the region written around 1630 by Abd al-Fattah Fumani, describes local resistance to the silk monopoly even under Abbas I.[76] This turn of events profited the ambitious Saru Taqi, who became grand vizier shortly after these events. In 1632 a VOC report states that most of Iran's silk trade was in the hands of Saru Taqi and a Jewish merchant, Khoja Davud.[77]

After the monopoly ended, Khoja Nazar continued to gather moneys from the Armenian silk trade and to deposit them in the *khassa*. Gold and silver imports were no longer handed to Muhibb Ali Bek, but rather to a new administration of *ghulams*. An edict of 1629 states that the eunuch Khwaja Sandal was to receive the sums due to the *khassa*.[78] As the Shah's silk factor was eliminated, the Armenians became the intermediaries for foreign sales. Letters from the Dutch and English factors show that they now hoped to buy from the Armenians on the Caspian shore.[79] The relationship between the Armenians and the English fluctuated wildly from mistrust to allegiance. These letters also make clear that the English had no source of information except Khoja Nazar and his messengers, whose information they had to accept.[80]

SILVER IMPORTS AND THE SALARIES OF THE *GHULAMS* IN THE MINTS

The Ottoman markets went through a period of silver debasement at the end of the sixteenth century. Iran, which depended heavily on the Ottoman transit of bullion, was no exception.[81] Importing bullion was crucial to the development of Iran's economy at the turn of the seventeenth century. The increased flow of bullion from the New World in the seventeenth century did not solve the constant scarcity of silver in Asia. The Ottoman markets remained the chief suppliers of silver and the Armenians its chief importers into Iran.

According to Jean-Baptiste Tavernier, the Armenians, chief importers of European silver from the Ottoman markets, deposited everything they brought in at the mints of Erevan or Tabriz.[82] Merchants could also choose to remit, for a fee, their silver further down the road, at the mint of Isfahan.[83] Silver and gold were turned into thread and local coins at the mints. During the previous century there were about seventy mints within Iran. The profits of minting went to local officials; before the reign of Shah Abbas the number was reduced to forty.[84] The heavy concentration of mints in Mazandaran and Gilan, the two main silk-growing regions, under Abbas I may well reflect the intensity of economic life in this region centred on the fully monetized silk trade.[85]

The aim of exercising court control over the mints through the *ghulams* has never been noticed. It parallels the attempt to control silk. That this Caspian region was newly controlled and governed by *ghulams* might well be a major factor in the consolidation of mints in this region under Abbas I. The *ghulam* viziers of the region were now the ones to profit from the minting in their provinces. They stood under the close supervision of the *mustawfi khassa*, the treasurer who controlled crown revenues.[86] The close association of the silk trade and of the mints under Abbas is perhaps best evident in the multiple functions held by the two high-ranking *ghulams* most prominent in the silk trade. Muhibb Ali Bek, better known as the tutor of the *ghulams*, also held several other titles: head merchant (*malik al-tujjar*) and controller of the assay (*mu'ayyir al mamalik*), as well as the title of mint master (*zarrabibashi*). Another *ghulam*, Mulayim Bek, also held all three titles.[87]

The ways in which silver revenues were channelled through the mints illuminate the financial links between the Armenian merchants and the *ghulams*. There were direct drafts on the mints for *ghulam* salaries, and part of the silver entering the mints was sent to the royal treasury in Isfahan for the purpose of the royal household's expenditure. Several *ghulams* who replaced the Qizilbash and the Persian landed notables as administrators of provinces required cash to pay an army of *ghulams* loyal to the Safavids in the provinces.[88] The salary of the *ghulams* in the army was taken from the royal treasury of the household. The silver and gold the Armenians imported into the mints provided the salaries and the incomes of the *ghulams,* as the following passage attests:[89]

> In the best years, when merchants brought from outside masses of *qurush*[90] coins and when, at the time of particular prosperity of Isfahan, 400 workers, all present, were daily employed in the Nine Departments of the Mint, and the fabrication of [plated] silver thread and copper coins was farmed out for 500 to 600, or 700 *tumâns*, the farm holder, on behalf of all the farm [given to him by the divan] used to send to the Treasury 1000 *ashrafis* [silver coins] and 100 *dastaja kila* [sic] [large *ashrafi* coins], which at the [given] rate were worth 250 *tumâns* approximately, and moreover used to pay 350 *tumâns* as salary to the Mu'ayyir, the *zarrabi-bashi* and other persons of the Private Household who were in possession of drafts (*arbab-i havalat*). Apart from the abovementioned sum, nothing else was sent to the Treasury. From ancient times until now, one sixteenth of the sum entering the Private [Royal] Household had been assigned to the Mu'ayyir al-mamalik [controller of the assay].[91]

The above excerpt from the *Tazkirat al-muluk*, a manual of Safavid administration, spells out exactly what sum went into the treasury of the royal household and the fact that certain officials were paid salaries directly by drafts at the mints. Other passages of the same manual show that the Shah profited directly, as he taxed all the coins minted. The controller of the assay was owed one-sixteenth of all the silver and gold entering the royal household as salary. He had several responsibilities, among them the reliability, weight and standardization of the coinage.[92]

The mints located at the frontiers such as the important ones in Armenia and Georgia continued to be very important under Abbas.[93] They were close to the Ottoman border, and since bullion imports came in from the Ottoman Empire and Russia, together with the mint at Tabriz they received the silver of returning merchants.[94] The Tiflis and Erevan mints were strategically located for silk traders; Tavernier goes on to explain that those who go to Gilan to negotiate silk go to the Tiflis mint, because the mint master there gives them two percent profit on their silver. He can manage this because the coinage he gives back is a little altered. They take it anyway because the coin is well accepted in Gilan.[95] This little aside is of further profit for them. The altered coin, which is what circulates in Gilan, is then used to purchase silk.

According to Zak'aria of Agulis, a merchant who was writing a diary in the middle of the seventeenth century, several Armenian mint masters succeeded each other at the important borderland mints of Tiflis and Erevan.[96] His own brother, Shemavon, was the agent for the khan of Erevan, one of the major tax-collecting stations, and head of the Erevan mint, one of the key stations for mandatory silver recoining. From Zak'aria's description, his brother's office was a very profitable one, and its tenure could be negotiated. Shemavon kept his office longer than the khan of Erevan. He retained his office at the mint under Najaf Ghuli, Abbas Ghuli and Safi Ghuli Khan.[97] It is clear from Zak'aria's description that his brother in the mints was a convert to Islam, while he himself remained Christian.

In his letters, Pietro Della Valle summarizes the role of the New Julfans: 'They are to the king of Persia like the Genovese are to the king of Spain, neither can they live without the king, nor the King live without them'.[98] That the Genoese were the bankers of the King of Spain is common knowledge, but that the New Julfan Armenians were the financiers of the Shahs has long escaped notice.[99]

CHRISTMAS WITH THE SHAHS

Silver and gold were also offered to the Shah and to the members of the royal household on the occasion of Armenian Christmas. The Shah's presence in New Julfa on Christmas Day marked his protection and was a day of tribute for the Julfans. Even though Christians were considered unclean (*najis*), sources such as the chronicle of the Carmelites mention that Abbas I broke the rules imposed by tradition and paid no attention to custom with the Julfan Armenians.[100] To mark the importance of the association of 1619, a few months after the auction Shah Abbas I granted the New Julfans the franchise of the land they lived on and attended Christmas.

On 6 January 1619, children as young as two months were baptized in the Zayanda River in the Shah's presence. Tavernier wrote:

> It is a wonder that these infants do not succumb to the cold when the season is a rough one. The king of Persia usually goes to this ceremony when he is in Ispahan and he goes to the riverbank on horseback accompanied by his grandees. After the ceremony he goes to Julfa, to the house of the kelontar, who is the governor or judge of the Armenians, where dinner is prepared.[101]

Tavernier witnessed two such events at the house of New Julfa's provost during the reigns of Shah Safi and Shah Abbas II. In these instances, the Shah's kitchen provided the feast itself, as had become the general rule since Abbas I. The Shah's gold tableware was transported to the host's house. Any host of appropriate rank wishing to invite the Shah gave the official in charge of the kitchens the sum of 20 tumâns (300 écus).

Pietro Della Valle was present at such a feast under Abbas. After the Christmas feast at the provost's house, a house described as covered with carpets and brocades, the Shah received magnificent gifts.[102] These were often purchased in Europe and worth at least 4000 or 5000 French écus, around 360 tumâns, according to Tavernier. The grandees of the royal household, in particular the eunuchs, also received gifts. Tavernier reveals that these were nothing compared to the principal gift, which went to the Shah's mother on Christmas Day. The value of these gifts may be measured by comparison with the salary of the chief of the harem, who earned 300 tumâns per year.[103] Furthermore, these enormous sums in cash, silver and gold were presented to the Shah in large gold basins. These gifts were in excess of the taxes on New Julfa. In a society where gifting remained a major economic factor, the gold and silver presented at Christmas were part of the exchange of patronage among the Armenians, the monarch and the courtiers.

THE DECLINE OF NEW JULFA AND
SILVER SHORTAGE IN IRAN

The financing of the *khassa* by the New Julfans was no longer as evident under Abbas II. The pivotal incident was the murder of Saru Taqi and the demise of the queen-mother, protector of New Julfa. The reign of Abbas II marked the height of the power of converted Armenians at court, yet it was a period of decline for the New Julfans. A *ghulam* of Armenian origin, Allah Virdi Khan, the son of Khusrau Khan, had been master of the hunt (*amir-shikar bashi*) for Abbas II since 1644, when the Shah was 11 years old. He arranged brilliantly organized *battues*, gaining the monarch's affection. He brought these strategic skills to the office of general of the *ghulams* or *qullar aqasi*, which he held until his death in 1663. This high position as head of the army gave him the power to install at court a Muslim-Armenian protégé, Muhammad Bek.[104]

Muhammad Bek was chosen because of his long-standing commercial experience as judge (*darugha*) of New Julfa, the second most important office after the provost. He was in contact with Allah Virdi Khan, as the master of the hunt was the official liaison between New Julfa and the court. The master of the hunt carried New Julfa's grievances to the Shah.[105] These two careers shed a new light on the political contacts there existed between the Muslim-Armenian *ghulams* and the Christians of New Julfa. In his rule of New Julfa the provost was seconded by *ghulams*. New Julfa, already in decline since the murder of Saru Taqi, did not fare well under the rule of these two *ghulams*, and was subjected to financial and political pressures, while Safavid Iran was experiencing an economic crisis. Saru Taqi's exactions, described in Chapter 1 had set a precedent.

Muhammad Bek became grand vizier in 1653. Previously, he had attained the post of *nazir*, the highest post in the *khassa*, having previously held the title of essayer of the mint (*mu'ayyir al mamalik*). During his tenure as grand vizier, he would take several measures in order to increase the flow of silver revenue to the Shah's treasury. He failed to curb the expenditures of the court and the army. He did enhance centralization with the integration of more crown lands (Hamdan in 1654, Ardabil in 1656–57 and Kirman in 1658), but it is believed that he did not manage to dictate adequate measures to the mints in order to adjust the coinage to the economic situation that was attributed to his mismanagement.[106]

Nevertheless, his failures should not mask the fact that during his tenure many of his family members successfully rose to occupy key financial posts both in the mint and for the export of silk and silver. Two of his brothers, Ushan Bek and Husayn Bek, were both *shah-bandar*, an office that controlled the important revenues of the port of Bandar Abbas. His brothers also held, but at different times, as he himself had before them, the title of essayer of the mint (*mu'ayyir al mamalik*). Later on Mohammad Bek's son, Amin Bek, was the assayer of the mint of Isfahan. One of his nephews held the post of vizier in the silk-producing region of Gilan and Lhaijan for as long as his uncle held the highest post in the country.[107] During most of the reign of Abbas II the commerce of silk and silver was controlled by Mohammed Bek and his family members. For the reign of Abbas II, there are no edicts to the New Julfans specifying the deposit of silver and gold in the *khassa*. The prominence of Armenian converts at court and their involvement in the financial administration of the realm is a token of the financial role played by this group of *ghulams* at court, as the role of the New Julfans seems to be eclipsed.

Muhammad Bek was made to step down as grand vizier in 1661. During the previous period, the orthodox *shari'a*-minded jurists greatly resented the rule at court of many Armenians converted to Islam.[108] Starting in 1645, and even more after 1661, the Caucasians in power at court, and the Julfan Armenians financially supporting this *ghulam* administration, became unwelcome as the power of the *ulama* grew at court.[109] There are other clear indications of yet another decline in New Julfa's status after 1661.[110] Although the grand vizier was made responsible for the economic crisis that was marked by a scarcity of silver, international factors were in great part responsible for the situation, as was the boycott of the mints on the northern borders of Iran by the New Julfans who stopped in Basra.

There was a general shortage of silver on the world market in this period. Ottoman prohibitions against its export never stopped the flow of silver to Iran.[111] In around 1640, the French, major importers of silver to the Ottoman markets, lost access to Spanish silver and started coining local silver coins that had very little silver content. They flooded the Ottoman markets with those debased coins.[112] Travellers have unanimously made fun of Ottoman credulity in accepting these coins, but Sevket Pamuk puts this silver shortage in perspective. There occurred a sizable decline in the output of silver from Ottoman mines, especially in the Balkans, and the coins were accepted in the absence of subsidiary coinage for daily exchanges on the market.[113] The debased coins on the Ottoman markets had an effect on Iran's economy during the reign of Abbas II, as it remained very dependent on the Ottoman markets. In addition, starting mid-century, the New Julfans seem to have taken most of their silver trade to Basra, in order to export it to India, where it fetched a higher price. They avoided the Safavid realm, which certainly contributed to the general economic crisis that the grand vizier failed to solve.[114]

Imports of silver and gold to Iran by the Armenians declined, because of both economic reasons (profit margins) and political causes. Though Safavid Iran experienced economic decline, the Armenian network continued to trade profitably – simply elsewhere.[115] It is possible that the Armenians' financial support of the *khassa* was already severed in the 1650s, when the last of the provosts of the Shafraz family ceased to rule over New Julfa and emigrated to Russia. It was clearly a family system, and Khoja Nazar's heir left Iran for Russia, which would become a new source of silver for Iran.

THE ECONOMIC ADMINISTRATION OF THE ROYAL HOUSEHOLD

As it has been done before, there is little need to describe the administrative organization of the *khassa*.[116] The administration of the royal household was separate from that of the state lands (*mamalik*).[117] Scholars believe that the formal separation of the two economic branches, the *khassa* administration and the *mamalik*, within the chancellery dates to the reign of Abbas I.[118] But many of these offices predate his reign. Grand viziers had control over the chancellery and the finance department within both the *khassa* and the *mamalik*.[119] Each of these two branches had an accountant that could be consulted, but the grand vizier was the one who had to seal and approve every transaction.[120] This may seem to underscore the power of grand viziers, yet, as will be made clear further, the grand vizier depended on the eunuchs in the harem, who held the seals.

The accountancy of the *khassa* was headed by the *mustawfi-yi khassa*, who ensured the flow of taxes and revenues from Isfahan and crown provinces like Gilan, Mazandaran and the ports of Bandar Abbas and Jarun. Since New Julfa was part of the *khassa*, this official would also receive the poll tax on the Armenians.[121] The *khassa* registry received, recorded and kept accounts for the revenues and expenditures of the royal household. The *mustawfi-yi khassa* was also in charge of seignorage and of the revenues of export and import, and therefore had many contacts with those involved in the silk trade, including foreigners such as the Dutch or the English.[122]

The economic department of the *khassa* was itself split into three different departments.[123] Chardin calls one of them the office of *Daftar kane tauzieh*, which is of interest here as it issued the drafts for payment of wages (*havala*) described above for the salaries taken from the mints. It also recorded the revenues of the Shah in great detail. Moreover, this department kept a record of who was in charge of administering which part of the revenue of the Shah and any changes in those revenues and assignations. Another office of the *khassa* organization is also of particular interest here. Chardin calls it *Defter kane lasker nuvis*; it was in charge of recording the names, the exact charges and the wages of all those employed in the royal household. Chardin uses the term *domestiques du roi*, the king's servants, and adds that the word *lasker* was used both for the army and the other administrative offices of the household.[124] The names of all the *ghulams* would appear in these records.

The pay scale of the *ghulams* serving in the army varied anywhere from 6 tumâns to 50.[125] Chardin is one among several sources to describe how slave soldiers and artisans serving the household were paid by the treasury of the *khassa*. He wrote that under Shah Abbas I the royal household had a *ghulam* force of ten thousand men. This army greatly diminished under Shah Safi and even more so under Abbas II. When he ordered a general review, according to Chardin, Abbas II saw the same men and the same horses march in front of him ten to twelve times. The soldiers were paid regardless of whether there was a war, or whether they ever even served. Young boys were entered in the payroll at age two, for the sum of half a tumân per year. They were presented to the Shah, who alone had the power to create a wage in perpetuity. According to Chardin, their wages were high.[126] This pay was assigned in drafts on specific locations, and in order not to travel to a mint or to the capital, the drafts were often sold by the *ghulams* for 50 percent of their value to obtain immediate cash and avoid the trip.[127] He also noted that in time of war the soldiers were given arms and ammunition but no provisions except for their pay in cash.[128] An army paid in cash depended on the court for wages. As discussed, cash was scarce under Abbas II. Since royal lands did not yield much cash, as many European travellers and the Persian administrative manual the *Tazkirat al-muluk* attest, the Julfan silver imports were imperative for maintaining this system. As discussed earlier, under Abbas II, the New Julfans were taking most of their silver directly to India via Basra, and New Julfan financing was no longer visible in Iran.

THE *NAZIR* AND THE ROYAL WORKSHOPS

Shahs Ismail and Tahmasb had already established several workshops for the weaving of silk and cotton at the beginning of the sixteenth century. The royal workshops (*buyutat*) were an integral part of the court, with some in the precinct of the palace itself and others located in the provinces. The royal workshops, *buyutat*, and the artisans employed in them, were units of the *khassa*. All of the workshops came under the authority of the superintendent of the royal workshops (*nazir-i buyutat*), with the exception of the mint, where the controller of the assay, also called the mint master, reported directly to court.[129] The pay of the artisans, the taxes they paid in goods or in labour and the quality of the goods they produced were all supervised by the *nazir*. This important post was held intermittently by a *ghulam* until the end of Abbas II's reign.[130] The superintendent (*nazir*) had to approve the goods produced annually by the workshops, thus controlling the consumption and expenditures of the household.[131]

He was responsible for fixing the price of the textiles produced, and summoned experts in order to determine this price. The Shah had to abide by that price.[132] It has been suggested that the *nazir* was the one responsible of fixing the price of the raw silk purchased by the Shah, and that this price was subject to negotiation, as with any other merchant.[133]

Much of Iran's best silk was sold within Iran and not exported. According to Chardin, the best silk workshops were in Yazd, Kashan and Isfahan, where various items of clothing, carpets and tents were produced. Other centres, such as Kirman, specialized in carpet production. Despite Abbas I's effort to curtail the domestic consumption of silk – he himself began to wear cotton as an example – courtiers and notables continued to indulge in this luxury. The quantity of silk used at court may be measured by the description of the vast size of royal tents and furnishings embellished with brocades of gold and silver thread.[134] The loss of all the Safavid accounting registers has masked the practice of keeping meticulous records of price and quality control for all 32 royal workshops at the court in Isfahan. The three accounting branches of the *khassa* recorded every entry, expenditure and salary.[135]

Although the *nazir* supervised the expenditures of the household, he depended on the grand eunuch who, according to Chardin, literally wore the key of the treasury around his neck.[136] The treasury in question was the storehouse for all precious objects of the court, such as jewels. Chardin, if we can believe him, describes a rare and rapid glimpse he was granted of the contents of the royal treasury, where he saw priceless pearls and rubies the size of eggs that no doubt would inflame the imagination of European readers for centuries to come. More importantly, while visiting in 1673, when the entry of silver into Iran was not at its height, he wrote the following: 'When I was at the Treasury, they drew a curtain in front of a wall, which I saw all covered up with bags, stacked upon each other all the way up to the ceiling. There could have well been three thousand bags, that I judged from their shape to be bags of silver.' He goes on to say that he was told that all the walls were similarly covered, and that each bag contained 50 tumâns of silver.[137] The important economic role played by the eunuchs, discussed in the previous chapter, has been overshadowed in European writings by the fantasies engendered by the harem. The royal treasury was the exclusive and reserved domain of the eunuchs; neither the grand vizier nor the *nazir* had any information about the actual contents of the royal treasury, because it was inaccessible to them. According to Chardin, in financial affairs the grand vizier took his orders from the eunuchs, who along with the queen-mother were the keepers of the seals necessary for validating documents. Keeping the seal was a function that would remain in the hands of eunuchs until the end of the seventeenth century.[138]

CONCLUSION

Scholars have already demonstrated a lack of social dichotomy between merchants and warriors in Mughal society, in which they have successfully brought down the firewall between the merchants and the military and the bureaucrats. Unlike in Europe, there was no distinct merchant class on this model, many rulers, administrators and land-owners were merchants themselves and people drifted in and out of trade. In addition, there was a structural interdependence between merchants and bureaucrats.[139] This social fluidity is very much the same in Iran.[140] Significant for establishing this fluid social model is not only the political status of the Julfans – as members of the *khassa*, and also as ambassadors and political representatives for the Shah abroad – but also the fact that some of the most important *ghulams* in administrative posts also held key commercial positions in the silk trade. Jean Aubin's work on Azerbaijan pointed the same way. It has demonstrated that major land-owners were also involved with commerce in India.[141]

The merchants of New Julfa were closely associated with the rise of *ghulam* administration in the first half of the seventeenth century through their financing of the *khassa*. Their silver imports were crucial and paid salaries and created profits for the *ghulams*. By the middle of the seventeenth century, the fortunes of New Julfa had begun to decline.[142] The murder of Saru Taqi in 1645 weakened the power of the queen-mother, Abbas II's mother, their protector. With them, New Julfa lost its main patrons at court and was subjected to conversions and economic hardships. Yet even under duress, only a few Armenian notables succumbed to conversion.[143] In addition to textual evidence, tombstones inscribed with the term *azat*, meaning 'free', testify to this fact. The word, of Iranian origin, was used in Sasanian times to denote class; it can be understood to mean 'noble or of noble origin'.[144] The seventeenth-century Armenian historian Arak'el states that the term was used on the tombstones of the notables of New Julfa to indicate that they were free citizens and not slaves.[145] Its use among the Armenians of New Julfa was intended to differentiate them from the *ghulam* members of the Safavid household, underscoring the predominance of the slaves in Safavid Iran's economy.

Given their ties to the *ghulams* and to the court, the Armenian merchants must be seen as an elite of Caucasian origin at the service of the Safavid shahs. Limiting our view of the Julfans to that of a Christian diaspora masks their crucial role in the political economy of the royal household. Part of that Armenian diaspora was Muslim, and there were ties between the two groups. In exchange for their skills and established international networks, the Armenians amassed wealth. Contrary to common belief, they constituted an elite embedded in the Safavid system, not merely a commercial bourgeoisie.[146] For the first half of the seventeenth century their interests converged with those of the slaves of the royal household.

The outlines of a planned political economy, which was structured on cooperation between Armenian merchants and *ghulams*, are difficult to trace after the middle of the seventeenth century. The different initiatives spelled out in a series of edicts (1619, 1629, 1631–32), discussed above, clearly demonstrate, at least in the case of the silk trade, that Iran's political economy depended on these two groups. New Julfa was granted a franchise in the same year – 1619 – as the Armenians successfully outbid the English for the Safavid silk trade. Simultaneously, the Armenians were granted the privilege of acting as the Shah's treasurer for silk traded in Ottoman territories. Abbas I had decreed (confirmed by Safi in 1629) that Armenians should deposit the silver reaped from the silk trade into the treasury for the administrators of the royal household. New Julfa was incorporated into the *khassa* by Shah Abbas and Safi's 1631–32 reinstatement, which continued their status within the same branch of government as the *ghulams*. Mid-century the prominence of the Christian Armenians is eclipsed as Muslim Armenian *ghulams* take central stage at court and in provinces crucial to the silk trade. Commerce and politics were closely intertwined, as the careers of several *ghulams* demonstrate. Some officials involved earlier in the silk trade, like Muhibb Ali Bek and Saru Taqi, were instrumental in the building of the capital of Isfahan, playing multi-faceted roles. The silver revenues of silk helped build one of the most beautiful capital cities in the world.

4

Launching from Isfahan:
Slaves and the Construction
of the Empire

This chapter redefines, through the intermediary of architecture, the *ghulams*' agency in the shaping of a cultural milieu. Forging relations between space and culture, it will demonstrate the ways in which the new composition of the royal household invested the *ghulams* with a leading role in the production of the built environment that both embraced and enunciated the authority and legitimacy of the reconfigured Safavid household, its political and military order and its economic infrastructure in the seventeenth century. Such a synthesis introduces into Safavid architectural studies a nexus among imperial, sub-imperial and provincial patronage. It further supplies ammunition to support our contention about *ghulam*hood in Safavid Iran. In this age of Safavid rule, *ghulam* patronage of architecture assumed substantial statistical and qualitative ascendancy over that of Qizilbash predecessors and contemporaries. Yet despite undertaking major imperial building projects, their claim to posterity remains, with a few exceptions, curiously understated. Powerful and wealthy *ghulams* built extensively, but rarely in their own name.

Because they were members of the ruling elite – the viziers, viceroys, governors, generals and other ranking court and government function-aries – the *ghulams*' architectural patronage in many ways paralleled that of other elites in preceding eras in Iranian history or in other Islamic lands. A normative feature of such patronage in pre- and early modern periods, whether funded by state treasury or by personal wealth, was the acknowledgment through titles of the reigning monarch under whose benevolent shadow the work was accomplished. Yet the patronage of the elite ordinarily extended well beyond building on behalf of the ruler, to include the charitable foundation of mosques, *madrasas*, tombs and even whole city quarters supplied with their own funds and carried out to their own glory. When funded from the individual's purse, the privilege of patronage, its extolling of the patron's piety, power and prestige, not to mention the legal protections of family fortunes under *waqf* (charitable) stipulations, was invariably advertised in either foundation inscriptions or contemporary historical sources. The extent to which the patronage of the *ghulams* in the seventeenth century conformed to or differed from this common formula reveals a different picture of the 'ties that bind'. As their predecessors and contemporaries had done, *ghulams* too exploited the potentialities of architectural patronage to inscribe the 'self' in the social space. Their agency, however, is chiefly manifest in the form of 'surrogate' patronage exercised on behalf of the royal household and its patriarch. Assuming anonymity in most such building projects, far from an expression of disempowerment, affirmed their links to the household, the generative locus of their elite status.

*Ghulam*hood inculcated loyalty and obedience in the service of the Shah. Regardless of the conditions preceding their entry into service or the vicissitudes of personal lives and careers, the *ghulams*, as we understand it, cohered into the Safavid royal household as into an extended family, with shifting balances and unpredictable alliances and outcomes just as in a biological family. Their precarious status as slaves notwithstanding, *ghulams* manifested their embrace of these familial ties not only in political and socio-economic terms, but also in the cultural spheres of art and architecture. In light of the family analogy, this chapter demonstrates how the *ghulam* members of the Safavid household, in that moment coinciding roughly with the first half of the seventeenth century, acted in unison to mould the Safavid vision of the 'City of Rule', to make Isfahan into the capital of the empire.

We understand the architectural and urban reconfiguration of Isfahan as one facet of the altered socio-military structure of the Safavid household. In this regard, the formation of Isfahan is conceptually analogous to that of Samarra, the new centre of Abbasid authority that was built in the ninth century on the foundation of the slave-military imperial household near the first Abbasid capital of Baghdad.[1] Samarra was a self-sufficient, gargantuan palace-city built to isolate and protect the caliph and his slaves from the dangers of Baghdad, where the rapidly growing and increasingly cosmopolitan population clashed with the imported slaves. Although its isolation as the capital of the Muslim commonwealth ended abruptly soon after its foundation, Samarra in its heyday was the preeminent centre of production for the political and cultural icons of the empire. Building types, such as the mosque, were transformed into lasting architectural forms, and new technologies, especially in ceramics and architectural decoration, reshaped the artistic landscape of the Islamic world. It was from Samarra that a unified language of art and architecture emanated and blanketed buildings and objects with a distinctive Islamic language of form and ornament, broadcasting symbols of the centralized empire.

The historical coincidence of building a new capital city and restructuring an imperial polity on the basis of a slave system recurred only in Safavid Isfahan.[2] The implementation of Shah Abbas I's vision of a divine kingdom on earth, its concomitant reforms and consolidation of the imperial household with its domestic, administrative and military slaves, also manifested itself in the shift to a new capital city and the shaping of its built environment. In 1590–91 CE (999–1000 AH), Shah Abbas I issued a royal decree to commence construction adjacent to the medieval city of Isfahan.[3] Unlike the Abbasid case, in which Samarra was built on virgin land and envisioned as a capital completely detached from Baghdad, Shah Abbas's new centre was built on a sparsely populated area adjacent to the old city, to which it was deliberately linked. Moreover, the new Isfahan was conceived as a city with a palace precinct, not a palace-city like Samarra.

The foci of the planned city, situated southwest of the old city, were a vast public square and a promenade (Fig. 2). The public life of the ruler and the ruled conjoined in the arena of the square (*maydan*), famed as the Maydan-i Naqsh-i Jahan or the Image of the World (Fig. 4). On its north side, an imperial bazaar complex (*qaysariyya*) linked the *maydan* to the ancient commercial centre of

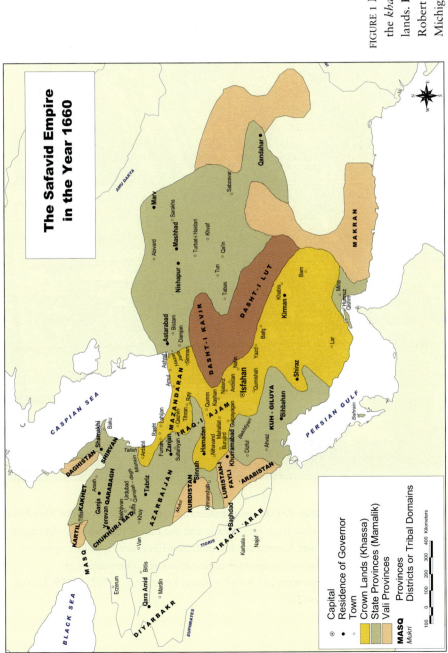

FIGURE 1 Map of Safavid Iran, the *khassa* and *mamalik* lands. Kathryn Babayan and Robert Haug, University of Michigan.

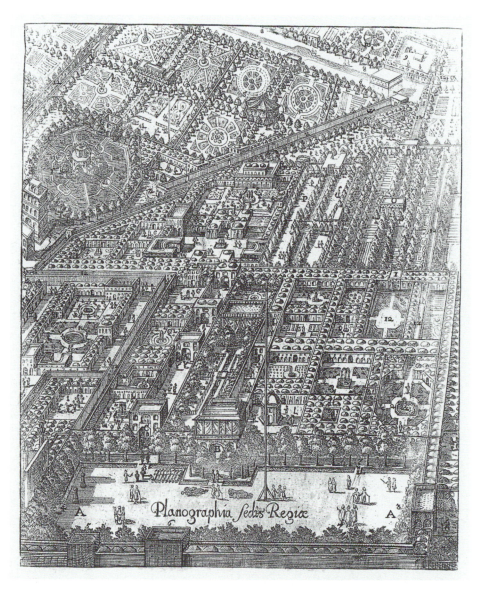

FIGURE 2 'Planographia Sedis Regiae', a seventeenth-century rendition of the Maydan-i
Naqsh-i Jahan, the Chahar Bagh promenade and the palace precinct (*dawlatkhana*)
of Isfahan; from Engelbert Kaempfer, *Amoenitatum Exoticarum, politico-physico
medicarum fasciculi, quibus continentur variae relations, observations et
descriptions rerum Persicarum et ulterioris Asiae*, Lemgovnia, 1712, p.179. Library
of Congress, Washington DC.

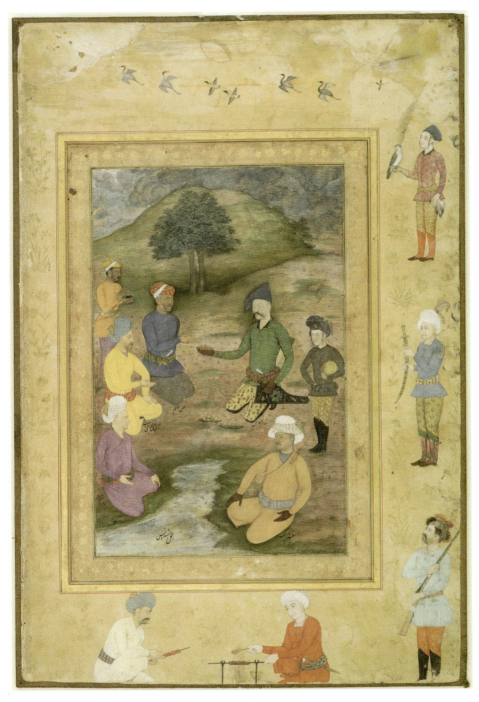

FIGURE 3 'Meeting of Shah Abbas and Khan Alam with Saru Taqi and Isa Khan' (Saru Taqi is seated on the lower left wearing a white turban), India, Mughal period, *ca.*1650, opaque watercolour and gold on paper. Boston, Museum of Fine Arts, Francis Bartlett Donation of 1912 and Picture Fund, 14.65.

FIGURE 4 Maydan-i Naqsh-i Jahan, Isfahan; view from the
qaysariyya with the Royal Mosque at the opposite end,
the Ali Qapu Palace on the right and the Shaykh Lutf-
Allah Mosque on the left. © Sussan Babaie.

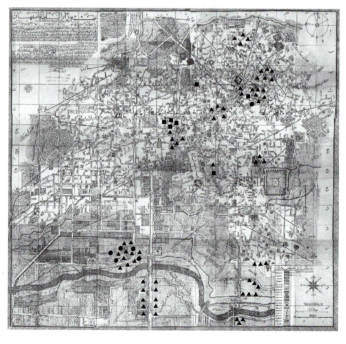

FIGURE 5 Map of
Isfahan with the
clusters of the
elite mansions,
culled from
descriptions by
Chardin in the
1660s and
1670s; after the
1924 map drawn
by Siyyid Riza
Khan. Sussan
Babaie and
Robert Haug,
University of
Michigan.

▲ houses of the *ghulams* and other government and court dignitaries
● houses of the wealthy merchants
■ houses of the high-ranking clergy

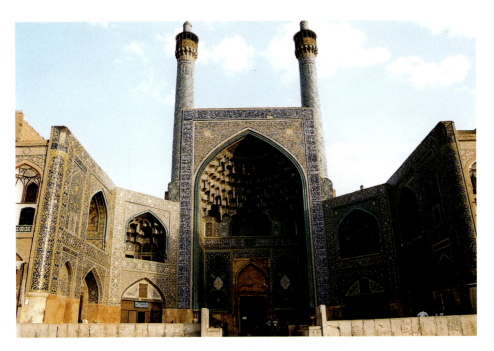

FIGURE 6 Royal Mosque, Isfahan, main portal. © Sussan Babaie.

FIGURE 7 Allah Virdi Khan Bridge, Isfahan. © Sussan Babaie.

FIGURE 8 Ganj Ali Khan Maydan, Kirman. © Sussan Babaie.

FIGURE 9 Ganj Ali Khan Mosque, Kirman, interior of the dome. © Sussan Babaie.

FIGURE 10 Saru Taqi
  Complex, lantern
  over the bazaar
  chaharsu and mosque
  portal, Isfahan. ©
  Sussan Babaie.

FIGURE 11 Ali Qapu
  Palace, Isfahan. ©
  Sussan Babaie.

FIGURE 12 'Standing Woman/Standing Man', two paintings mounted as an album page, inscribed (left) Sadiqi, seal impression, 'Abbas, slave of the king of Holiness', inscribed (right) to Ustad Muhammad Qasim, Iran, Qazvin (?) *ca.* 1590, opaque watercolour, ink and gold on paper. Washington DC, Arthur M. Sackler Gallery, Smithsonian Institution, S1987.305.

FIGURE 13 'The Assembly of Birds', from a manuscript of the *Mantiq al-tayr* ('Conference of the Birds') by Farid ad-Din Attar, present-day Afghanistan, Herat, 1486, rebound with four Safavid paintings, Isfahan, *ca.* 1600, opaque watercolour, ink and gold on paper. New York, Metropolitan Museum of Art, Fletcher Fund 1963 (63.210.11).

FIGURE 14 'Timur Padishah
Enthroned', from a copy of the
Habib al-Siyar ('Beloved of
Chronicles'), vol. 3, Iran, Qazvin,
1579–80, opaque watercolour and
ink on paper. Washington DC,
Arthur M. Sackler Gallery,
Smithsonian Institution, S1986.47,
folio 321r.

FIGURE 15 'Sea Battle off Hormuz
(Jarun) in 1623', from a copy of the
Jarun-nama ('Book of Jarun'), Iran,
1697, opaque watercolour and ink
on paper. London, British Library,
Add. 7801, folio 43a.

FIGURE 16 Three plates, China, early fifteenth century, porcelain with cobalt under colourless glaze. Tehran, Museum of Islamic Art.

FIGURE 17 Bottle, China, early
fifteenth century (with the
names of Bihbud and
Qarachaqay), porcelain with
cobalt under colourless glaze.
Tehran, Museum of Islamic Art.

FIGURE 18 'Royal Reception Scene',
right half of a double-page
composition, Iran, ca. 1620,
opaque watercolour and gold on
paper. Baltimore, Walters Art
Museum (10.691).

FIGURE 19 'Virgo', from a manuscript of the *Tarjuma-yi suwar al-kawakib* ('Translation of the Book of Stars'), Iran, Mashhad, 1631–33, colour wash, ink and gold on paper. New York, Public Library, Spencer Collection, Pers. ms. 6, folios 106v–107r.

FIGURE 20

'Sagittarius', from a manuscript of the *Tarjuma-yi suwar al-kawakib* ('Translation of the Book of Stars'), Iran, Mashhad, 1631–33, colour wash, ink and gold on paper. New York, Public Library, Spencer Collection, Pers. ms. 6, folio 121r.

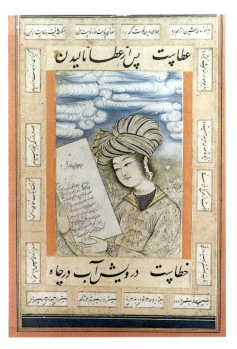

FIGURE 21 'Youth Holding a Folio', signed
by Muhammad Qasim, Iran, *ca*. 1630s,
opaque watercolour, ink and gold on
paper. Tehran, Gulistan Palace Museum,
Album 1629.

FIGURE 22 'Solomon and Bilqis
Enthroned', left half of a
double-page frontispiece, from a
manuscript of the *Shahnama*
('Book of Kings'), Iran,
Mashhad, 1648, opaque
watercolour and gold on paper.
England, Royal Library,
Windsor Castle, MS Holmes
151 (A/6), folio.

FIGURE 23 'Zal at Rudabah's Palace', from a manuscript of the *Shahnama* ('Book of Kings'), Iran, Mashhad, 1648, opaque watercolour, ink and gold on paper. England, Royal Library, Windsor Castle, MS Holmes (A/6), folio 55v.

FIGURE 24 'Zal at Rudabah's Palace', from a manuscript of the *Shahnama* ('Book of Kings'), Iran, Mashhad (?) 1645–55, opaque watercolour, ink and gold on paper. Tehran, Gulistan Palace, MS. 2239.

FIGURE 25 'Shah Abbas II and Nadr Muhammad Khan' (detail),
wall painting in the main audience hall of the Chihil Sutun,
Isfahan, *ca.*1647. © Sussan Babaie.

FIGURE 26 'Outdoor Drinking Party' (detail), wall painting
in one of the lateral rooms of the Chihil Sutun, Isfahan,
ca. 1647. © Sussan Babaie.

the city. A kettledrum house (*naqqarakhana*) above the entrance to the *qaysariyya* provided the traditional royal prerogative of fixing, with martial music, the time of daily and occasional rituals. Two-storey arcades with shops and coffeehouses formed the peripheral walls of the *maydan*. Directly across the royal bazaar stood the imperial congregational mosque, Masjid-i Jadid-i Abbasi, better known as Masjid-i Shah or the Royal Mosque. On the western and eastern sides of the *maydan*, a small private mosque for the royal household, Masjid-i Shaykh Lutf-Allah, and a five-storey palace known as the Ali Qapu (Lofty Gate) faced each other. Beyond the Ali Qapu lay the sprawling royal precinct (*dawlatkhana*). The promenade of Chahar Bagh (Four Gardens), to the west of the *dawlatkhana*, stretched for several miles, traversing the Zayanda River (running south of the city) over the Allah Virdi Khan Bridge and ending at the suburban royal palace of Hizar Jarib or Bagh-i Abbasabad. The Chahar Bagh functioned both as an artery linking the city with its new suburbs and as a space for public leisure.

Built over several decades, the city articulated Abbas I's principal impulse, as recorded by all the contemporary sources, to make Isfahan a true capital and to make it a throne-worthy abode.[4] In the decades following Abbas I's plans and constructions, the city expanded further, with additional residential quarters east of the river, and acquired a second major bridge and several new palaces.[5] While keeping the master plan of Abbas I remarkably intact, these projects, sponsored by Shahs Safi I (1629–42) and Abbas II (1642–66), further consolidated in the image of Isfahan the Safavid vision of centring the empire.

Open public spaces, mosques, marketplaces, arteries, residential quarters and royal precincts embody in their locations, shapes and linkages the conceptualization of Isfahan as the pivot of the reshaped Safavid universe. The grand urban plan conveyed this notion of centring in a number of ways. At the physical and symbolic heart of the new capital, the *maydan* had to rival and eventually eclipse the medieval urban centre of the city, where a powerful business district had grown around the venerated Great Mosque of Isfahan, a singular building renowned throughout the Islamic world and a point of enormous pride for the denizens of Isfahan. The old marketplace of Isfahan, known as Maydan-i Harun Vilayat, featured prominently in Abbas I's urban renewal plans, for he initially intended to modernize and rebuild those markets through royal commercial investments.[6] His initiative, however, was rebuffed by local land-owners, whose formidable resistance was anchored by their ancestral property, commercial capital and prominent civic roles in the city.[7] Robert McChesney has suggested that Abbas I, who may have originally envisioned the new *maydan* as a ceremonial, religious and entertainment arena, now had to incorporate the commercial facet of his centralizing plan into the built environment of the Maydan-i Naqsh-i Jahan. In order to compete with the long-established medieval religious and economic centre, the Shah had to unleash the prerogatives of his station.

On the economic side, the project entailed considerable capital investment, for purchasing vast tracts of property and construction on a massive scale, as well as long-term subsidies for the maintenance of the commercial facilities. The resistance of the wealthy local notables may indeed have led to the inclusion of the peripheral shops in the new *maydan*, but the fact that the royal bazaar ensemble of the *qaysariyya* was an integral part of the master plan affirms that some measure of economic hegemony had already been conceived as part of the reforms of Abbas I in the Isfahani phase. The final form of the *maydan* represents the full spatial articulation of the commercial interests of the royal household and its monopolizing tactics.

On the architectural side, the attractiveness and improved utility of a new shopping district coexisted with the more important attempt to manipulate the experience of the space. Placing the imperial mosque at the south end increased traffic through the *maydan*, especially during the obligatory noontime congregational prayer on Fridays. Subtler but no less effective was the location of the two lateral buildings (the Ali Qapu Palace and the private mosque), placed not in the centre but two-thirds down the length of the *maydan*. At the time of the construction of the *maydan*, the people of Isfahan entered its space through the cavernous, albeit lively, maze of the bazaar. And throughout the history of Isfahan as the capital, the formal entry point for all foreign visitors was from the northern flank. Seen from this vantage point, the principal buildings in the *maydan* are cast into a theatrical perspective, forming a visual climax for those about to traverse its length.

The *maydan* indeed became the theatre for staging imperial drama. There the court sponsored daily market displays, polo matches, fireworks, mock battles, state executions, military parades and royal processions, thus articulating a perpetual dialogue between the spectator and a panorama of imperial regalia, both human and material. Moreover, the siting of the towering palace of Ali Qapu on the threshold between the public square and the royal precinct encoded the actual as well as the imagined presence of the monarch.

Maydans have long been an urban fixture in Iranian cities, as elsewhere in much of the Islamic world. It is, however, in comparison to earlier *maydans* in Iran and other Islamic cities that the particular articulation of the arena for ritual and interaction in the new *maydan* of Isfahan comes into sharper socio-political focus. Abbas I's urban-renewal plan constitutes a significant facet of the debate in Safavid studies on the question of the very meaning of a capital city in the Iranian context. In the sixteenth century and prior to the transfer of the capital to Isfahan, the Safavids ruled first from the northwestern city of Tabriz, which proved vulnerable to repeated Ottoman invasions, and second from Qazvin in north-central Iran. While both cities were recognized as the 'seat of rule' (*dar al-saltana*), in Safavid administrative terminology the designation was neither fixed nor exclusive. The seat of rule was where the itinerant Shah resided, even if temporarily. This multiplicity of centres reflected the heritage of a tribal system of governance in which the base of authority was nomadic and hinged upon shifting balances between the monarch and the tribal confederacy of the Qizilbash, which provided both military and economic support.

As discussed in Chapter 2, these Turkman tribes had not only helped install the Safavid dynasty on the Persian throne in the first place, but also continued to sustain their hegemony by occupying key roles within the empire. By the time Abbas I ascended the throne in 1587, two civil wars had been fought in an attempt to define the Safavid–Qizilbash balance, nearly unravelling the Safavid dynastic fabric. Abbas I contained the political crisis by implementing reforms that curtailed the tribal authority of the Qizilbash, introducing military and administrative corps of slaves loyal to the Shah and the royal household rather than to tribal solidarities. The monarch, along with his slave corps, his patronized clergy and his protected Armenian merchant community, could now centralize his domain, and Isfahan was conceived of in this sedentarized chapter of Safavid history as the pivot from which Abbas I could rule.

In comparison to Tabriz and Qazvin, the urban development of Isfahan inaugurated a new chapter in the spatial articulation of Iranian cities, one in which, moreover, the centralizing tendencies of Abbas I and his successors came to be expressed in the built environment. The little we know about Safavid Tabriz relies on literary evidence, and much of Safavid Qazvin has fallen prey to destruction.[8] As in all medieval Persian cities, *maydans* framed some of the chief royal, administrative, religious and economic functions of the city. Yet there is no precedent for the full consolidation of all the social enterprises of the city such as that devised for the *maydan* in Safavid Isfahan. In Tabriz the principal *maydan* of Shah Ismail (1501–24) was inherited from the city of the deposed Aqquyunlu dynasty. By the middle of the sixteenth century the *maydan* was delineated by three mosques, *naqqarakhana* and, apparently, the outer walls of the royal palace gardens (containing the Aqquyunlu Hasht Bihisht pavilion as the main royal residence). Its open space, like that in Isfahan, served for court-sponsored festivals such as those marking the end of the month of fasting ('*Id al-fitr*), for ritual enactment of the expression of loyalty to the Shah by Qizilbash devotees and for polo and other equestrian entertainments. As an assemblage of both old and new buildings, however, the *maydan* in Tabriz never assumed the architectural definition that was to characterize the Isfahan *maydan*.

In transferring the seat of rule to Qazvin, Shah Tahmasb (1524–76) constructed a royal precinct with ceremonial, governmental and residential functions of the court distributed among pavilions set in gardens. The precinct obliquely bordered on a vast rectangular *maydan* known as Maydan-i Asb-i Shahi (royal equestrian square). Here again the court sponsored festivals, military parades, executions and equestrian shows. The *maydan* in Qazvin also served as a space for the mobilization of the cavalry in preparation for wars. As Maria Szuppe has noted, the Safavids in the sixteenth century departed from the tribal practices of preceding eras by bringing this generally extramural function of the army into the centre of the city.[9]

Most scholars contend that Qazvin provided the prototype for the *maydan* in Isfahan. There are indeed several aspects of the *maydan* in Qazvin that would support such a view: its large size and rectangular shape, the proximity of the palace and some of the functions this open space came to serve. Yet, lacking peripheral structures such as mosques, bazaars or other institutions architecturally to define its boundaries or specify its functions, the *maydan* in Qazvin remained a relatively undifferentiated space for royal and military performances.

Compared to Qazvin, the architectural, functional and ritual differences in the conception of the *maydan* in Isfahan signify a radical transformation in the evolving notion of the city centre. The precise architectural definition of this city square and the deliberate juxtaposition of the major institutions that anchored the centralized empire invest the *maydan* in Isfahan with unprecedented clarity of purpose and intensity of expressive meaning. With its mixed uses carefully interwoven, the *maydan* configured the stage for a wide spectrum of action and interaction ranging from commerce to piety to ritual, thus ensconcing community and arbitrating social life at the core of the capital and, by extension, the empire.

The *maydan* area, however, forms only one facet of the notion of centring represented in the built environment of Isfahan. New suburban residential quarters constitute the other significant zone of imperial design. During the first two decades of the seventeenth century, urban development extended to housing the displaced merchant families from Tabriz southwest of the city on the northern banks of the Zayanda River, and the Armenian community on the southern bank. In time the Tabrizi quarter, or Abbasabad, grew into a thriving neighbourhood, with some of the wealthiest long-distance traders building their mansions in this well-appointed quarter.[10] The Armenian suburb of New Julfa developed into a self-sufficient satellite city with churches, markets and other services as well as thousands of houses, among which could be counted some of the stateliest mansions in all of Isfahan. Their proximity to the court in urban terms and their conspicuous display of wealth, especially telling for their echoes of the palatial architectural and decorative features, underline the privileged status and the pivotal economic role of the Armenian merchants, as discussed in Chapter 3.

The Chahar Bagh promenade provided the arterial linkage for these new quarters to the centre of commerce, politics and piety. Like all the renowned boulevards of major cities of the world, the Chahar Bagh served multiple urban functions: it was a space for transition from residential to public arenas; it was a place of leisurely strolls, picnics and social intercourse; and it marked the potential for prime property. The latter potential, however, was the purview of the Shah. Soon after the construction of the Chahar Bagh, Abbas I commanded court and government dignitaries to build their mansions in adjoining parcels of land along the portion of the avenue south of the river. Here, facing one another, stood magnificent gateways, each leading to sprawling gardens with pavilions and mansions of the most notable functionaries and servants of the court. Powerful and wealthy slaves of the household, such as Qarachaqay Khan, the converted Armenian *ghulam* governor of Khurasan, and Allah Virdi Khan, the commander-in-chief, resided in this area. Other mansions are known by the official positions or titles of their owners to have belonged to *ghulams* and eunuchs.[11] Although not all *ghulams* lived in the Chahar Bagh area, the deliberate clustering of the new elites in these upscale, planned neighbourhoods visibly manifested the structuring of the imperial household and its base of power and authority (Fig. 5). The fact that governors of provinces would feel the urge, or were expected, to maintain a stately residence at Isfahan further underscores the city's centrality as the capital of the empire. Such an urban strategy, too, is unprecedented in Iranian history.

Besides constructing suitable mansions to make visible their exalted status, the *ghulams* helped fashion an imperial architectural agenda that encompassed a wide range of building types. As discussed below, their architectural agency ranged from mosques and palaces to building the infrastructure with bridges, roads and dams, to mass housing projects, commercial centres and even brand-new cities. Whether in the capital or the provinces, *ghulams* carried out large-scale architectural and urban plans both on behalf of the monarch and independently, while always remaining surrogate patrons loyal to the vision of the Shah.

Although it took more than three decades to complete, the master plan of Isfahan and its principal architectural features remained remarkably intact for the next one hundred years of Safavid history, while much of the subsequent royal architecture in Isfahan focused on the building of palaces. Beyond the record of the Shahs' patronage, the history of Safavid Isfahan has left us little about the individuals who helped materialize the architectural expression of this imperial vision. Most of the architects and engineers remain unknown, so understanding the creative and practical processes of design and construction depends largely on conjecture. Yet the role of the *ghulams* in the building of Isfahan illuminates not only the corporate nature of the production of architecture, but also more importantly, the role of this new elite in Safavid architectural patronage. Their building record reveals and corroborates their emerging function in the Isfahani phase of Safavid politics and economy.

A *farman*, or royal decree, issued in September 1614 CE (Sha'ban 1023 AH) for the construction of a cathedral in New Julfa, the Armenian suburb south of the river, offers remarkable insight into the parameters of the *ghulam*-patron's job.[12] According to the decree, and in order to show royal favour to his Armenian and Christian subjects, Abbas I ordered a lofty church to be built on a plot of land granted by the Shah himself. The cathedral was to house some remaining sacred stones from the ruined church of Edjmiazin near Erevan, which the Shah had ordered to be transported to Isfahan for this purpose.[13] He appointed the alderman (*darugha*) of Isfahan (traditionally a Georgian prince-*ghulam* of the royal household) and the tutor of the *ghulams*, Muhibb Ali Beg Lala, to choose a suitable site and take royal architects to survey the land and begin the project. The decree further stipulated that the building design was to be devised jointly by Muhibb Ali Beg Lala, the vizier of Isfahan, and the (unnamed) architects; the blueprints, on wood panels and paper, were to be sent for the Shah to review; then the master builders could begin their work.[14]

Although the decree appears to leave the cost of construction to the church fathers to bear, it clearly reveals the degree of interest and involvement of the Shah. This was to be a major church in the newly constructed Armenian suburb. The land was a royal gift, and the Shah had intended to invest the church with heightened sacral importance by ordering the transfer of the revered stones from Erevan.[15] What is particularly significant here is the exertion of royal control over the design of the building.[16] Surely the Armenians knew how to build a church; yet it was the *ghulam* Muhibb Ali Beg Lala (and his unnamed *ghulam* partner) who was entrusted with the task of overseeing the plans and the project.

The political sword of Muhibb Ali Beg Lala had a double edge. Not only was he the all-important tutor of the *ghulams*; he was also the 'supervisor of the royal buildings in Isfahan' (*sarkar-i imarat-i khassa-yi sharifa-yi Sifahan*).[17] At the height of his career during the first two decades of the seventeenth century, and in his capacity as the chief official for royal building campaigns, he was put in charge of the housing project for the refugees from Tabriz.[18] Under his supervision (*bi sarkari*), five hundred houses were constructed in four quarters surrounding an intersection of bazaars (*chaharsu*) in the Bagh-i Jannat area west of the Chahar Bagh avenue and north of the river.[19] Furthermore, he acted as the chief supervisor for the hydraulic project to divert water from Kuhrang Mountain to Isfahan, until he was replaced in 1620 by another *ghulam*, Imam Quli Khan, the son of Allah Virdi Khan and his successor to the governorship of Fars.[20] And at least one caravanserai in Isfahan bears the name of the tutor of the *ghulams*.[21]

Muhibb Ali Beg Lala is, however, best known for his personal involvement in the construction of the Royal Mosque, the first congregational mosque to have been built in the city since the Saljuq Great Mosque of Isfahan (Fig. 6). It was situated strategically on the south side of the great public square (*maydan*), and the foundation inscription on its portal, dated to 1616, records Muhibb Ali Beg Lala as the contractor or supervisor (*mushrif*).[22] Robert McChesney has suggested that the principal responsibilities of Muhibb Ali Beg were probably to procure land, to organize labour and building supplies, and to ensure the steady progress of construction.[23] Various traditions concerning the acquisition of the land for the mosque indicate that many high-ranking court functionaries benefited from the clearing of the surrounding area, among them Muhibb Ali Beg Lala, who seems to have had a residence in the vicinity of the mosque.[24] Muhibb Ali

Beg's role in the organization of labour and construction materials, on the other hand, depends on a reasonable analogy with another supervisory task recorded for a 1593 building of a temporary residence on the edge of the palace precinct.[25] Rather exceptionally in the case of the Masjid-i Shah, sources attribute the building plans (its design and engineering) to two named individuals: Ali Akbar al-Isfahani, whose name is inscribed on the foundation plaque, and Badi' al-Zaman Tuni, who is identified with the early stages of the design in one of the contemporary chronicles of Abbas I's reign.[26]

As is evident from the cases of the church and the mosque, the tutor of the *ghulams* would certainly not have been equipped to devise and execute the mosque's design. Yet what is so clear as to be obvious, but still needs to be stated, is that no building of such scale and importance would have gone up without the 'creative' engagement of the persons in charge. Admittedly, it would be difficult to measure the creative input of the supervisor/contractor, especially since in the normative art-historical approach, we tend to credit only patron and architect. Middlemen such as Muhibb Ali Beg Lala remain just that, bridges to facilitate the materialization of somebody else's vision. Nevertheless, the outlines of the architectural side of Muhibb Ali Beg Lala's career (between 1611 and 1619) point to a more engaged presence than that of a mere contractor. In the mosque project, he was not simply attending to his 'job'. Rather, he had made a considerable personal investment by donating no less than 30 percent of the total endowment of properties and revenue from various sources, thus trailing only the Shah himself in his *waqfs* (endowments) for the mosque.

More importantly perhaps, Muhibb Ali Beg Lala was also appointed administrator (*mutivalli*) of the endowments, an office that in the sixteenth century was either reserved for blood members of the Safavid family, as in the Ardabil shrine, or entrusted to religious notables, the *ulama*. And although Muhibb Ali Beg was not alone in residing near the mosque, his mansion's location close to the court, his sphere of political influence and his prominent role in the construction and maintenance of the new congregational mosque, where his name appears on the portal inscriptions, communicate the symbolic and practical charge of this *ghulam*'s status.

His substantial gift to the chief congregational mosque of the new city should be understood as an expression of the loyalty of a household slave whose ambitious acts of piety and generosity further confer, as well as emanate from, his status as a member of an elite of the realm. His case parallels that of Qarachaqay Khan, the Armenian *ghulam* governor of Khurasan, who donated (or was forced to donate) his own collection of porcelain to the Safavid ancestral shrine at Ardabil. Qarachaqay Khan's patronage and collections are discussed in the next chapter of this book. Here it suffices to note that these *ghulams* offered such gestures of piety and generosity in unison with the family patriarch. Shah Abbas I himself initiated the act of giving by making the entire *maydan* area a *waqf* in the name of the Fourteen Infallibles (the 12 Shi'i imams, the Prophet and his daughter Fatima) and by donating his own collection of books and porcelain to the Ardabil shrine.[27]

As is evident from his multifaceted role – the chief royal buildings' superintendent, the supervisor of the mosque project, the endower of a major portion of funds for the mosque and a loyal servant of the Shah – Muhibb Ali Beg had every incentive to shepherd the construction to its best possible architectural outcome. In other words, it would be reasonable to assume some creative input on the part of the *ghulam* functionary, although its proof may not be forthcoming in the sources. Similarly significant in this regard is the role of the superintendent of royal architectural works, through whose office Abbas I ensured the suitability of the design – and its royal source of patronage – of the Armenian church. In this light, one wonders whether the appropriation of the building and decorative style of local Isfahani architecture in the New Julfan churches, in general, is not, at least in part, a reflection of such measures of creative control.

A significant portion of public architecture in the first half of the seventeenth century involves the *ghulams* in a supervisory capacity akin to Muhibb Ali Beg Lala's. The magnificent bridge linking the Chahar Bagh avenue with the suburbs south of the Zayanda River bears the name of Allah Virdi Khan, the famous converted Georgian *ghulam* general of Abbas I (Fig. 7).[28] Completed in 1607, the bridge deservedly counts among the masterpieces of Persian architecture and engineering. Until recently, there was no record of the bridge's professional builders and designers. Thanks to Charles Melville, however, we now have the name of the architect, Mir Jamal al-Din Muhammad Jabiri.[29] As in most such cases, little is known about this architect to whose genius the brilliant engineering must chiefly be owed. Nevertheless, Allah Virdi Khan was entrusted with its construction (*ihtimam-i sakhtan-i an*). As the surrogate patron, acting on the orders of the Shah and on his behalf, it would be reasonable to assume that he too, like the tutor of the *ghulams*, played a substantial role in all stages of design and construction of the bridge.

Allah Virdi Khan is furthermore credited with several important building works in Fars and elsewhere: a large double dam near Sarab to conduct water to Shiraz (known as Nahr-i Abbasi);[30] a fortification around a village in Fars; a large *qaysariyya*, or royal market, in Lar, which Figuera, the rather haughty Spanish ambassador to the court of Abbas I, praised as so beautiful as to compete with the best of European buildings; and a stately house near Nahavand for Abbas I.[31] Allah Virdi Khan also initiated the construction of a spacious, and architecturally notable, theological college known as Madrasa Khan in Shiraz as a teaching base for the famed scholar Mulla Sadra.[32] The *madrasa* was completed in 1615 by his son Imam Quli Khan, who succeeded his illustrious father as governor of Fars.[33] Clearly, many of these constructions were intended to invigorate the governor's appointed province and to concretize the extent of his power and wealth. Yet the patronage of a converted *ghulam* for a high-calibre centre of teaching, for example, serves to illustrate the degree to which *ghulams* came to participate in the dissemination of the religious policies of Abbas I.[34] The *ghulam*-governors' other building works also reflect the concerted centralizing efforts of the Safavids in that, unlike their Qizilbash counterparts, much of their architectural patronage remained in the realm of public amenities and infrastructure, thus bringing the commercially and strategically significant province of Fars firmly into the imperial orbit.

Allah Virdi Khan's distinction may be gauged by the location and architectural elegance of his own tomb in Mashhad.[35] Abutting the northeastern wall of the domed shrine of Imam Riza, the *ghulam*-general's tomb is a two-storied octagonal structure with marble slabs and tiles sheathing the interior. Iskandar Beg Munshi records that a few days before Allah Virdi Khan's death in May 1613, his appointed supervisor for the building of the tomb met with the ailing general. Allah Virdi Khan inquired about the progress of work on his tomb, to which the supervisor, a 'simple Turk', responded that all was beautifully carried out and awaiting the general's arrival. The Turk's premonition aside, his humble status, noted by the historian, does not warrant much creative credit to this supervisor, for the tomb is architecturally and decoratively quite inspired. Instead, the anecdote, far from detracting from the significant role of the supervisor, should highlight Allah Virdi Khan's own involvement in the design and execution of his tomb. Having already overseen architecturally magnificent projects such as his namesake bridge, he brought to his tomb the personal edge that one expects for the fashioning of a final resting place, especially considering that his tomb was one of only two such private mausoleums in the sacred precinct, a site reserved for royalty.[36] In building a tomb for himself and in such a symbolically and religiously charged site, Allah Virdi Khan stands alone among his fellow *ghulam* functionaries of Safavid Isfahan. His tomb manifests the lofty position he held in the eyes of Abbas I, who in fact respected him as a father-figure. Such familial bonds guaranteed a trusted status that was denied his Qizilbash peers but was in principle shared by other notable *ghulams* of this age.

One such loyal servant was Ganj Ali Khan Zek, a Kurdish *shah-sevan* devotee of Abbas I, and his appointed governor to the province of Kirman.[37] In Safavid history, Ganj Ali Khan is memorialized by his construction of a remarkable *maydan* complex in Kirman that decisively altered the face of the city and enhanced its trade functions. A Kurd by origin, Ganj Ali Khan grew up in Herat with Abbas I when, as a prince, Abbas Mirza was entrusted to the care of Ali Quli Khan Shamlu, the Qizilbash governor of Khurasan. The memory of their childhood friendship lived on into adulthood when Abbas ascended the throne in 1587. In forging bonds of brotherhood, Ganj Ali Khan tirelessly accompanied the Shah on nearly all his military campaigns until his own death in 1624.

In 1596, Abbas I appointed Ganj Ali Khan governor of Kirman. Both the timing and the choice for the governor are crucial to our discussion. Kirman in the sixteenth century had become the domain mainly of the Afshar tribe. As was the norm for much of the first century of the Safavids, Qizilbash overlords, including the Afshars of the province of Kirman, enjoyed considerable autonomy. In fact, Biktash Khan, the last governor of Kirman before Abbas I had succeeded to the throne, was so independent and powerful that he assumed complete control over the two provinces of Yazd and Kirman, entertained the annexation of Fars into his dominion, and amassed legendary wealth. Biktash Khan's resistance to the central-izing policies of Abbas I coincided with similar reactions by Ya'qub Khan, the Zu'lqadr governor of Fars. Together, these two governors presented Abbas I with a rebellious front that was subdued only by the elimination of the opposing parties at the conclusion of the second civil war.[38]

The appointment in 1595 of Allah Virdi Khan as governor of Fars, and in 1596 of Ganj Ali Khan as governor of Kirman, should be seen as evidence of the Shah's sustained efforts to regain full control over the south and the principal links to the maritime trading ports on the Persian Gulf. As such, both men participated in Abbas's dismantling of the Qizilbash hegemony. Ganj Ali Khan's *shahsevani* sentiments, his long years of loyal service and his close ties with Abbas I's household must have rendered him a safe choice to succeed the unruly Afshar tribal chiefs. As a gauge of Abbas's confidence in Ganj Ali Khan, his Kirman post in fact fades in comparison to his appointment as governor of Qandahar after Abbas's conquest in 1618 of that commercially and politically sensitive city, over which intense rivalries had been raging among the Safavids, the Mughals and the Uzbeks.[39]

Like Allah Virdi Khan and Qarachaqay Khan, the other surrogate brothers of the Shah, and the high-ranking *ghulam* functionaries, Ganj Ali Khan too maintained a residence in Isfahan. But his was even more privileged in that his multi-storied octagonal pavilion was located on the southern bank of the Zayanda River, along the side where only royal retreats were to be found; a parallel case to the tomb of Allah Virdi Khan in Mashhad.[40] More revealing, however, is the *maydan* of Ganj Ali Khan in Kirman, a project that preserves the most remarkable remains of Safavid town planning outside Isfahan (Fig. 8). His *maydan* can further serve as an indicator of the architectural and urban sophistication of other towns built at the command of Abbas I, such as those in Mazandaran, no longer extant, the construction of which was supervised by the eunuch-*ghulam* Saru Taqi (more on him below).

Ganj Ali Khan's ensemble comprises a rectangular space articulated on three sides by the rhythmic march of an elegant arcade and on its eastern side by a two-storey caravanserai.[41] The caravanserai side houses a few shops opening directly onto the *maydan* as well as a small mosque, adjacent to and accessible from inside the caravan-serai on the northeastern side. Vaulted inner passages, behind the arcade, give way to spacious shops and form a linked bazaar around the other three sides of the *maydan*. Each flank is further marked by a major building set back behind the vaulted bazaar artery and serving public and governmental functions: the *zarrabkhana* (mint) on the north, the famed *hammam* (bath house) on the south, and a cistern, built by Ganj Ali Khan's son, on the west. In its essential operative features, both facilitating and concentrating the commercial flow of the city, Ganj Ali Khan's *maydan* resembles the new *maydan* in Isfahan. Although nearly sixteen times smaller in area (the Isfahan *maydan* measures more than eighty-five thousand square metres; the one in Kirman about five thousand) and streamlined in its architectural and functional articulation, Ganj Ali Khan's *maydan* closely parallels the *maydan* in Isfahan in its conceptual formalization of public space.

Yet Ganj Ali Khan's patronage exercises a degree of restraint that once again indicates the particularities of the familial relationships between such loyal servants and the patriarch. Devoid of any architectural pretence to exaggerated images of power or authority – lacking any royal or ceremonial space on the *maydan* itself – Ganj Ali Khan's *maydan* nonetheless includes a superbly refined and elegantly decorated reception porch inside the caravanserai located on the side of the inner courtyard that is directly across from the entrance gate.[42] Similarly royal in conception is the little mosque on the side of the caravanserai, where a simple doorway, set deep inside a vaulted hall, hides the exquisitely proportioned interior space of the mosque, with its soaring central dome, a small royal balcony and intensely painted mural decorations (Fig. 9). As if cognizant of the potential for royal displeasure should he flaunt his personal wealth and local status, Ganj Ali Khan brought in these touches of discreet architectural glamour signifying his personal status at the same time that he provided a suitable venue for royal reception. What is also noteworthy is Ganj Ali Khan's employment of artists from Isfahan, such as the celebrated calligrapher Ali Riza Abbasi, whose designs graced the two royal mosques on the Maydan-i Naqsh-i Jahan. Similar interface in *ghulams'* patronage between the centre and the provinces characterizes the arts of the book produced for the family of Qarachaqay Khan discussed in the next chapter.

In light of the timing of the appointment of Ganj Ali Khan and his relationship to the Shah, the conception of the *maydan* complex in Kirman may be recast not so much as a personal initiative by Ganj Ali Khan as one facet of the new governor's efforts on behalf of the Shah to bring the newly recovered city and province in line with the centrally inspired intentions of the imperial household. The similarity in spatial composition of the *maydan*'s shopping arcade to that of the *maydan* in Isfahan may testify to this flow of inspiration from the centre outward. Moreover, Ganj Ali Khan's complex recalls Shah Abbas's ensemble in some other unexpected ways as well. A *waqf* document dated 1605, in which the khan calls himself the slave of the imperial house, *ghulam-i dargah-i shahi*, records the endowment of the entire complex and other property of the khan's family.[43] The complex was made *waqf* in the name of Imam Riza, the administration of the *waqf* was to be in the hands of the khan and his male descendants, and the *maydan* area had forcibly to be cleared of the original shops, inns and houses that surrounded it. In all its important features, this *waqf* deed parallels the one Shah Abbas made for the Maydan-i Naqsh-i Jahan and its buildings. The Isfahan *waqf*, also made in 1605, was in the name of the Fourteen Infallibles; the Shah himself and the Safavid shahs to rule after him were to be the executors, and some of the land was purchased forcibly.

In considering the architectural patronage of *ghulam* dignitaries, however, none compares to that of Mirza Muhammad Taqi, known as Saru Taqi (d. 1645) – so nicknamed by Abbas I because of his fair hair.[44] Building works by Saru Taqi – construction of brand new towns and major commercial roads, restoration and refurbishment of the venerated Shi'i shrine of Imam Ali in Najaf (present-day Iraq), completion of a *madrasa* in Qazvin, a fundamental alteration to the Ali Qapu Palace in Isfahan, two mansions, two mosques and a caravanserai, also in the capital, among other construction – bespeak an extraordinary degree of royal trust and personal influence.

Raised in a Muslim family of noted administrators from Tabriz, Saru Taqi in his youth entered the military in Isfahan. His future, however, lay in administrative posts: he began as financial comptroller for the governor of Ardabil and rose as high as grand vizier toward the end of his life. Saru Taqi's flourishing career during the reign of Shah Abbas I, his castration by order of the Shah, his status as a eunuch-*ghulam* and his ascent to the second-highest position in the Safavid polity have been discussed in Chapter 2. Here we consider his building works and architectural patronage.

It was in his capacity as the governor of Mazandaran that Saru Taqi seems to have begun his distinguished career as a patron of architecture (Fig. 3). In 1615, while still acting as the regent of Qarabagh, Saru Taqi was appointed governor of Mazandaran and entrusted with the construction of the new towns of Farahabad (near Sari) and Ashraf (present Bihshahr), the initial planning for which had already begun in 1611–13.[45] Farahabad, the first of the two nearby cities, was planned as the provincial capital, with networks of streets and public amenities (mosques, bath houses, bazaars etc.) and residential quarters. Ashraf, on the other hand, was conceived as the royal retreat, comprising palaces and pavilions for the Shah and stately mansions for courtiers and dignitaries.

Little survives from these cities where Abbas I's vision of royal retreat merged with imperial politico-economic designs. Mazandaran was not only the Shah's matrilineal homeland but also the region to which he often retired for its restorative air, verdant nature and plentiful prey for hunting. Despite the emphasis, in both contemporary and modern literature, on the natural appeal of the place, contemporary sources relate a more politically charged agenda in the decision to build new towns in this region. Iskandar Beg Munshi reports that, three years after the initial construction began, and coinciding with Saru Taqi's appointment, Abbas I ordered the transfer to Mazandaran of some fifteen thousand families from northwestern frontiers of Safavid domains, the majority of them Armenian. Promoting the silk business must have loomed large in the royal mind, as Armenians were not only skilled merchants (and already resettled in Isfahan) but also well-suited as silk workers, whose labour was especially needed in the silk-producing Caspian region. The Armenian role in the centralized economy of the Safavids, discussed in Chapter 3 of this book, also illustrates, if obliquely, the close network of intentions, actors and actions. Saru Taqi played a crucial role in these imperial designs. The resettled populations were drawn from the region in northwestern Iran that was under his supervision, and he himself was placed in charge of creating towns that would give shape to the politico-economic agenda of the Shah.

Contemporary European and Persian sources praised Saru Taqi's work in constructing major roads that linked this agriculturally rich strip of land to the interior of the country.[46] More impressive were the towns themselves, which elicited unanimous praise from visitors and guests of the Shah. The urban schemes of these towns, however, cannot be reconstructed. Nor do we have enough evidence to assign the plans or individual buildings to a single person or a recognizable group of architects. Saru Taqi's role then becomes a matter of conjecture but one that, in retrospect and in light of his other works, draws upon his future career as a patron of architecture. As in the case of the other *ghulam* grandees, his supervisory role entailed more than the procurement of land, labour and material.

The remains of at least two palatial complexes in Ashraf and a large mosque in Farahabad indicate planning on a grand scale of well-proportioned and finely wrought architectural units that were especially responsive to the local building traditions and took advantage of the natural environment. In the planning of the palaces in particular can be detected the adoption of architectonic elements that incorporated open vistas (and strategies for circulation of air in a humid climate) into the fabric of the buildings, taking into account the mountains and the plentiful bodies of water (the Caspian Sea, the smaller lakes and the rivers).[47] For example, roofed wooden pillared spaces open to the environs (*talar*), a feature derived from Mazandaran vernacular, were turned into vast royal gathering halls suitable for feasting and entertainment. As noted below, such architectural units and their particularity of function were soon adopted in the palatine ensembles of the imperial capital of Isfahan.[48] And Saru Taqi was instrumental in the transition from a provincial to an imperial architectural vocabulary.

The inception of these new towns in 1611–13 coincided with a series of major architectural works in key centres of the Safavid domain. All these came in the wake of the decisive victory in 1611 against the invading Ottoman armies and the signing of a peace treaty in 1612.[49] The diverse building campaigns of this period signal a renewed confidence in the military capability and structural efficacy of the reformed Safavid polity. Immediately after the re-conquest of Tabriz, the last time the city was to be wrenched from Ottoman control, Abbas I appointed Manuchihr Beg, a *ghulam* of the household, as the master of the ceremonies of the harem (*ishik aqasi-yi haram*), in charge of constructing a new fortified citadel in the famous Rab'-i Rashidi, an early fourteenth-century quarter built by the grand vizier of the Ilkhanid ruler. Here a new palace, bath house and cistern served as the seat of the provincial government. Then in 1611, Muhibb Ali Beg, the tutor of the *ghulams*, began two major campaigns in Isfahan on behalf of the Shah. His housing project, like Saru Taqi's building and populating of Farahabad, aimed at economic revival and consolidation. His involvement in the construction of the Royal Mosque on the south side of the *maydan* in Isfahan gave shape to the transformation of the capital city into the religious heart of the realm, grafting imperial omnipotence onto matters of religious authority and making visible the Shah's role as the master of the new Ka'ba.

A corollary to this magnified display of the twin prerequisites of piety and authority was the urban overhaul of the holy city of Mashhad.[50] A new thoroughfare, with a water-channel running at its centre, similar to the Chahar Bagh of Isfahan, facilitated the flow of water and traffic to the sacred precinct, and the shrine itself was refurbished with a fresh architectural scheme in which the redesign of the main courtyard and the addition of at least two magnificent *iwans* (entrance porches) formalized the centuries-long accumulation of haphazardly constructed sections. As far as can be ascertained, the Mashhad project lacks documentation on the particular persons, *ghulams* or otherwise, who were entrusted with the task.[51]

The cases of Tabriz, Isfahan and Farahabad (and possibly Mashhad) serve to illustrate the ways in which *ghulams'* agency in architectural and urban campaigns of Shah Abbas I were interwoven with the reconfigured structure of the household and its reformed policies in the early years of the seventeenth century. There is indeed no parallel in the history of Islamic Iran to the kind of systematized and centralized architectural sheathing of the empire that we encounter in this period. Only the *ghulams*, the servants of the Shah, his adopted sons and brothers whose loyalties transcended tribal ties of the Qizilbash grandees, could have acted in unison as the all-embracing arms of the monarch in order to implement and concretize these imperial designs.

Saru Taqi's role in this regard extends well beyond the reign of Abbas I. While still the governor of Mazandaran, Shah Safi I dispatched Saru Taqi to Najaf in 1631 to undertake repairs of the neglected shrine of Imam Ali. Abbas I had regained the Mesopotamian territories from the Ottomans in 1623–24 and had sent the royal *ghulam*, the alderman of Isfahan (*darugha*), Khusrow Mirza Gurgi (the Georgian) to refurbish Baghdad. Saru Taqi's assignment, only two years into Safi's reign, not only activated the competing sentiments of the Shi'i Safavids against Sunni Ottomans through laying claim to the symbolically charged and highly venerated shrine of 'Ali but also gained much recognition for the *ghulam* surrogate-patron.

According to Iskandar Beg Munshi and his collaborator Muhammad Yusuf Muvarrikh, Saru Taqi's record in Mazandaran earned him royal trust in this politically most important architectural project of Safi's reign.[52] The vizier of Mazandaran, equipped with royal (*khassa*) funds and expertise (architects and engineers employed by the court in Isfahan), enlarged the sanctuary, replaced the shrine's dome and built a canal to conduct water from the Euphrates to the shrine. From at least one source, we also learn that Saru Taqi contributed some of his own funds for this project. A parallel case of personal investment is Muhibb Ali Beg's endowment for the Royal Mosque of Isfahan. Yet an even more telling link between the two projects was the topos of timely divine intervention. The miraculous discovery of a marble quarry near Isfahan had rescued the construction of the Royal Mosque in Isfahan from failure.[53] Saru

Taqi, surely cognizant of the iconographic significance of such miracles, constructed a scenario of near doom and eventual rescue by the holy emanations of the sacred shrine when he too found a suitable marble quarry to allow the completion of the repairs he had envisioned.[54] The role of Saru Taqi in the Najaf campaign is emphasized by the inclusion of his name in the long panegyric on Safi and the Najaf shrine by the court poet Sa'ib-i Tabrizi: 'Taqi, the dust on the path of the Twelve Imams Has fashioned the terrestrial abode with the pen of righteousness'.[55] This is a most exceptional instance, since royal patronage is rarely mixed with sub-imperial patron names. As such, it also signifies that Saru Taqi was a partner in the realization of a major imperial project, not a mere supervisor.

Most of the extant buildings of Saru Taqi date to the period between his appointment in 1634 to the post of grand vizier (Safi I's reign) and his murder in 1645 (Abbas II's reign). Saru Taqi entered the political stage in Isfahan in the wake of the internal positioning for power after the Bloody Massacre of 1632. His rise to the lofty position of grand vizier through his harem connections, especially with the concubine queen-mother of Abbas II, Anna Khanum, is outlined in Chapter 2. Saru Taqi actively contributed to the demise of his predecessor, Mirza Talib Khan Urdubadi, which led to the latter's murder. He then not only succeeded to his post but also inherited Talib Khan's paternal mansion.[56] According to Chardin, Saru Taqi made a substantial investment, both monetarily and creatively, to complete and refurbish the mansion into what the French observer considered to be among the most beautiful buildings in Iran. Here at his mansion the grand vizier entertained foreign ambassadors and kings on behalf of the Shah.[57] Adam Olearius, secretary of the Holstein Embassy in 1637, describes the reception hall of the mansion, with a central fountain and walls covered with mirrors on the lower zones, crowned by portraits of women in different costumes painted in a European style.[58] As fate would have it, Saru Taqi himself was assassinated beside the fountain in this same hall.[59]

The taste for such interior mural decoration and especially portraits of diverse ethnic groups rendered in European representational modes was set at the palaces first in Mazandaran and then in Isfahan. Other mansions (belonging both to courtiers and to the chief Armenian merchant families) followed suit, indicating the dissemination of new trends from the court. Olearius's description, however, predates most others outside the palaces and further highlights Saru Taqi's particularly good connections and his involvement in imperial architectural and decorative strategies during the reign of Safi and his successor. Echoes of this relationship are also found in Saru Taqi's mosque complex.

His mansion was located in the Hasanabad quarter southeast of the *maydan*, where in 1643 he also completed a mosque and a bazaar. The mosque, now largely altered, preserves its domed sanctuary. Relatively large in size, the dome is distinguished from other sub-imperial Safavid mosques in the city by its interior decoration – a painted and gilded sunburst pattern in a style that recalls interior domes of royal edifices. Nothing remains from the adjacent bazaar except a lantern turret, which marks the location of the recessed alcove of the mosque portal. Sectioned *muqarnas* units (concave cells) of brick that lead to a central shallow vault are supported on double-fork type arches, a composition that makes this lantern the only Safavid structure to resemble the lantern turret on the fifth floor of the Ali Qapu Palace (Fig. 10). A tiled inscription band on the mosque portal, penned by Muhammad Riza al-Imami, whose designs graced imperial monuments, serves as the foundation inscription, further underlining the importance of the building and its patron.

The inscription is unusual in that it not only records the standard references to the reigning monarch (Abbas II), the date (1643) and the calligrapher (Muhammad Riza al-Imami), but more importantly it spells out the credentials of the patron. His position as the grand vizier (*itimad al-dawla*) and his full name together with his nickname (Mirza Muhammad Taqi famed as Saru Taqi) are accompanied here by a strikingly boastful phrase, 'the master of the emirs and the servant of the poor (*makhdum al-umara va khadim al-fuqara*.)' The linguistic twists in this phrase on the notions of service, the servant and the served cannot be accidental considering that by 1642 the youthful new king, Abbas II, was no more than a mask for the real masters of the court and government, the concubine queen-mother and the eunuch-*ghulam* Saru Taqi.[60] Evocations, in decorative and structural forms in his mosque-bazaar complex and in the nearby mansion, of royal edifices, and the prominently displayed expression of his lofty status distinguish Saru Taqi's architectural patronage from that of his fellow *ghulams*.

In fact, the political circumstances of the first three years of Abbas II's reign (1642–45), during which Saru Taqi assumed extraordinary powers, correspond to an accelerated building activity by the *ghulam* grand vizier. Besides his mosque-bazaar, Saru Taqi began constructing one of the largest caravanserai in the main bazaar of Isfahan.[61] Situated in the bazaars on the northeast side of the *maydan*, the caravanserai, now badly altered and neglected, was based on an unusual plan: an elongated rectangle composed of series of double-storey rooms along a large courtyard on one side and along two smaller courtyards on the other. One of its two entrances opens to an elegantly proportioned *chaharsu* (domed intersection of bazaar arteries) where, on the opposite side, stands the entrance to a small mosque. Inscription bands on the facing façades of the caravanserai and mosque are once again penned by Muhammad Riza al-Imami; they date the completion of the construction to 1646 and lament, in Persian verse, the murder of Saru Taqi a year earlier.

Saru Taqi's active patronage of architecture during this period seems to have been recognized widely. The anonymous author of a text known as *Dar danistan-i caravansara-yi Isfahan* ('On Knowing the Caravanserai of Isfahan') attributes the construction of the Jadda (Grandmother) caravanserai, one of the largest in the city, to Saru Taqi's term as the vizier (*dar zaman-i vizarat-i Saru Taqi sakhta shuda*).[62] Furthermore, as Saru Taqi's name appears twice in this record on Jadda caravanserai, it seems plausible to consider his patronage in this case to extend beyond encouragement; for the grandmother in question was Dilaram Khanum, Safi's Georgian concubine-mother and Abbas II's grandmother.[63] The recognition of the vizier's tenure in matters of patronage, and not the Shah's reign, is highly unusual in Safavid history.

As the only grand vizier and *ghulam* to have been able to forge such direct bonds with the royal household (thanks to his castration), Saru Taqi appropriated architecture as a means of enunciating his social standing well beyond the boundaries of Isfahan. In Qazvin, he completed a *madrasa* attached to a shrine known as Buq'a

Paygham-bariyya (Prophet's Shrine). The small complex, probably dating to the time of Shah Tahmasb and Qazvin's heyday, has been altered and does not seem to have been architecturally notable to begin with.[64] Yet its religious significance must have been recognized, because it originally stood just outside the walls of the royal precinct on a major artery and because in local memory it is especially venerated on the belief that four Quranic prophets had been buried here. An inscription at the entrance to the *madrasa* records its date as 1644 and states that the building was completed during the reign of Abbas II, the slave of Imam Ali (*ghulam*), by the grand vizier, the slave (*banda*) of the Shah (and here he spells out his full name but omits his nickname). Once again, Saru Taqi's acutely observed self-image *vis-à-vis* his royal patron occasions a verbal play on the meaning and stages of *ghulam*hood, in this case linking him with the first Shi'i imam through the intermediary of the Shah.

Unlike his last buildings in Isfahan, where the expressive intent of his patronage found voice in functional significance or prime locations, his patronage outside Isfahan seems to focus attention on the symbolic charge of the location itself. In Qum, the second most holy city in Safavid Iran, he constructed a cistern (in 1645) adjacent to the shrine of Fatima Massuma, the sister of Imam Riza, which was one of the most venerated Safavid sites.[65] Shah Safi and, later, Shah Abbas II were buried in the shadow of the shrine's holiness. The choice of a cistern, an architecturally indistinct edifice, relies for its impact on the cultural significance of facilitating the supply of water in an area that suffered from lack of readily accessible sources: an act of charity and piety. Saru Taqi seems to have literally tapped into the symbolic supply.

The tiled foundation inscription, by the same Muhammad Riza al-Imami, on the lintel above the entrance to the subterranean cistern provides the most potent enunciation of Saru Taqi's construction of his identity. Here his claim to be 'the master of the emirs and the servant of the poor (*makhdum al-umara va khadim al-fuqara*)' is further aggrandized by the addition of lengthy attributes lauding the reigning monarch (Abbas II) as not only the king of kings but also the propagator of the Shi'i creed (both standard phrases, here given a more hyperbolic edge) and his lofty government (*dawlat*), of which

Saru Taqi is spelled out as the trustee. Two tiled quatrains, in Persian, in the spandrels above the entrance, expand on the meaning of Saru Taqi's patronage here. According to the poems, he had intended the blessings of the cistern to extend to Shah Safi, a rare case of the expression of loyalty and devotion extending beyond the life of the patriarchal master (the Shah).[66] Furthermore, the function of the building as a cistern is given an intricate literary web of meanings by the way the poem construes the drinking of every drop of water from the cistern as a means of memorializing Imam Husayn, the third Shi'i imam, who was martyred in Karbala and whose thirst in that desert became a centrepiece in Shi'i exegesis and ritual practice. The chronogram in the quatrain heightens the symbolic charge of the message by cursing Yazid, the instigator of the martyrdom of Imam Husayn, his companions and Yazid's tomb, an apt contrast to the blessed tomb of Fatima Massuma.[67]

As if mindful of the locus of power that invested him with his unique prerogatives, Saru Taqi ensured that his late buildings collectively manifested his loyalty as a *ghulam* and his devotion as a Shi'i at the same time that they expressed his increased confidence, stemming from an uncommon access to the royal household. Whether in appropriated royal architectural features, in buildings of culturally recognized functional significance, or in epigraphic condensation of constructs of identity, Saru Taqi proves to have been the most astute patron of architecture in the Safavid period, one who merged his realization of the potential of his *ghulam* status with an equally deliberate exploitation of the lasting powers of architecture in enunciating this status and identity.

Despite the apparent focus on these self-generated latter-day architectural outbursts, Saru Taqi continued to serve as a trusted agent of the Shah and a surrogate patron after the 1631 Najaf project of Safi's reign. The works in Mazandaran and Najaf belonged to the period of his provincial governorship. In Isfahan, he stepped in as the *ghulam* grand vizier and indeed left his indelible architectural mark at the physical centre of power, the palace precinct itself. Here in 1644, two years into the reign of the 12-year-old Abbas II, Saru Taqi was entrusted with the construction of the *talar*, the wooden pillared porch, in front of the Ali Qapu Palace (Fig. 11).[68] Vali Quli

Shamlu, the historian of Abbas II, records that the *talar* and its substructure were completed in a short time 'under the supervision of the master of the noble emirs, Mirza Taqi, the grand vizier (*bi sarkari-yi makhdum al-umara al-akram Mirza Taqi vazir-i a'zam*)'.[69]

From its inception, the Ali Qapu was part of Abbas I's master plan for the *maydan*. Begun as a two-storey gateway into the royal precinct, by 1615 the building had become a mixed-use five-storey tower, housing the judiciary office and the special guards on the ground floor, and a storage space and service area on the second floor, providing a suitably grand audience hall with a shallow viewing stage onto the *maydan* (the *iwan*) on the third floor, with private rooms for the harem women overlooking the audience hall where they could secretly observe the royal receptions on the fourth floor, and surmounted by a series of magnificently decorated rooms for private royal entertainment on the fifth floor. A vast, sheltered stage with commanding views over the *maydan*, the *talar* greatly expanded the ceremonial space of the Ali Qapu, while at the same time its substructure projected its mass into the public zone, making its presence felt literally.[70] The addition of the *talar* magnified the conceptual and functional significance of the Ali Qapu as the most visible arena for the performance of the ruler's multifarious tools of kingship, standing as it were on the threshold between the public world of the *maydan* and the royal zone of privilege.

As a timber architectural unit and a sheltered open space, the *talar* is an alien concept in the brick vernacular of central Iran and especially in the Isfahan region. Its architectural homeland in Iran is Mazandaran, where we have already encountered, through descriptions, its adoption in the structures at Abbas I's two new cities of Ashraf and Farahabad and where Saru Taqi served as the supervisor of construction. The *talar* in the Ali Qapu was in fact the third instance of its appearance in palatine architecture of Safavid Isfahan. The first two, the Talar-i Tavila (Hall of the Stables) and the Ayinakhana (Hall of the Mirrors), were constructed during the reign of Safi between about 1635 and 1642, that is during the grand vizierate of Saru Taqi. Both were conceived as ceremonial palaces with a series of enclosed rooms and halls connected to a vast *talar* as the principal reception hall of the palace and its façade.

Until a full art-historical analysis of the *talar* in Mazandaran and Isfahan has been published, it suffices to note here the fundamentally different architectural conception of the ceremonial space in seventeenth-century Safavid palaces from the preceding palatine traditions of Iran.[71] What needs emphasis, however, is the intermediary role that Saru Taqi seems to have played in the transmission from a provincial to an imperial idiom of a uniquely Safavid architectural feature. The Mazandaran connection, his position as the eunuch-*ghulam* grand vizier, and the fact that he is recorded to have built the Ali Qapu *talar* help anchor the facilitation of this transmission to Saru Taqi.

Architectural patronage in the case of Saru Taqi spans a wide range: from privately funded to imperial sponsorship, from small to palatial scale, and from religious foundations to roads and canals. The extent and variety of his architectural career is an apt commentary on his extraordinary political power and social standing. In his expertise and propensity for building, Saru Taqi, however, was not alone, as is evident from the structures sponsored by other *ghulams* such as Muhibb Ali Beg Lala and Allah Virdi Khan. Although architectural patronage by the elites was not a new phenomenon in Iran, that of the *ghulams* was of a different sort, one that found its closest parallels in other early modern slave systems, such as in the Ottoman dominion.

Construction of substantial buildings in key cities of rule by the grandees of the empire has a long history. Isfahan itself bears the glorious marks of such patronage. Nizam al-Mulk's south dome (1086–88) over the *mihrab* of the Great Mosque of Isfahan and Taj al-Mulk's north dome (1088) in the same mosque, a masterpiece of Persian architecture, were the fruits of rivalry between the two viziers of the Saljuq Malik Shah.[72] Similarly grand were the architectural patronage of the two Ilkhanid viziers, Rashid al-Din, the founder of the vast suburban quarter of Rab'-i Rashidi or Rashidiyya in Tabriz (early fourteenth century), and Taj al-Din Ali Shah, whose name-sake mosque (1310–20) in Tabriz is among the most important Ilkhanid buildings.[73]

The pillars of the Timurid government in the fifteenth century also sponsored large-scale building projects in the principal cities of the empire. Among them the works of Ali Shir Nava'i, the celebrated vizier of the last Timurid sultan, Husayn Bayqara, surpassed all competition in number if not, in some instances, in grandeur. One of his foundations was a complex of charitable institutions in Herat inspired by the Rashidiyya in Tabriz (begun 1475/76).[74] Yusuf Khwaja, governor of Qum under Shah Rukh, built the Madrasa Du Dar (1439) adjacent to the shrine complex of Imam Riza in Mashhad.[75] Ghiyas al-Din Pir Ahmad Khwafi, the most influential vizier of Shah Rukh, constructed the outstanding Ghiyasiyya Madrasa in Khargird (1444).[76]

While all such sub-imperial patronage defers, in epigraphic and historical records, to the protection and glory of the reigning monarch, none fails to spotlight the prominence of the patron and his acquisition of prestige through the act of building. In most cases, in fact, the construction is funded independently from the royal purse and is on land belonging to the patron, as in Rashid al-Din's property in Tabriz and Khwafi family lands in Khargird and elsewhere.

The sixteenth-century situation is fundamentally the same, with the distinct exception that the first century of Safavid rule displayed a considerable slowing of building activity. Two important extant buildings to consider are the neighbouring shrine of Harun-i Vilayat and the Masjid-i Ali in Isfahan.[77] Harun-i Vilayat was and remains the principal shrine in Isfahan. Its inscriptions ascribe the foundation to Durmish Khan, the Qizilbash governor of Isfahan, and to his vizier, Mirza Kamal al-Din Shah Husayn Isfahani, originally an architect/builder. Ten years later, this same Shah Husayn Isfahani founded (or completed) the Masjid-i Ali, this time in his own capacity as the vizier and viceroy (*vakil*) of Isfahan. The foundation inscriptions of these buildings celebrate the reign of Shah Ismail (1501–24), a topos in all such cases, yet claim the construction for the patrons (*bi iqbal*) and as a memorial to the architect (*yadgar*).[78] Durmish Khan and Mirza Kamal al-Din Shah Husayn present a sixteenth-century parallel to the patronage of such *ghulams* as Muhibb Ali Beg, who supervised the construction of the Royal Mosque in the new *maydan* in Isfahan a hundred years later. The Qizilbash governor and his successor, however, neither built on behalf of the Shah nor were active in such imperial-scale architectural campaigns in the principal Safavid centres of authority.

In fact, the most crucial site for the architectural manifestations of Safavid authority and piety, their ancestral shrine at Ardabil, displays no significant marks of sub-imperial patronage.[79] Rather, members of the royal family – the shahs, princes and princesses – are the primary patrons at the Ardabil shrine and the other two Shi'i repositories of political ideology and pietistic veneration at Qum and Mashhad.[80] And when a royal construction appeared to have been implemented for the Shah by a person outside the imperial line, such as a pavilion built for Shah Ismail's arrival at the old royal precinct in Qum, it was initiated by a former regent of Qum whose office had expired before Ismail's ascent to the throne.[81]

The absence of major architectural campaigns by the Qizilbash grandees in the sixteenth century, much less in the first half of the seventeenth century, as well as the ascendance of the *ghulams* as the primary agents of the shahs in constructing the capital city in Isfahan and the infrastructure of the empire, underlines the crucial political and economic role of this new elite.[82] In contrast to the all-pervasive tradition of building in one's own name and to one's own glory, *ghulams* of the Isfahani phase of Safavid rule displayed relatively little that was entirely funded by them and bore their own names. Replacing the traditional elites, the *ghulams* instead assumed the lion's share of a widely divergent imperial programme of building. Not only did they build bridges, roads and cities; they also engaged in construction of the religious symbols of the empire. Where in the past the founding of mosques, shrines and *madrasas* was the venue for manifesting largesse, power and personal piety, in the age of the *ghulams*, the architectural embodiment of the wish to acquire prestige in this world and blessings in the next was channelled through the imperial foundation of religious institutions. Far from being stripped of the privilege, as Muslims (converted or otherwise), to manifest piety through architecture, they participated in the collective spiritual gains of the royal household by facilitating imperial projects.

In this sense, to read the historical record of their supervisory role (*mushrifi, sarkari* and *ihtimam*) at face value would be to miss the significance of the *ghulams'* positioning as the arms of the household. Indeed, engineers and architects (*muhandissan va mi'maran*) must have supplied the designs and constructed the buildings. Yet the job of the supervisor, *sarkar* or *mushrif*, as the evidence for the *ghulams* in the Isfahani age demonstrates, entailed engagement well beyond the organization of labour and materials. As in the cases of Muhibb Ali Beg, Allah Virdi Khan, Ganj Ali Khan and Saru Taqi, the *ghulams* ensured the enforcement of imperial canons and controlled the suitability of the designs and their associated significations. It was through the benevolence of the patriarch and the household, however fickle it may have been, that these men had been groomed for service and were positioned as the pillars of the empire. And it was through them, and not the caged and impotent princes or the dismantled Qizilbash hierarchy, that the centralization of the empire came to materialize conceptually and architecturally.

In the early modern age of Muslim empires, the Ottoman slave system presents the closest parallel to the Safavids. The famed palace schools in Istanbul, where young boys and girls were recruited from non-Muslim subject populations, were converted and trained as administrators of the empire and as royal concubines and potential wives of the new household elites, is exactly the same phenomenon as we encounter in Safavid Isfahan, albeit vastly better-documented than the Persian case. Ottoman slave-elites, like their Safavid counterparts, facilitated the dissemination of the imperial icons of authority through the full spectrum of architectural projects.[83] The mosque in particular was favoured in the Ottoman territories as the quintessential vehicle for the manifestation of the sultan's omnipresence in all the conquered lands. Sinan, the greatest master of Ottoman architecture, was a converted Christian slave of the household who rose in rank to become the chief administrator of all buildings and maintenance of the empire.[84] His architectural genius effectively advanced the centralized imperial policies by creating canonical building types throughout the empire, branding cities and territories as far-flung as Mecca and Belgrade as Ottoman domain.

In contrast to the well-preserved buildings and documents for the Ottomans, the Safavid patronage of the slave-elites of the household is glimpsed mostly through literary and epigraphic sources. The considerable destruction of individual buildings and whole towns has left scant material evidence. Nonetheless, the careers of prominent *ghulams* of the household – like Saru Taqi, Muhibb Ali Beg Lala,

Allah Virdi Khan and Ganj Ali Khan – underscore their crucial role in architecturally crafting the new capital and the centralized empire. Their agency is not confined to the organization of labour and materials but rather should be viewed as embracing all the characteristics and expectations of a patron. Theirs, however, was a surrogate form of patronage, one in which they essentially built on behalf of their sovereign, to whom they were tied through the new familial codes of *ghulam*hood. The articulation of their role and their peculiar form of patronage in constructing the key monuments of seventeenth-century Isfahan, Mazandaran, Kirman and Shiraz, offer a glimpse of some of the mechanisms involved in formulating Safavid imperial architecture in this period. Focusing on their contributions, and not merely limiting our inquiry to royal titular patronage, further allows us to evaluate and refine the place of the *ghulams* as a new elite in shaping the locus of their power and influence within the familial network of the Safavid royal household.

Our focus on the *ghulams* has not been at the expense of other social elites. Safavid Isfahan indeed provided a fertile environment for upward mobility. The fruits of global trade and long-distance ventures in search of fortune and fame had fattened enough merchants and doctors in the seventeenth century, for example, to fill the city with a conspicuous concentration of wealth in mansions and houses. A converted Jewish court physician acquired enough fame and fortune to be able to memorialize himself in the largest, architecturally most notable mosque, known as Masjid-i Hakim, built in Isfahan completely independently of the royal sphere of influence. In a study of the urbanization of Isfahan in the seventeenth century, Masashi Haneda has identified and sorted a list of the religious buildings constructed in this period.[85] This roster of religious buildings demonstrates a noticeable rise in patronage of other social elites for the period between 1590 and 1714, when Isfahan was the capital. Out of a total of thirty-one buildings known both by the patron's name and by date to have been constructed in this period, the most significant were three royal foundations; the rest were sponsored by women of the royal household (three), artisans (four), wealthy families (six) and court functionaries (fifteen). Of the fifteen instances of patronage by court functionaries throughout the seventeenth century, the majority fell under the sponsorship of *ghulams* of the household from the first half of the century, including Saru Taqi. More importantly, nearly all privately founded sub-imperial patronage in this chronological framework, in Isfahan or elsewhere in Iran, remained modest in both scale and architectural significance. With the exception of Saru Taqi's personally funded buildings in Isfahan or the Grandmother's caravanserai, for example, the rest comprise small local mosques, *madrasas*, caravanserai and the like.

Architectural patronage necessitates substantial funds, material resources and labour, and the *ghulams* had the privilege of access to the royal purse (the *khassa*, in the full meaning of the term). As members of the royal household, the partnership between the *ghulams* and the Armenian merchants facilitated the flow of cash that funded the imperial construction projects. Their particular form of patronage allows us to paint a richer picture of the Safavid architectural landscape in which the royal household exerted its vision of authority through its adopted sons and brothers by building extensively at both the core of the empire and its satellite nodes.

This synthesis of the evidence demonstrates the shift away from the traditional patterns of patronage, in which one's status was made visible through privately funded buildings, to a pattern in which the individual's patronage was channelled through large-scale projects built on behalf of the monarchs. It was not for lack of influence, wealth, ambition or piety that the new elites of Isfahan did not invest in substantial building projects of their own. Rather, we suggest, the explanation lies in the altered nature of the patron–client relationship between the shahs and the *ghulams* within the new order that was forged in the first half of the seventeenth century. The Shah was the pivot of the centralized and sedentarized Safavid universe, and Isfahan in its built environment articulated this notion of centring. Building for the Shah in Isfahan came to signify participation, through architecture and, as we shall see, through the arts, in the creation of the cultural ethos of this universe.

5

Military Slaves in the Provinces: Collecting and Shaping the Arts

By the early seventeenth century, *ghulams* had joined the royal library-cum-atelier (*kitabkhana*) as painters and calligraphers, and some had also become active patrons and collectors of illustrated manuscripts and other luxury objects. Before long, they eclipsed the rival Qizilbash as patrons of the arts of the book and contributed towards the formulation of a new pictorial language that reached its culmination in the mid-seventeenth century.[1] As is illustrated in the previous chapter, several prominent *ghulams* supervised and actively supported religious, civil and commercial architecture in Isfahan and the provinces. Patronage of the luxury arts, on the other hand, was limited to a select few. The most notable among these patrons was the Armenian *ghulam*, Qarachaqay Khan, and his descendants, who served as successive governors of the city of Mashhad in north-eastern Iran from 1617 to 1665. The relatively small, but highly important corpus of works associated with this family has been generally discussed in the context of the capital Isfahan. Both literary and artistic evidence indicates, however, that the creation of these illustrated texts can be linked to Mashhad at a time when the city replaced Herat, the chief political and artistic centre under the Turkoman Shamlus in the northeast, as the new locus of power. This chapter will examine the nature and impact of artistic patronage sponsored by the *ghulams*, in particular Qarachaqay Khan and his descendants, within the larger framework of the political order forged by Shah Abbas I and his successors.

When Abbas I succeeded to the throne in 1587, patronage of the arts of the book, traditionally centred at the royal court, was largely dominated by the Qizilbash nobility, who had set up their own libraries in the provinces. Shah Tahmasb's growing orthodoxy in 1540s,[2] compounded by the political turmoil of the reigns of Shah Ismail II (1576–77) and Shah Muhammad Khudabanda (1577–87), who was virtually blind, provided an ideal opportunity for the Qizilbash to consolidate their role as principal patrons of illustrated manuscripts.[3] Although some artists remained in Qazvin, many gravitated towards the provinces, where they found ready support among the Qizilbash.

One such centre was Shiraz, the capital of Fars. From the 1560s to the 1580s, Shirazi manuscripts, created under the patronage of members of the Zu'lqadar tribe, became increasingly luxurious, rivalling some of the finest works associated with Tahmasb I's court.[4] Farhad Khan Qaramanlu, the governor of Azerbaijan, and later Fars, was another leading Qizilbash patron, whose library staff included two of the most celebrated Safavid calligraphers, Ali Riza Abbasi and Mir Imad.[5]

In 1576, when Abbas Mirza, the future Shah Abbas I, arrived in Herat as royal governor of the province, his Turkoman guardian (*lala*) Ali Quli Shamlu established one of the premier libraries in the city and employed several leading poets and artists, including the painter Muhammadi, who later joined Shah Abbas I in Qazvin.[6]

Notwithstanding genuine Qizilbash interest in the arts of the book, their patronage also fulfilled an important political objective. Sponsorship of lavishly illuminated and illustrated texts and deliberate emulation of the Safavid court style helped the Qizilbash to strengthen their cultural status and present themselves as formidable rivals of the Safavid household.[7]

Shortly after his accession to the throne in 1587, Shah Abbas I decided to revive the royal library and appointed Sadiqi Beg, a painter of Qizilbash descent, as head librarian. Historically, the library-cum-workshop represented an integral ideological and physical part of the court. It served both as a repository for texts defining the political, cultural and religious ideals of a ruler/patron and as a workshop where these works were formulated, recorded, revised and illustrated, lending literary and visual credence to the patron's objectives and ideology. The promptness with which Abbas I re-instituted the royal library/painting atelier at Qazvin suggests his awareness of the *kitabkhana*'s importance as a royal appendage. The decision can also be viewed as part of the Shah's systematic effort to restore the city's role as the Safavid administrative and cultural centre and further counter Qizilbash influence.

During his governorship in Herat, the future Abbas I had already appropriated the painter Habibullah of Sava from Husayn Khan Shamlu, and now ordered Farhad Khan to relinquish his two prized calligraphers, Ali Riza Abbasi and Mir Imad.[8] These men joined other luminaries, such as the celebrated Aqa Riza (later known as Riza Abbasi), Muhammadi, Sadiqi Beg and Siyavush at the library in Qazvin. In addition to commissioning and collecting individual drawings and paintings (Fig. 12), the Shah ordered a copy of Firdawsi's *Shahnama*, Iran's national epic and the most potent literary expression of kingship and legitimacy. The text was copied between 1587 and 1597 under Sadiqi Beg's supervision and includes some fifty illustrations of the first half of Firdawsi's text. Although the manuscript was never completed, its scale and luxurious illustrations were clearly intended to bolster the Shah's political authority and confirm his rightful claim to the Persian throne, especially in view of persistent Qizilbash threats.[9]

When the capital was transferred from Qazvin to Isfahan in 1590–1, a new library and painting studio was established within the royal precinct. Both physically and administratively, it was considered one of the royal workshops (*karkhanaha-yi saltanati*) and stood together with several storehouses and the treasury in the *dawlatkhana* area, identified on Engelbert Kaempfer's drawing of the palace grounds (Fig. 2). According to Chardin's description, it was a rather small space, measuring only 22 by 12 feet, where the books were organized according to size rather than subject-matter. They stood on their side in niches that were protected by curtains.[10]

Ali Riza Abbasi (not to be confused with the painter, Riza Abbasi), the Shah's favourite calligrapher, replaced Sadiqi Beg as head librarian in 1596–97. He completed an album of calligraphies and paintings in 1599–1600, but is primarily known for the design of numerous monumental architectural inscriptions, such as those of the Masjid-i Shah, the Masjid-i Shaykh Lutf-Allah and the Safavid additions to the Imam Riza shrine at Mashhad.[11]

During his tenure as head librarian, Ali Riza also supervised in *ca.* 1600 the addition of four paintings to a 1486 Timurid copy of Attar's *Mantiq al-tayr* ('Conference of the Birds') (Fig. 13).[12] The illustrations have been attributed to the artist Habibullah, whom the Shah already knew while serving as governor in Herat. Adopting a Timurid pictorial idiom, Habibullah's work shares far greater stylistic affinity with late-fifteenth-century Herati paintings than with contemporary illustrations created for Abbas I's *Shahnama*. Interestingly, Safavid fascination with Iran's Timurid past was not limited to Abbas I's personal taste, for contemporary chronicles, such as Qazi Ahmad's *Khulasat al-siyar* ('Selection of Chronicles') also underline Safavid–Timurid historical and ideological links as a means to strengthen Safavid legitimacy.[13]

With the move from Qazvin to Isfahan, Abbas I's attitude towards art and architecture seems to have undergone a noticeable transformation. He became increasingly preoccupied with the capital's monumental architectural projects and, in response to the changing artistic and cultural landscape of Isfahan, his taste in the arts of the book expanded to include new forms and styles of pictorial expression. Instead of commissioning traditional illustrated text of Persian classics, Abbas I showed greater interest in individual drawings, paintings and calligraphic exercises, intended for albums (*muraqqa'*). Some of these sheets must have been created specifically for him, while others were probably already in the royal collection or may have been appropriated by the Shah to establish his own artistic identity and enlarge his personal holdings (Fig. 12).

The presence of a large Christian Armenian community in Isfahan, as well as the arrival of European diplomats, merchants and missionaries, meant that Abbas I also amassed through gifts, as well as special requests, Western works of art. One of the most important such gifts was a medieval French Picture Bible, presented to the Shah in 1608 by the Carmelite fathers on behalf of the Bishop of Krakow. Intrigued by the manuscript's cycle of biblical illustrations, Abbas I instructed one of his clerics to provide Persian glosses for each of the images.[14] Such European works seemed to have become readily available in Isfahan at the time, for Sadiqi Beg also created a series of drawings and paintings inspired by Flemish and Italian religious and mythological imagery, completed between the 1580s and 1609. Such works affirm the growing interest of Safavid painters and patrons in new pictorial sources and the popularity of novel artistic conventions and subjects as early as the late sixteenth century.[15]

The Shah's preference for single sheets and fascination with European works of art, coupled with his preoccupation with Isfahan's architectural transformation, must have contributed in part towards a broadening and 'democratization' of artistic patronage in the early seventeenth century. Court painters such as Sadiqi Beg and Riza Abbasi began to enjoy the freedom to work for patrons outside the court, such as affluent physicians, merchants and fellow artists. In reference to the calligrapher Mawlana Baba Shah, Iskandar Beg Munshi maintains that his work was avidly collected by the wealthy and fetched high prices when available.[16] Artists also sold their work on the open market, both in Iran and abroad, and Sadiqi Beg boasted about the large sums of money paid for his work in India.[17]

Once members of the Safavid household, however, painters and calligraphers of the royal workshop appear to have retained their status and remained, at least nominally, members of the court.[18] When Sadiqi Beg was dismissed as head librarian in 1596–97, he was allowed to retain his title and salary. In 1603, the Shah awarded the painter Riza with the honorific title 'Abbasi' (that is of Abbas), which he kept after his temporary departure from the court shortly afterwards. The calligrapher Ali Riza was honoured with the same title, while Shaykh Abbasi, active during the reign of Abbas II (1642–66), signed his compositions with the unusual phrase, 'it [the work] has gained value because it/he became the Shaykh of Abbas' (*baha girift chu gardid Shaykh Abbasi*), emphasizing the bond between artist and patron.[19]

By the late sixteenth century, several *ghulams* were also recruited into the royal library. Chief among these was Siyavush, the 'Georgian'. Captured in *ca.* 1544 during one of Shah Tahmasb's raids into Georgia, Siyavush was brought to Tabriz, where he was schooled at court. As a member of the royal household, his education in the arts began at an early age. According to the Safavid historian Bitlisi, in addition to the religious and natural sciences, horsemanship, polo and archery, *ghulams* were instructed in civility (*ansaniyat*), humanity (*adamgari*) and painting (*sanat-i naqashi*). These subjects were considered essential to the development of taste (*saliqa*) and constituted an integral part of court education.[20]

Reportedly, Siyavush's artistic talents caught Shah Tahmasb's attention and, after assigning him to the library, the Shah became personally involved in his training. Under the guidance of Muzaffar Ali, one of the court's most gifted artists, Siyavush developed into a meticulous (*daqiqa-kar*) painter and excelled in figural compositions (*majlis-sazi*), as well as in the depiction of armies and mountain scenes (*sipah va kuh pardazi*). Following Tahmasb's death in 1576, Siyavush continued to enjoy royal support. He contributed to Shah Ismail II's *Shahnama* (1576–77) and in 1579 illustrated with Sadiqi Beg a copy of the *Habib al-Siyar* ('Beloved of Chronicles') by Khandamir (Fig. 14). Siyavush must also have benefited from Abbas I's patronage as is evident from two of his signed drawings, in which he refers to himself as the 'the slave of the King of Holiness' (*ghulam-i shah vilayat*), stressing his status and allegiance to his royal master.[21] Shortly after 1597, Qazi Ahmad claims that the aging artist left the court and joined his Georgian countrymen in Shiraz, where he served the officials (*yasaqiha*) of the city but remained master of his art (*ustad-i fan*). He died around 1616.[22]

By Siyavush's 'countrymen', Qazi Ahmad is undoubtedly referring to Allah Virdi Khan, a Georgian slave and Abbas I's trusted friend, who was appointed governor of Fars in 1595. For the first time, a member of the royal household had replaced a tribal governor, in this case a member of the powerful Zu'lqadar tribe, who were regarded as one of the principal instigators of the second civil war. Their defeat in 1590 is generally acknowledged as the turning point in Safavid–Qizilbash relations.[23]

Allah Virdi Khan is primarily associated with patronage of architecture in Isfahan, as discussed in the previous chapter, but during his governorship, the arts of the book continued to flourish in Fars.[24] One of the most fascinating illustrated manuscripts from this period is a copy of the *Futuhat-i Humayuni* ('Royal Conquests'). Compiled by the historian Siyaqi Nizam, it recounts Abbas I's first major military success in 1598–99 against the Uzbeks in Khurasan, a campaign in which Allah Virdi Khan also played a central role. The undated, illustrated copy was probably completed sometime between 1605 and 1610 in Shiraz. It opens with a double-page composition of the Shah and his trusted general leaving for battle, an image that links the two both visually and conceptually to the struggle for Khurasan and the defence of the Safavid throne. Although the patron of the manuscript is unidentified, it cannot be coincidental that the text was copied and illustrated during Allah Virdi Khan's governorship. The *Futuhat Humayuni* visually commemorates both Abbas I's first important military victory and the ascendancy of the slave nobility, in particular Allah Virdi Khan, whose role in the campaign was central to its success.[25]

Like his father Allah Virdi Khan, Imam Quli Khan was considered one of the most distinguished *ghulams*. In 1610, he was appointed governor of Lar and, following his father's death in 1613, became the governor of Fars and spent the rest of his administrative career curbing Portuguese power in the Persian Gulf. Imam Quli Khan's capture of the strategic Portuguese fort on the island of Qashm was commemorated in 1622–23 in the *Jangnama-i Qashm* ('Qashm Book of War'), written in verse by the poet Qadri from Fars. Reportedly, a copy of this text was owned by the Italian traveller Pietro Della Valle; it is now housed in the Vatican Library.[26] Shortly afterwards, Qadri composed another *mathnavi* (a narrative work written in couplets), known as the *Jarun-nama* ('Book of Jarun', that is, Hormuz), relating Imam Quli Khan's final siege and capture of Hormuz in 1622. The only extant illustrated version of the *Jarun-nama* is dated 1697 and includes a later section on the murder of Imam Quli Khan and his family in 1633 at the behest of Shah Safi (Fig. 15). The patron of neither text is identified, but Imam Quli Khan, known for his support of artists, calligraphers and poets at his court, seems the most likely candidate to have commissioned both works. Like his father's *Futuhat-i Humayuni*, the two accounts highlight Imam Quli Khan's military prowess and, by extension, underline his status within the new Safavid administrative system.[27]

The influential grand vizier Saru Taqi was also known as an accomplished poet and supporter of the arts of the book. The only extant text associated with his patronage is a sumptuous copy of the Quran, which he dedicated as endowment to Shah Safi's tomb in Qum.[28] According to the *Tazkira-yi Nasrabadi*, he employed a certain Musavvir, a poet and painter from Kashan, who is identified as the son-in-law (*damad*) of the celebrated painter Riza Abbasi, a native of the same city.[29] Thus, by the early seventeenth century, *ghulams* such as Saru Taqi and Allah Virdi Khan supported not only architectural projects, but also historical chronicles and religious texts, and even composed their own poetry. None of these activities was either new or unusual among members of the Safavid elite, but for the newly converted slaves, artistic patronage must have played an important role in bolstering their standing and help counter the Qizilbash's long-established political and cultural influence. Although certain Qizilbash emirs, such as Hassan Khan Shamlu, the governor of Herat, continued to maintain a library and commission illustrated manuscripts, by the 1630s their patronage no longer dominated Safavid arts of the book as in the past.[30]

Among the *ghulams* Qarachaqay Khan and his descendants stand out as the most active patrons and collectors of portable luxury arts in the first half of the seventeenth century. As discussed below, the first Qarachaqay Khan succeeded in amassing a remarkable collection of Chinese porcelain, while his son, Manuchihr Khan, and grandson and namesake, Qarachaqay Khan (II) became two of the most influential Safavid patrons of illustrated texts.

Qarachaqay Khan's rise to power followed the patterns of several other first-generation royal slaves. A Christian Armenian from Erevan, he was captured as a child and raised with the other *ghulams* and princes at court. He began his career in the royal tailoring workshop (*qijaijigari*) and was soon promoted to head a battery of artillery (*mir-i tupkhana*) in 1602–3. Qarachaqay Khan became commander of a regiment of musketeers (*tufangchian*) and in 1605 assisted Allah Virdi Khan in defeating the Ottoman forces at Sufiyan near Tabriz, thus temporarily securing Safavid control over the province of Azerbaijan.[31]

Shortly after this important battle, Abbas I embarked on one of the most highly publicized and politically charged acts of his reign, in which the trusted Qarachaqay Khan also played an important role. Sometime between 1606 and 1607, the Shah decided to establish an endowment to the Fourteen Immaculate Ones. The *waqf* included several of the newly constructed monuments around the *maydan* in Isfahan and the Shah's personal collection of luxury objects. His Qurans and religious manuscripts, including those on jurisprudence (*fiqh*), traditions (*hadith*) and commentaries (*tafsir*), were given to the shrine of Imam Riza at Mashhad. The Safavid ancestral shrine of Shaykh Safi al-Din at Ardabil received the Shah's volumes on history and poetry, his collection of carpets, jewels, gold and silverware and rare Chinese porcelain.[32] The choice of gifts for Mashhad and Ardabil was clearly not an arbitrary one, but was based on a conscious decision to lend each site its own distinct identity: The collection of Qurans and religious texts were intended to transform Mashhad into the undisputed religious, and by extension Shi'i, symbol of Iran, while Ardabil's remarkable holdings of secular manuscripts and luxury goods reinforced its status as the Safavid ancestral shrine.[33] The two sites may have already carried different ideological significance prior to the 1606–7 *waqf*, but these were still relatively fluid, for in 1561 Mahin Banu Sultan, Shah Tahmasb's daughter, left her jewellery, paintings and Chinese porcelain collection not to Ardabil but to Mashhad.[34]

Apart from the far-reaching political and religious implications of Shah Abbas I's gift to Ardabil, the range and quality of the objects were truly remarkable. The Chinese porcelain collection, one of the two most important outside of China (the other is presently housed in the Topkapi Palace Museum, Istanbul) comprises some of the finest extant examples of late-fourteenth- and fifteenth-century white ware and celadon, but is particularly celebrated for its blue-and-white porcelain from the late Yuan and Ming periods (Figs. 16 and 17). According to John Pope, it is 'the most complete and well-rounded collection of blue and white from about 1350 to 1600 to be found in one place'.[35]

The monumental scale and splendid decoration of the *chini-khana*, which became the repository of the Chinese porcelains and Persian manuscripts, underline the importance of the gift. Adam Olearius, the head of a diplomatic mission from Schleswig-Holstein, who arrived in Ardabil in 1634, was the first European to describe the structure. He maintains that the porcelain pavilion ('Tzenetserai') was a large, vaulted space with deep niches, which served as the library.

> The books, locked up in different chests, were not in order but laid flat; they consisted primarily of Arabic, but also Persian and Turkish volumes, some were written neatly either on parchment or paper. The historical manuscripts were illustrated, the bindings covered with red cloth and decorated with applied gold floral and vegetal motifs. In the vaulting, one could also see at least a hundred porcelain vessels, some of which could be filled with at least ten jugs of water.[36]

According to the *Tarikh-i Abbasi* ('Abbasi History'), the Shah instructed Mullana Muhammad Husayn-i *hakak* (engraver) to add his endowment deed (*waqfnama*) to each object, which reads, 'The slave of the King of Holiness [Imam Ali], Abbas endowed [it] to the threshold of Shah Safi' (*banda-yi shah vilayat Abbas vaqf bar astana-yi Shah Safi nimud*).[37]

Some twenty vessels are inscribed with the words, 'Bihbud', 'Quli', 'Abu Talib' and 'Naringi'. Except for the term 'Naringi', which refers to the colour orange and the word for citrus fruit in Persian, the others are personal names and titles.[38] The largest group of extant vessels other than those associated with Shah Abbas I are inscribed with the name 'Qarachaqay'. Numbering at least ninety-four,[39] the superb collection comprises Ming blue-and-white porcelain from the early fifteenth century. Most of the vessels range from small to medium-sized serving bowls and dishes, embellished with a variation of vine, peony and chrysanthemum designs. The group also includes four impressive vases, known as *mei-p'ing,* and a large *yü-hu-ch'un-p'ing*, a bulbous bottle decorated with a dragon painted in reverse against a deep blue ground.[40]

One of the most striking characteristics of Qarachaqay Khan's porcelain collection is its formal and visual uniformity, not to mention its consistently high quality. Even if Islamic literary sources, such as Ali Akbar's *Khataynama* ('Book of China'), a description of China completed in 1516, stress the importance of practical rather than aesthetic considerations of Chinese porcelain for Muslim patrons, Qarachaqay Khan's collection suggests that, at least for him, shape, design and artistic refinement also served as important criteria.[41]

Most of the vessels with the name 'Qarachaqay' are also engraved with Abbas I's *waqf* inscription, which raises the question of ownership at the time of the dedication. Qarachaqay Khan's name is different in both style and execution from that of the Shah, suggesting that it was probably added by an engraver other than Mullana Muhammad Husayn and at a different time than in 1610–11. It would seem likely that Qarachaqay Khan established his ownership of the porcelain pieces when he first acquired them. Several possible scenarios come to mind. As a slave of the royal household, Qarachaqay Khan's life and possessions, in principle, belonged to the Shah, who could have appropriated his collection or ordered him to relinquish it as a supplement to the royal endowment. It seems more likely, however, the Armenian *ghulam* voluntarily offered his holdings to Abbas I prior to 1610–11, perhaps after learning of the Shah's intention to give away his own collection to Ardabil. Such lavish gifts to the ruler occurred on a regular basis and served both as tributary and a means to secure favours and special privileges.[42]

Qarachaqay Khan's contribution towards the endowment of the Ardabil shrine parallels Muhibb Ali Beg's support for the construction of Isfahan's Masjid-i Shah. Both projects were motivated by political and religious considerations and relied on the participation of two powerful royal household slaves. As discussed in the previous chapter, Muhibb Ali Beg, better known as Lala Beg, was responsible for supervising the construction of the congregational mosque and also donated significantly to its endowment. In both Ardabil and Isfahan, the *ghulams* supported the Shah's political, religious and cultural initiatives, which in turn facilitated their ascendancy within the Safavid administration.

Although the popularity of Chinese porcelain in Iran dates back to the late Ilkhanid period (1256–1353) and reached its zenith under the Timurid dynasty in the fifteenth century, little is known about the range and scope of individual collections.[43] As a highly valued and relative easily portable commodity, Chinese porcelain was one of the most desirable types of booty or gift. Following the battle of Chaldiran in 1514, for instance, Selim I transported 64 porcelain pieces from the Hasht Bihisht palace and elsewhere in Tabriz to Istanbul. According to Ottoman sources, the Safavids were also the only foreign power to have sent regular gifts of porcelain to the sultans.[44] Curiously, the Ottomans did not reciprocate in kind, but

Abbas I received Chinese porcelain from other rulers, such as a white bowl bearing the Mughal emperor Jahangir's seal, which he presented to the Ardabil shrine.[45]

Shah Abbas I probably inherited much of his collection and received additional pieces as gifts or through confiscation. But how did Qarachaqay Khan amass his impressive holdings? Based on the stylistic uniformity of the vessels, it can be argued that Qarachaqay Khan obtained the core of the collection all at once, perhaps as booty on one of his military campaign in the east. Others may have been added over time. At least one of the vessels is inscribed with the names of Qarachaqay Khan and Bihbud, suggesting that it must have changed hands between the two.[46] Collectors such as Qarachaqay Khan may have also benefited from sales of private holdings of the deceased, as was popular in Ottoman Turkey. According to the French traveller Tavernier, at the Ottoman court, the chief merchant (*bazarganbashi*) would fix the prices of the porcelain, usually at half of its market value. The head gatekeeper would offer the best pieces to the leading members of the court, while the pages of the treasury would get the second choice.[47] While the methods of acquisition of porcelain in Iran still demands further study, Qarachaqay Khan was clearly financially able to amass a remarkable collection during the early years of his administrative career or was in a position to claim such a valuable booty. Moreover, his holdings confirm not only the continuous availability of high-quality late Yuan and Ming porcelain in seventeenth-century Iran, but also its desirability as an economic and social status symbol among the elite.

Qarachaqay Khan's devotion and generosity to the Shah did not go unrewarded, for shortly afterwards he was honoured with the title of 'intimate of the illustrious' (*muqarab al-hazrat*), reserved for the Shah's close companions. In 1616, he also received the title 'khan' and was appointed commander-in-chief of the army (*sipahsalar*), thus joining the highest rank of the Safavid administration. A portrait of the Armenian *ghulam* is included in the right half of a double-page composition, where he is identified as Qarachaqay 'Khan', suggesting that the painting was completed sometime after 1616 (Fig. 18). Tall of stature with a prominent handlebar moustache, he is standing on the right in a red coat. Two other figures, one identified as Alpan Beg, Abbas I's aide-de-camp in 1604–5 and the other as Allah Virdi Khan, the *ishik aqasi bashi*, are also included in the composition. Each wears an elegant white turban wrapped around a short staff. The headgear, which was introduced during the reign of Abbas I, recalls the distinctive shape of the *taj-i haydari*, the turban associated with Shah Isma'il, the founder of the dynasty. While the new headgear must have signalled certain rank and status among the ruling elite, it probably also symbolized the Shah's commitment to Shi'ism, the unifying force of the Safavid dynasty.[48]

Following his defeat of the Ottoman Khalil Pasha in 1617 at Cerebrum, Qarachaqay Khan was appointed governor of Tabriz and the entire province of Azerbaijan. Shortly afterwards, Abbas I recalled Qarachaqay Khan from this post and sent him as governor to the northeastern province of Khurasan. Iskandar Beg maintains that the *sipahsalar*'s removal from Azerbaijan was meant to reassure the Ottomans of Abbas I's peaceful intentions. At the same time, however, it may have been prompted by the Shah's decision to distance the *ghulam* from his homeland Armenia and thwart the formation of possible alliances between the converted *ghulam* and his countrymen.

During much of the sixteenth century, the province of Khurasan played a central role in Safavid politics, as battleground for both the Safavid heir apparent, Abbas Mirza (the future Abbas I) and for Persian and Uzbek rivalry. After subjugating the Uzbeks in 1598, Abbas I began a systematic campaign to transform Mashhad, the burial site of the eighth Shi'ite imam, Imam Riza, into the dynasty's religious icon and as an alternative pilgrimage destination to Mecca and the Shi'i shrines in Iraq.[49] Following his celebrated journey on foot to Mashhad in 1601, he established a *waqf* the next year, ensuring the availability of more cemetery space for the shrine. In 1612, he ordered major restoration of the harem precinct and the construction of an irrigation channel. To accommodate the growing number of pilgrims, merchants and other travellers, new caravanserais were erected along the routes to Mashhad.[50] Qarachaqay Khan's appointment, like Allah Virdi Khan's governorship of Fars or that of Ganj Ali Khan's in Kirman, was emblematic of Abbas I's efforts to shift the balance of power away from the Qizilbash emirs and, with the help of the *ghulams*, create a new Safavid political system.

Apart from its religious and strategic importance, Mashhad, together with Kirman, was also revived as a centre for Persian ceramic production in the first half of the seventeenth century. Inspired by Chinese prototypes, Persian blue-and-white ware was created for local consumption as well as for export to Europe. According to seventeenth-century observers, their quality was so high that they would be mistaken for Chinese originals.[51] Whether Qarachaqay Khan's interest in Chinese porcelain directly effected the resumption of ceramic production in Mashhad is unclear, but the city's thriving religious and commercial life under his governorship and that of his descendants must have created the necessary conditions for the revival of this important art form and lucrative commodity.

Until his death in 1623, Qarachaqay Khan continued to serve as both commander-in-chief of the army and governor, two of the most important posts within the Safavid government. When he and one of his sons, Imam Virdi Khan, were killed during the Georgia campaign, their bodies were brought back to Mashhad and, like Allah Virdi Khan, were buried within the shrine complex. As a sign of respect for his loyal *ghulam*, Abbas I appointed Qarachaqay Khan's other son, Abu'l Fath Manuchihr Khan, who was head (*yüzbashi*) of an artillery unit, to the governorship (*hakim* or *beglarbegi*) of Mashhad.[52]

It is unclear whether Manuchihr Khan shared his father's passion for Chinese porcelain, but he and his younger brother, Ali Quli Khan, were clearly among the Safavid cultural and intellectual elite.[53] Both men are referred to as 'men of knowledge and integrity' (*ahl-i fazl u kamal*) and 'of illustrious acts and deeds' (*sahib-i mua'sir u asar*). Ali Quli Khan studied with a number of notable scholars in Qum and wrote several important theological and literary works. He also served as the overseer (*mutavalli*) of the city of Qum – a remarkable achievement for the son of a converted *ghulam*. In 1641, he was appointed head of the royal library, further affirming his status among the Safavid literary and religious class.[54]

Manuchihr Khan expressed his intellectual curiosity by commissioning one of the finest illustrated manuscripts of the period – a Persian translation of Abd al-Rahman ibn Umar al-Sufi's *Suwwar*

al-kawakib ('Book of the Patterns of the Stars') (Figs. 19 and 20).[55]
The text opens with a lengthy preface by the author Hasan ibn Sa'd
al-Qaini, a mathematician-astronomer. He maintains that Manuchihr
Khan was keenly interested in astronomy and commissioned a translation of al-Sufi's Arabic treatise into Persian. As discrepancies were
noted between the measurements in the original and those that
could be observed in the heavens, al-Qaini was instructed to make
necessary corrections so that the longitude and latitude of the stars
corresponded to those in the year 1631. The manuscript was copied
by Muhammad Baqir al-Hafiz, whose name appears together with
dates ranging from 1630 to 1632 in seventeen short colophons.

According to al-Qaini, once the text was completed, every star or
constellation was illustrated by one of Manuchihr Khan's painters,
Ustad Malik Husayn. Referring to him as the 'rarity of his time'
(nadir al-asr), the author states that he was particularly renowned
for his drawing and painting (tasvir va naqashi), and was also
knowledgeable in the science of astronomy. His illustrations were
exact representations of the stars visible in the skies in 1630–32,
an important factor for those who planned to copy the work in the
future.[56]

Manuchihr Khan's 'Translation of the Book of Stars' is notable
for a number of reasons. It represented the first Persian translation
of al-Sufi's text since Nasir al-Tusi's in 1250, and its illustrations
offered a new pictorial style.[57] Conforming to the traditional layout
of Islamic astronomical treatises, each entry is accompanied by two
images, one showing the stars as they appear on a celestial globe and
the other their configurations in the heavens. In comparison to earlier
illustrated al-Sufi texts, the finely painted images are unusually large
and occupy much of the surface of the folios; several are even executed
on foldout sheets of cotton and extend well beyond the confines of
the manuscript (Figs. 19 and 20). Instead of the schematized drawings
found in most earlier al-Sufi texts, Malik Husayn's figures have been
meticulously rendered and their contours accentuated with light
washes of colour and delicate shading, lending them a sense of
volume.[58] Malik Husayn's experimentation with the techniques of
modelling and shading was probably inspired by both European and
Indian pictorial sources.

During the 1640s and 1650s, several younger artists, such as Muhammad Qasim, Muhammad Yusuf and Muhammad Ali, Malik Husayn's son, became even more preoccupied with selectively integrating Western artistic principles into traditional Persian artistic idiom. Interestingly, most of them worked for the Armenian governors of Mashhad, who must have encouraged this new particular style of painting, which enjoyed considerable popularity in the mid-seventeenth century.[59]

Among the al-Sufi illustrations, the figure of Sagittarius is of particular interest (Fig. 20). Depicted on one of the large foldout sheets, the bearded figure is wearing the same type of turban as Qarachaqay Khan in the reception scene discussed earlier. On the basis of his carefully individualized features and distinct headgear, Barbara Schmitz has proposed that the figure depicts the patron of the manuscript, Manuchihr Khan.[60]

The sign of Sagittarius also carries additional significance. According to Jallal al-din Munajjim, Abbas I ordered the construction of his new capital towards the beginning of Safar 1000, corresponding to mid-November 1591, which also falls under the sign of Sagittarius.[61] By inserting himself into the pictorial cycle, Manuchihr Khan was embracing a well-established Persian practice and underscoring his role as a patron of the manuscript. His portrayal as Sagittarius may also denote his own birth sign, which would have identified him with Isfahan, the new centre of Safavid political, religious and cultural power.[62]

Manuchihr Khan's project to revise, translate, transcribe and illustrate al-Sufi's treatise certainly required a highly skilled team of artists, who either were part of a permanently staffed library-cum-atelier or may have been temporarily employed for the project. The 17 colophons, which span a period of three years, attest to the manuscript's grand scale. Its purpose was equally ambitious. As the preface implies, the text was intended not simply as Manuchihr Khan's personal copy, but like the *Zij Gurkani* ('Gurkanid Ephemeries'), commissioned by the Timurid prince Ulugh Beg in *ca.* 1440 in Samarqand, as a model for subsequent generations of scientists, artists and presumably patrons like him.[63]

As Manuchihr Khan had hoped, the *Tarjuma-yi suwwar al-kawakib* inspired at least two other illustrated works. One manuscript, dated

1633–34 and now in the Egyptian National Library, Cairo, is almost contemporary with the present text. Its illustrations share a marked similarity to the 1630–33 al-Sufi text, suggesting that it may also have been produced in Mashhad, perhaps even in the governor's library, or by painters familiar with Malik Husayn's work, if not by the artist himself. A second, probably slightly later version, in the Malik Library, Tehran, attests to the continuous artistic and scientific importance of Manuchihr Khan's manuscript.[64]

Although no other illustrated manuscripts commissioned by Manuchihr Khan have been identified at this time, the *Tarjuma-yi suwwar al-kawakib* ('Translation of the Book of Stars') ranks among one of the most innovative illustrated texts of the first half of the seventeenth century, establishing him as a leading patron of the arts of the book. Manuchihr Khan's interest in illustrated texts seems all the more important, for few other securely dated works from the 1630s are known and none can be linked directly to the patronage of Shah Safi (1629–44), Abbas I's son and successor. The manuscript's association with the Armenian *ghulam* and, by extension, the city of Mashhad, also supports the emergence in the 1630s of a manuscript centre other than Isfahan.[65]

When Manuchihr Khan died in 1636, his son Qarachaqay Khan, named after his illustrious grandfather (and hereafter referred to as Qarachaqay Khan II) succeeded him as governor. Relatively little is known about Qarachaqay Khan II's political career, but he seemed as committed as his father to supporting the arts of the book, in particular Persian literary texts.[66] His first commission was a copy of Vahshi's *Farhad u Shirin*, completed in 1636, the very year of his appointment as governor.[67] The present whereabouts of the manuscript are unknown, but its four paintings, notable for their carefully outlined figures and finely stippled surfaces, have been attributed to Muhammad Qasim, an accomplished painter and poet of the first half of the seventeenth century.[68]

The artist's relationship to Qarachaqay Khan II is further illustrated by an unusual tinted drawing of a young man holding an inscribed folio, which reads as follows (Fig. 21):

> He the magnificent Khan, may God extend his eternal shadow, I who invoke blessing upon you, Muhammad Qasim Musavvir, am one of your devoted

servants. May the Almighty Bestower protect your Highness' nobility and graciousness, worthy of the highest epithets, and protect your Lordship from all evil. As this humble one considers himself a novice (*javan*) among those already invoking blessings upon you, by sending an image (*tasvir*) as a letter of appeal (*ariza*), [I hope] to be considered among your servants and beg to be received among your subjects; I hope to be exalted by your acceptance of this letter and to be referred to for a service, the execution of which would be the greatest honour. And salutations.[69]

Unlike several of Muhammad Qasim's other full-length portraits of youths holding inscribed folios of poetry,[70] the image is cropped below the figure's shoulders to focus attention on the inscribed sheet, which is clearly intended as a petition. Although the addressee is simply referred to as a 'Khan', the text implies that he already employed other artists, who were 'invoking blessings' on him. In view of Muhammad Qasim's subsequent association with Qarachaqay Khan II, it can be safely argued the petition was intended for the new governor of Mashhad.

The practice of submitting petitions as an integral part of a painting or drawing was not a new one. Two of the most celebrated sixteenth-century painters, Mir Sayyid Ali and Muzaffar Ali, had already used this device to draw attention to their personal and professional needs.[71] Their requests, however, were addressed to the ruler and members of his immediate family, while Muhammad Qasim is the first Safavid painter to seek the support of a non-royal patron, in this case a member of the slave household. Their sponsorship of manuscripts must have offered artists, such as Muhammad Qasim or Malik Husayn, an alternative source of patronage to that of the royal court, the Qizilbash emirs or to working independently, further broadening and diversifying the Safavid system of patronage.

In 1643–44, Abbas II temporarily removed Qarachaqay Khan II as governor of Mashhad for his reported arrogance (*bad suluki*) and appointed Murtiza Quli Khan, the governor of Marv, a Turkman Qizilbash, to the post. When Murtiza Quli Khan became commander-in-chief of the army (*qurchi bashi*) in 1645–46, Qarachaqay Khan II was restored to his former post, serving as governor of Mashhad until 1664–65.[72] Not long after his reinstatement, he embarked on his most ambitious artistic project – a monumental copy of the *Shahnama* (Figs. 22 and 23), now in the collection of the Royal Library at Windsor Castle, England.[73]

According to the colophon signed by Muhammad Hakim al-Husayni, the scribe of the *Tarjuma-yi suwwar al-kawakib*, the large and sumptuously illustrated *Shahnama* was completed by the order of Qarachaqay Khan II, the *beglarbegi* of Mashhad, in his library in May 1648. Only two of the 148 paintings are signed; the name of Malik Husayn the artist of Manuchihr Khan's al-Sufi manuscript, appears on a finely painted double-page frontispiece, depicting Solomon and the Queen of Sheba (Fig. 22). The other signed composition is by Muhammad Yusuf (folio 320v), one of the most prolific artists of the period, who executed the majority of the illustrations (Fig. 23) On stylistic grounds the other illustrations have been attributed to Muhammad Qasim, who continued to enjoy the governor's favours. A third painter, Muhammad Ali, Malik Husayn's son, may have also contributed to the project.

Qarachaqay Khan II's reliance on some of the same painters and calligraphers employed by his father implies that he must have either inherited Manuchihr Khan's library staff or re-assembled it to complete his monumental *Shahnama*. The newcomer, Muhammad Yusuf, was probably a local artist or at least associated with Mashhad, as is evident from a signed drawing dated 1657–58 and completed in the city.[74]

In addition to its scale and sumptuousness, Qarachaqay Khan II's manuscript is notable for its content, which comprises the post-*Shahnama* epic, the *Burzunama*, an account of the adventures of the legendary hero Burzu, Suhrab's son and Rustam's grandson.[75] The 13 illustrations underscore the importance of the paladin Rustam, his descendants, and the conflict between the Iranians and the Turanians in the narrative cycle. By incorporating the *Burzunama* in his copy of the epic, Qarachaqay Khan II perhaps intended to draw a parallel between his loyalty to Iran and that of the mythical Rustam, especially in light of his recent temporary fall from royal favour. The inclusion of the post-*Shahnama* epic can also be interpreted as a reference to the bitter battle between the Safavids and Uzbeks for Khurasan, a province that had served as the family's power base for decades.

Unlike Vahshi's relatively unknown work, Firdawsi's text, under-scoring universal concepts of courage, loyalty and the Persian ideals of kingship, was an obvious choice for illustration. Qarachaqay

Khan II's commission, however, may have also been prompted by a more personal reason. Upon Abbas II's accession to the throne in 1642, the *qurchi bashi* Murtiza Quli Khan, who had temporarily replaced him as governor of Mashhad, had ordered a monumental illustrated copy of the *Shahnama* as a gift to the new Shah. The manuscript, which was not completed until 1651, is the only other contemporary illustrated text to rival the Windsor Castle *Shahnama* in both size and grandeur.[76] Qarachaqay Khan II's temporary dismissal from the prestigious governorship of Mashhad must have inspired a sense of resentment and animosity between him and Murtiza Quli Khan, as well as the need to re-establish his reputation and reaffirm his loyalty to the Shah. His decision to embark on such an ambitious rival project highlights the importance of illustrated manuscripts as symbols of status, especially among the *ghulams* and the Qizilbash elites continuously vying for power and royal recognition.

Qarachaqay Khan II's 1648 *Shahnama* shares a number of striking characteristics with an unsigned and undated copy of Fridawsi's text, now in the Gulistan Palace Library (Fig. 24). Almost identical in size, the Gulistan manuscript also includes the *Burzunama*, and its 97 illustrations, attributable to Muhammad Yusuf and Muhammad Qasim, rely on the same bold, often schematized compositions, bright, saturated colours combined with dark outlines, and an even greater use of shading and stippling.[77] A third, earlier and smaller copy of the *Shahnama*, datable to the early 1640s, includes a painting by Muhammad Yusuf, who probably executed the rest of the pictorial cycle.[78] The close stylistic similarity of these manuscripts and the thematic correlation of the Windsor and the Gulistan *Shahnamas*, in particular, raise a number of interesting issues. Just as Manuchihr Khan's 'Translation of the Book of Fixed Stars' served as a model for a number of subsequent manuscripts, can we assume that Qarachaqay Khan's *Shahnama* inspired other copies of Firdawsi's text?[79]

An important factor in support of a Khurasani provenance is the marked stylistic difference of these illustrated texts and contemporaneous paintings associated with Isfahan. These include the work of painters such as Mu'in Musavvir, Riza Abbasi's most renowned student. In addition to several copies of the *Shahnama*, created for anonymous patrons, Mu'in is primarily known for his large body of single-page drawings and paintings. His delicately outlined figures, soft shades of purple and orange, and insistence on flat, broad surfaces stand in sharp contrast to the stiffer, more accentuated drawing and vivid palette favoured by Muhammad Yusuf, Muhammad Qasim and Muhammad Ali.[80] Other Isfahani painters, such as Shafi Abbasi, who focused primarily on bird-and-flower compositions inspired by European and Indian pictorial sources, or Shaykh Abbasi, responsible for developing a new 'Indianized' style, worked in a new artistic idiom altogether.[81] The more hybrid, 'international' style of these Isfahani artists suggests that they were responding to the taste and aesthetic preferences of a different group of patrons, such as Qarachaqay Khan.

When considered as a whole, the work of contemporaneous Safavid painters, such as Mu'in Musavvir, Shaykh Abbasi and Muhammad Yusuf, reveals considerable stylistic and thematic variety. Instead of adhering to a strictly codified and homogenised pictorial mode, as in the case of seventeenth-century Mughal painters, for instance, these artists drew on new visual sources or refined traditional ones to forge their own personal and distinct style. Painters tried and developed new styles, formats and subject-matter in an effort to forge their own individual artistic 'signature'.

The different, at times hybrid, pictorial idioms that flourished simultaneously in seventeenth-century Iran, however, cannot be simply explained according to a central, court style and its provincial or sub-imperial variations. For one, the illustrated manuscripts of Manuchihr Khan and Qarachaqay Khan II equalled – if not surpassed – in scale and sumptuousness paintings associated with royal patronage. Instead of supporting painters such as Shafi Abbasi or Shaykh Abbasi, whose single-page compositions were particularly favoured at court, the *ghulams* commissioned illustrated historical, scientific and literary texts, and repeatedly relied on a small group of artists who represented a different mode of painting. Unlike the Qizilbash in the late sixteenth century, the *ghulams* neither emulated the court style nor competed for the same artists. It can be argued that European or Indian pictorial sources may not have been as readily available in Mashhad as in Isfahan or that Qarachaqay Khan and his descendants had to rely on local, more traditional talent for their patronage of the arts of the book. By commissioning illustrated texts of Persian classics or collecting Chinese porcelain, however, they clearly expressed their awareness of long-established Persian cultural norms of the ruling elite. As loyal servants of the Shah and an extension of the royal household, they encouraged a parallel and equally important pictorial tradition, thus contributing to the court's efforts towards the formulation of a new, more diverse and 'international' artistic language that echoed the new cosmopolitan nature of Safavid society. The new pictorial identity is best exemplified in the wall paintings of the Chihil Sutun Palace in Isfahan.

Built by Abbas II in 1647 as the Safavid ceremonial showcase, the palace's public reception area is decorated with historical scenes depicting Safavid rulers and their neighbours. Executed in a new style that fused Indian, European and Persian pictorial conventions, these large, politically charged wall paintings served as visual reminders of the power and authority of the Safavids (Fig. 25). They are juxtaposed with idealized scenes of intimate gatherings and well-known literary themes, rendered in a more traditional Persian idiom with its preference for idealized figures also found in contemporary single-page compositions (Fig. 26).[82] Finally, throughout the public and private spaces, naturalistically rendered floral designs, inspired by Indian models, integrate the entire programme of wall decoration. Although none of the images is signed, they were clearly executed by a team of artists, some of whom worked in a style associated with Manuchihr Khan's and Qarachaqay Khan II's painters in Mashhad, while others favoured the more Europeanized and Indianized visual modes, fashionable in Isfahan. In the Chihil Sutun Palace, different themes and pictorial idioms have been carefully integrated, offering a comprehensive, multifaceted repertoire of images and styles, affirming the new Safavid artistic identity. The painting programme for Abbas II's palace is the most public manifestation of later Safavid pictorial language and patronage, formulated primarily at the court in Isfahan and by members of the *ghulams* in the provinces.

Qarachaqay Khan II's *Shahnama* is the last major project associated with this family of *ghulams*. According to the *Abbasnama*, because of his renewed bad conduct, Qarachaqay Khan II was removed from his post in 1664 and replaced by Safi Quli Beg, the Lord of High

Justice (*divanbegi*), thus terminating the association of this prominent *ghulam* family with Mashhad.[83] The only other member of Qarachaqay Khan's family who is mentioned as a patron is Mihdi Khan, the son of Ali Quli Khan, Qarachaqay Khan II's brother, who built the Khan Madrasa in 1713 in Qum.[84]

As discussed in Chapter 1, with Abbas II's death in 1666, the power and influence of the *ghulams* began to erode, which also undermined their role as patrons of both art and architecture. Among the painters associated with Qarachaqay Khan II, Muhammad Yusuf was still active in Mashhad in 1658, as confirmed by his signed and dated drawing, mentioned earlier, while Muhammad Qasim died in 107[0] AH/1659–6[0] CE and was buried in the Takht-i Pullad cemetery in Isfahan.[85] By the 1660s, the idiosyncratic style of these artists, which had enjoyed considerable popularity during the past two decades, appears to have fallen out of fashion. The next generation, represented by Shaykh Abbasi, Muhammad Zaman and Ali Quli Jabbadar, drew more heavily on both European and Indian artistic concepts and subject-matter in an effort to innovate Persian painting even further. Among them, Ali Quli, a painter of European, probably of Albanian, descent, deserves special mention. Already active in the late 1640s, Ali Quli's signed compositions frequently include the epithet *jabbadar* or 'keeper of the arsenal', suggesting that he was associated with that particular branch of Safavid military, which was controlled by the white eunuchs.[86] As Ali Quli also identified himself as *ghulamzada-yi qadimi* (the son of the old slave), Abolala Soudavar has proposed that it was the painter's father who worked for the arsenal. Ali Quli's foreign descent, his identification as the son of a *ghulam*, and the family's association with the arsenal confirm that, like the late sixteenth-century painter Siyavush, he was also of slave origin. Ali Quli's numerous formal portraits of Shah Sultan Husayn (r. 1666–94) and visiting dignitaries attest to the privileged status he must have held at court.[87] In addition to Ali Quli's work, a group of full-length oil paintings, attributed to the last quarter of the seventeenth century, depict Armenian and Georgian dignitaries. These elaborately painted images, inspired by European oil paintings, further suggest the continuing influence of the slave-elite in late seventeenth-century Safavid Iran.[88]

As some of the most active patrons and collectors of portable luxury arts, the *ghulams* add a fascinating dimension to our understanding of Safavid artistic patronage in the first half of the seventeenth century. Entrusted with some of the highest administrative offices, they reciprocated in part by supporting Safavid artistic and cultural life. Qarachaqay Khan's ability to amass an impressive collection of Chinese porcelain within a relatively short time suggests his highly refined taste and, more importantly, his adoption of Persian cultural ideals, which must have secured his status both among the existing and the new elites. By presenting the collection as a gift to Abbas I and supplementing Ardabil's significant endowment, he also affirmed his devotion and generosity to his royal master. For Allah Virdi Khan and his son, Imam Quli Khan, the patronage of the portable, luxury arts, in particular illustrated manuscripts, held a more commemorative function. The historical chronicles associated with the two eminent *ghulams* celebrate in word and image their military triumphs and, by extension, that of Abbas I. The accounts must have also served as apt reminders of the slaves' steadfast support in the struggle for Safavid political and military hegemony, in contrast to the disloyalty and treachery of some of the rival Qizilbash emirs. As a genre, these texts recall a particular group of Ottoman illustrated manuscripts, also devoted to local campaigns by viziers and other high-ranking dignitaries, such as the 1594 *Tarih-i Feth-i Yemen* ('History of the Conquest of Yemen'), an account of Sinan Paşa's conquest of Yemen in 1570 and that of Tunisia in 1574.[89] Representing the second and third generation of converted slaves, Manuchihr Khan and his son Qarachaqay Khan II chose to give their full attention to the arts of the book to reinforce their Persian identity. As the case of Qarachaqay Khan II's and Mirza Quli Khan's *Shahnama* projects suggests, illustrated texts continued to play an important role for both the *ghulams* and the Qizilbash to affirm loyalty and devotion to the Shah.

Under the governorship of Manuchihr Khan and his son, Mashhad flourished into a significant religious and commercial centre and became an important locus for manuscript production with its own distinctive style equal in importance to that of Isfahan. Rather than competing with the court, as in the case of the Qizilbash in the late sixteenth century, the arts of the book in Mashhad developed as a parallel artistic tradition, further broadening Safavid pictorial language. Like Safavid poetry, the new aesthetic depended on what Paul Losensky has termed the creative interaction of tradition, imitation and innovation and, as argued earlier, finds its fullest expression in the decorative program of the Chihil Sutun Palace in Isfahan.[90]

The association of the *ghulams* with both Chinese porcelain and illustrated manuscripts perhaps also held a particular significance within seventeenth-century Safavid culture. Singled out as the most prized possessions, Abbas I gifted his personal collections of secular texts and porcelain to Ardabil to underline Safavid dynastic power. *Ghulams*, such as Qarachaqay Khan and his descendants, could do no better than follow the royal example and support Safavid political, cultural and artistic ideals.

Appendix

These charts appear in Kathryn Babayan, 'The Waning of the Qizilbash', PhD dissertation (Princeton University, 1993)

A. DISTRIBUTION OF COURT FUNCTIONS BETWEEN TAJIKS, TURKMAN, *ULAMA* AND *GHULAMS*, 1629–66

	Sultan al-Ulama	Mirza Talib	Saru Taqi	Saru Taqi	Sultan al-Ulama	Muh. Bek	Mirza Mahdi
Grand Vizier	Tajik *Ulama*	Tajik	*Ghulam*	*Ghulam*	Tajik *Ulama*	*Ghulam*	Arab *Ulama*
Sipahsalar	Turkman	*Ghulam*	*Ghulam*	Vacant	Turkman *Ghulam*	*Ghulam*	Turkman
Qurchi Bashi	Turkman	Turkman	Turkman	Turkman	Turkman	Turkman	Turkman
Qullar Aqasi	*Ghulam*	*Ghulam*	*Ghulam*	*Ghulam*	*Ghulam*	*Ghulam*	*Ghulam*
Ishik Aqasi Divan	Turkman	Turkman	Turkman	Turkman	Turkman *Ghulam*	Turkman	Turkman
Ishik Aqasi	*Ghulam*	*Ghulam*	*Ghulam*	Turkman	Turkman	Turkman	Turkman
Divan Begi	*Ghulam*	*Ghulam*	*Ghulam*	Turkman	Turkman	Turkman *Ghulam*	*Ghulam*
Tufangchi Aqasi	*Ghulam*	*Ghulam*	*Ghulam*	Turkman	Turkman	Turkman	Turkman
Sadr	Tajik *Ulama*	Arab *Ulama*	Arab *Ulama*	Arab *Ulama*	Arab *Ulama*	Arab *Ulama*	Tajik *Ulama*
Nazir-i Buyutat	*Ghulam*	*Ghulam*	*Ghulam*	*Ghulam*	*Ghulam*	*Ghulam*	Turkman
Mustawfi Mamalik	Tajik	Tajik	Tajik	Tajik	Tajik	Tajik	Tajik
Mustafwi Khassa	Tajik	Tajik	Tajik	Tajik	Tajik	Tajik	Tajik
Majlis Nivis	Tajik	Tajik	Tajik	Tajik	Tajik	Tajik	Tajik
TOTAL	*Ghulam* 5 Tajik 5 Turkman 3 *Ulama* 2	*Ghulam* 6 Tajik 5 Turkman 1 *Ulama* 1	*Ghulam* 7 Tajik 3 Turkman 2 *Ulama* 1	*Ghulam* 3 Tajik 3 Turkman 5 *Ulama* 1	*Ghulam* 2/4 Tajik 4 Turkman 6/4 *Ulama* 2	*Ghulam* 5 Tajik 3 Turkman 5 *Ulama* 1	*Ghulam* 2 Tajik 4 Turkman 5 *Ulama* 2

* Tajik *Ulama* are included under both Tajiks and *Ulama*

B. THE REIGN OF SHAH SAFI, 1629–42
I. Sultan al-Ulama's Administration 1629–32

Function	Functionary
Grand Vizier	Sultan al-Ulama
Sipahsalar	Zaynal Khan Shamlu
	Rustam Bek (1630)
Vakil	Zaynal Khan Shamlu
Qurchi Bashi	Isa Khan Shaykhavand
Qullar Aqasi	Khusraw Mirza/Rustam Khan
Tufangchi Aqasi	Zaman Bek
Sadr	Mir Rafi al-Din Muhammad
Divan Begi	Rustam Khan
Ishik Aqasi of the Divan	Zaynal Khan Shamlu
	Ughurlu Khan (1630)
Ishik Aqasi of the Harem	Abul Qasim Bek
	Evoghlu Chelebi Bek Evoghlu (1630)
Majlis Nivis	Mirza Talib Khan Urdubadi
Nazir-i Buyutat	Zaman Bek
Rish Safid of Harem	Khwaja Muhibb
Shaykh al-Islam of Isfahan	Mirza Qaz
Mustawfi al-Mamalik	Mirza Abul Husayn Bek Urdubadi
Mustawfi al-Khassa	Mirza Qasim Isfahani

II. Mirza Talib Khan's Administration 1632–34

Function	Functionary
Grand Vizier	Mirza Talib Khan Urdubadi
Sipahsalar	Rustam Bek
Vakil	Vacant
Qurchi Bashi	Chiragh Khan Zahidi
	Amir Khan Zulqadr (1632)
Qullar Aqasi	Siyavush Bek
Tufangchi Aqasi	Rustam Bek
Sadr	Mirza Habibullah Karaki
Divan Begi	Rustam Bek
Ishik Aqasi of the Divan	Ughurlu Khan
Ishik Aqasi of the Harem	Chelebi Bek Evoghlu
Majlis Nivis	Mirza Muhammad
Nazir-i Buyutat	Husayn Bek
Rish Safid of Harem	Khwaja Muhibb
Shaykh al-Islam of Isfahan	Mirza Qazi
Mustawfi al-Mamalik	Mirza Sa'id
Mustawfi al-Khassa	Mirza Qasim Isfahani

III. Saru Taqi's Administration 1634–42

Function	Functionary
Grand Vizier	Saru Taqi
Sipahsalar	Rustam Bek
Vakil	Vacant
Qurchi Bashi	Amir Khan Zulqadr
	Jani Bek Shamlu (1637)
Qullar Aqasi	Siyavush Bek
Tufangchi Aqasi	Mir Fitah
Sadr	Mirza Habibullah Karaki
Divan Begi	Rustam Bek
	Ali Quli Bek (1635)
Ishik Aqasi of the Divan	Imam Quli Bek Inanlu-Shamlu
	Jani Bek Shamlu
	Murtaza Quli Bek
	Bijarlu-Shamlu (1637)
Ishik Aqasi of the Harem	Chelebi Bek Evoghlu (d. 1637–38)
	Haydar Bek Evoghlu
Majlis Nivis	Mirza Muhammad Taysar
	Mizra Abul Fath Taysar
	Mizra Ma'Sum (1634)
Nazir-i Buyutat	Husayn Bek (d. 1639–40)
	Muhammad Ali Bek Isfahani
Rish Safid of the Harem	Khwaja Muhibb
Shayk al-Islam of Isfahan	Mirza Qazi
Mustawfi al-Mamalik	Mirza Sa'id
Mustawfi al-Khassa	Hashim Bek Tihrani
	Mirza Muhsin Isfahani

C. THE REIGN OF SHAH ABBAS II, 1642–66
I. Saru Taqi's Administration 1642–45

Function	Functionary
Grand Vizier	Saru Taqi
Sipahsalar	Vacant
Vakil	Saru Taqi*
Qurchi Bashi	Jahni Khan Shamlu
Qullar Aqasi	Siyavush Bek/Khan
Tufangchi Aqasi	Mir Fitah
	Qalandar Sultan
	Chulah Chagatay (1643)
Sadr	Mirza Habibullah Karaki
Divan Begi	Murtaza Quli Bek Bijarlu-Shamlu
Ishik Aqasi of the Divan	Murtaza Quli Bek Bijarlu-Shamlu
Ishik Aqasi of the Harem	Haydar Bek Evoghlu
	Mirza Ali Qubad Bek
	Chulah Chagatay (1643)
Majlis Nivis	Mirza Ma'sum
Nazir-i Buyutat	Muhammad Ali Bek Isfahani
Rish Safid of the Harem	Khwaja Muhibb
Shayk al-Islam of Isfahan	Mirza Qazi
Mustawfi al-Mamalik	Mirza Sa'id
Mustawfi al-Khassa	Mirza Muhsin Isfahani

* Saru Taqi is referred to as Vakil in only one source: Muhammad Tahir Vahid, *Abbasnama*, 50–54.

II. Sultan al-Ulama's Administration 1645–54

Function	Functionary
Grand Vizier	Sultan al-Ulama
Sipahsalar	Murtaza Quli Khan Qajar
	Ali Quli Khan (1648)
Vakil	Vacant
Qurchi Bashi	Murtaza Quli Khan Shamlu
	Murtaza Quli Khan Qajar (1649)
Qullar Aqasi	Siyavush Bek/Khan (d. 1651)
	Allah Virdi Khan
Tufangchi Aqasi	Qalandar Sultan
	Chulah-Chagatay
Sadr	Mirza Habibullah Karaki (d. 1653)
	Mirza Muhammad Mahdi Karaki
Divan Begi	Ughurlu Bek Qajar Ziyadoghlu
Ishik Aqasi of the Divan	Mahdi Quli Khan Shamlu
	Firaydun Bek (1652)
Ishik Aqasi of the Harem	Mirza Ali Qubad Bek
	Chulah Cagatay
Majlis Nivis	Muhammad Tahir Vahid
Nazir-i Buyutat	Muhammad Ali Bek Isfahani (d. 1649)
	Muhammad Bek
Rish Safid of Harem	Khwaja Sandal
Shayk al-Islam of Isfahan	Shayhk Ali Shirazi
Mustawfi al-Mamalik	Mirza Sa'id
Mustawfi al-Khassa	Mirza Muhsin Isfahani

III. Muhammad Bek's Administration 1654–61

Function	Functionary
Grand Vizier	Muhammad Bek
Sipahsalar	Ali Quli Khan
	Allah Virdi Khan (1658–59)
Vakil	Vacant
Qurchi Bashi	Murtaza Quli Khan Qajar
Qullar Aqasi	Allah Virdi Khan
Tufangchi Aqasi	Qalandar Sultan Chulah-Chagatay
Sadr	Mirza Muhammad Mahdi Karaki
Divan Begi	Ughurlu Bek Qajar Ziyad-Oghlu
	Safi Quli Bek (1657)
Ishik Aqasi of the Divan	Mahdi Quli Khan Shamlu
Ishik Aqasi of the Harem	Mirza Ali Qubad Bek
	Chulah-Chagatay (d. 1661)
Majlis Nivis	Muhammad Tahir Vahid
Nazir-i Buyutat	Safi Quli Bek/Khan
Rish Safid of Harem	Khwaja Sandal
Shayk al-Islam of Isfahan	Shaykh 'Ali Shirazi
Mustawfi al-Mamalik	Mirza Sa'id (d. 1662)
	Mirza Sadr al-Din
	Muhammad Jabiri
Mustawfi al-Khassa	Mirza Muhsin Isfahani

IV. Mirza Muhammad Mahdi's Administration 1661–66

Function	Functionary
Grand Vizier	Mirza Muhammad Mahdi Karaki
Sipahsalar	Ali Quli Khan (dismissed in 1665)
	Zaman Bek Qajar
Vakil	Vacant
Qurchi Bashi	Murtaza Quli Khan Qajar (dismissed in 1663)
	Husayn Quli Khan Shamlu (1664)
Qullar Aqasi	Allah Virdi Khan (d. 1662)
	Jamshid Khan
Tufangchi Aqasi	Qalandar Sultan
	Chulah Chagatay (1661–62)
	Budaq Sultan Chulah-Chagatay
Sadr	Mirza Qavam al-Din
	Muhammad (1661–64)
Divan Begi	Safi Quli Bek/Khan Avaz Bek (1663)
	Abbas Quli Bek (1664)
Ishik Aqasi of the Divan	Mahdi Quli Khan Shamlu
	Ughurlu Khan Shamlu (1663–64)
Ishik Aqasi of the Harem	Abdal Bek Chulah-Cagatay
Majlis Nivis	Muhammad Tahir Vahid
Nazir-i Buyutat	Safi Quli Bek/Khan
	Zaman Bek Qajar (1665)
Rish Safid of Harem	Khwaja Sandal
Shayk al-Islam of Isfahan	Shaykh Ali Shirazi
Mustawfi al-Mamalik	Mirza Sadr al-Din
	Muhammad Jabiri
Mustawfi al-Khassa	Mirza Muhsin Isfahani

D. PROVINCIAL GOVERNORS UNDER SAFI AND ABBAS II
I. Safi (1038–52/1629)

Qandahar	Ali Mardan Khan (1633–38)
Amir al-Umara	Nazar Bek Zik Mughul (1637–38)
Herat	Hasan Khan Shamlu (d. 1641–42)
Amir al-Umara/Beglarbegi	Abbas Quli Khan Shamlu
Azerbaijan	Pir Budaq Khan Purnak Turkman (1635–36)
Amir al-Umara/Beglarbegi	Rustam Khan (*Ghulam* Sipahsalar)
	Pir Budaq Sultan (dismissed) (1640–41)
Erevan	Tahmasb Quli Khan Qajar (1635–36)
Amir al-Umara/Beglarbegi	Kalb Ali Khan
	Muh. Quli Bek Chagatay (1640)
Qarabagh and Ganja	Imam Quli Khan (*Ghulam*) (d. 1633)
Amir al-Umara/Beglarbegi	Muh. Quli Khan Ziyadoghlu Qajar
Beglarbegi	Murtaza Quli Khan Ziyadoghlu Qajar
Astarabad	Khusraw Khan (*Ghulam*) (1636)
Amir al-Umara/Beglarbegi	Qazaq Khan (*Ghulam*) (1636–39)
	Husayn Bek (Nazir-i Buyutat)
	Mihrab Bek (*Ghulam*) (1641–42)
Kuh-Giluya	Naqdi Khan Shamlu (d. 1638–39)
Amir al-Umara/Beglarbegi	Zaynal Bek Shamlu
Kirman	X. Zulqadr (1628–29)
Beglarbegi	Jani Khan Shamlu (1637–39)
Marv-i Shahi Jahan	Murtaza Quli Khan Qajar in (1641–42)
Beglarbegi	
Qalamraw-i Ali Shikar	???
Amir al-Umara/Beglarbegi	
Mashhad	Manuchahr Khan (*Ghulam*) (1633–34)
	Qarachaqay Khan (*Ghulam*)
Qazvin Darugha	Shah Virdi Bek Turkman

II. Abbas II (1642–66)

Qandahar	Ali Mardan Khan (1642–43)
	Mihrab Khan Qajar (d. 1648)
Amir al-Umara	Haji Manuchahr Bek Qajar
	Utar Khan (1652)
	Zulfaqar Khan (1658–63)
	Kartasb Bek (*Ghulam*)
Shirvan	Arab Khan (d.1643–44)
	Khusraw Khan (*Ghulam*)
Amir al-Umara	Zul Faqar Khan (1652–53)
	Manuchahr Khan Qajar (1660)
	Muhammad Khan Qajar (1661)
	Najaf Quli Khan Charkas (1662–63)
Herat	
Amr al-Umara/Beglarbegi	Abbas Quli Khan Shamlu (1664–65)
Azerbaijan	Siyavush Khan (*Ghulam*)
	Ali Quli Khan (*Ghulam*)
Amir al-Umara/Beglarbegi	Murtaza Quli Khan Qajar (1658–59)
	Pir Budaq Khan (1663–64)
Erevan	Kaykhusraw Khan Charkas (*Ghulam*)
	(1645–)
Amir al-Umara/Beglarbegi	Abbas Quli Khan Qajar (1663)
Qarabagh and Ganja	Murtaza Quli Qajar (1646)
Amir al-Umara/Beglarbegi	Urghurlu Bek Ziyadoghlu (1664)
Astarabad	Mihrab Khan Qajar (1646)
(Dar al-Marz)	Muh. Quli Khan (*Ghulam*) (1651)
Amir al-Umara/Beglarbegi	Jamshid Khan (*Ghulam*) (d.1660–61)
Kuh-Kiluya	Zaynal Khan Shamlu (imprisoned in 1645–46)
	Siyavush Bek (*Ghulam* Qullar Aqasi)
	Pir Budaq Khan Turkman (1663–66)
Amir al-Umara/Beglarbegi	Muhammad Zaman Khan
Kirman	Murtaza Quli Khan Qajar (Qurchi Bashi and
Beglarbegi	Sipahsalar) (1648)
Khassa from 1655–59	Abbas Quli Khan (1651)
Marv-i Shahi Jahan	Murtaza Quli Khan Qajar
	Ali Quli Khan (*Ghulam*) (1645)
Amir	Qurkhams Khan
	Aslan Khan (1658–29)
Qalamraw-i Ali Shikar	???
Mashhad	Qarachaqay Khan (*Ghulam*)
	Manuchahr Khan (*Ghulam*)
Beglarbegi	Safi Quli Khan (*Ghulam*) (1666)
Qazvn Darugha	Karjasi Bek (*Ghulam*) (1645–46)

Notes on the Text

Chapter 1

1 Mullah Salih Qazvini, *Muhazirat al-udaba va muhavirat al-shuara va al-bulaqa*, cited in Rasul Jafariyan, *Safaviyya dar arsa-yi din, farhang, va siyasat*, vol. 2 (Qum: Pajuhishkada-yi Hawza va Danishgah, 2000): 792.

2 Our panel was entitled 'New Elites of Isfahan: Patronage, Aesthetics and Power in Safavid Iran', Second Biennial Conference on Iranian Studies (SIS/AIIS), Washington DC, May 1998.

3 For Samarra and slave armies, see Matthew Gordon, *The Breaking of a Thousand Swords: A History of the Turkish Military in Samarra (AH 200–275/815–889 CE)* (Albany: State University of New York Press, 2001).

4 See David Ayalon, 'Mamlukiyyat', in *Outsiders in the Lands of Islam: Mamluks, Mongols and Eunuchs* (London: Variorum, 1988): 321–49.

5 See Bibliography.

6 For one such comparative study see Orlando Patterson, *Slavery and Social Death* (Cambridge: Cambridge University Press, 1982); this is an attempt to place Islamic slavery within global paradigms of slavery drawn from a rich body of scholarship on North America, South America, Africa, Europe, Far East and Russia.

7 The concept of *shahsevan* may have been already introduced during the reign of Muhammad Khudabanda (r. 1578–87).

8 By the term individual we do not mean to convey hyper-individuality but rather a distinction between tribal solidarities and other group interests.

9 For an analysis of this pilgrimage's narrative, see Charles Melville, 'Shah 'Abbas and the Pilgrimage to Mashhad', in Charles Melville (ed.), *Safavid Persia: The History and Politics of an Islamic Society* (London: I. B. Tauris, 1996): 191–229.

10 See Robert McChesney, '*Waqf* and Public Policy: The *Waqf* of Shah 'Abbas, 1011–1023/1602–1616', *Asian and African Studies*, 15 (1981), 169–70.

11 Jean Chardin, *Les Voyages du Chevalier Chardin en Perse et autres lieux de l'Orient* (Paris: Le Normant, 1811): vol. 5, 308 and vol. 6, 24 and 40–42.

12 Vladmir Minorsky, *Tazkirat al-muluk* (London: Gibb Memorial, 1943): 127, n.4, has suggested that there may be some confusion regarding this house and the *anbar-i ghulaman* (the storehouse of the slaves).

13 For the important role of the Georgian *ghulams* see Hirotake Maeda, 'The *Ghulams* of Safavid Dynasty: The Case of Georgian Origin', *Toyo Gakuho*, 81 (1999), 1–32 and 'The Innovation of the Political System under the Safavid Dynasty: The Historical Role of the Gholams', *Shigaku–Zasshi* (57: 1998), Rudolph Matthee, 'Georgians in the Safavid Administration', *Encyclopaedia Iranica*, vol. 10, 493–96, Giorgio Rota, 'The Shah's Janissaries: Safavid *Ghulams* (1587–1722)', unpublished paper presented at Middle Eastern Studies Association Annual Conference, 1997.

14 Anonymous, *Safarnama-yi manzum-i Hajj*, Rasul Jafariyan (ed.) (Qum: n.p., 1995): 24.

15 Chardin, *Les Voyages*, vol. 5, 433 as cited in Minorsky, 127.

16 We would like to thank Gülru Necipoğlu for pointing out this significant difference between Safavid and Ottoman slave patronage.

Chapter 2

1 For the metaphor of slavery as 'social death', see Orlando Patterson *Slavery and Social Death: A Comparative Study* (Cambridge, MA: Harvard University Press, 1982). The term *ghulam-i khassa-yi sharifa* enters Safavid discourse by the end of Shah Tahmasb's reign.

2 See David Ayalon, *Eunuchs, Caliphs and Sultans: A Study in Power Relationships* (Jerusalem: Magnes Press, 1999).

3 See Ayalon on his coining of the term *great triangle* to depict the collaboration among eunuchs, concubines and military slaves in Muslim systems like that of the Mamluks in Egypt and Ottomans, where the institution of slavery was the main form of rule.

4 See *Encyclopaedia Iranica* 2 articles, '*Ghulam*', by D. Sourdel, C.E. Bosworth, P. Hardy and H. Inalcik, '*Abd*', by R. Brunschvig. Also see *Encyclopaedia Iranica* article on '*Barda and Bardadari*', by M.A. Dandamayev, M. Macuch, C.E. Bosworth and W. Floor, *Slavery In the Islamic Middle East*, *Princeton Papers*, Shaun Marmon (ed.), vol. 7, 1999.

5 The categorization of the eunuch as a third gender in Muslim societies has been discussed by Shaun Marmon, *Eunuchs and Sacred Boundaries in Islamic Society* (New York: Oxford University Press, 1995).

6 See David Ayalon, *Eunuchs, Caliphs and Sultans* (295, 317–25) on eunuchs who did get married and have children, as well as those who were still sexually active, engaging both in same-sex and heterosexual intercourse.

7   See the *Dastur al-muluk* and the *Tazkirat al-muluk*, two Safavid admin-
     istrative manuals from the early eighteenth century, as well as my article
     in *Encyclopaedia Iranica*, on 'Eunuchs under the Safavids'.

8   See Willem Floor, *The Safavid Government Institutions* (Costa Mesa, CA:
     Mazda Publishers, 2001): 167–75, on the *ghulams*. Floor, quoting from
     Iskandar Bek Munshi, claims that *ghulams* were first recruited from among
     the Chagatay, Arab and Persian population of Khurasan, Azerbaijan and
     Tabaristan. As a cautionary note it is important to distinguish between
     the Safavid usage of the term *ghulam* as a common rendering of allegiance
     to the household and the particular category of slaves of the royal
     household.

9   Nasir al-din Tusi, *The Nasirean Ethics*, trans. G.M. Wickens (London:
     George Allen & Unwin Ltd, 1964): 182.

10   Nizam al-Mulk, *The Book of Government*, trans. H. Darke (London:
     Routledge & Kegan Paul, 1960): 121. This quote is cited by David Ayalon,
     'Aspects of the Mamluk Phenomenon', *The Mamluk Military Society*
     (London: Variorum Reprints, 1979): 216.

11   See Dick Davis, *Epic and Sedition* (Fayetteville: University of Arkansas
     Press, 1992) as well as his recent translation of sections from Ferdowsi's
     Shahnama that deal with the theme of *Fathers and Sons* (Washington,
     DC: Mage Publishers, 2000).

12   See Leslie Peirce, *The Imperial Harem, Women and Sovereignty in the
     Ottoman Empire* (New York: Oxford University Press, 1993) for a parallel
     development in the Ottoman empire.

13   See Patricia Crone, *Slaves on Horses: The Evolution of the Islamic Polity*
     (London: Cambridge University Press, 1980); and Fred Donner's review
     of Crone's book in the *Journal of the American Oriental Society*, 102
     (1982), 367–71. Jürgen Paul in *The State and the Military: The Samanid
     Case*, Papers on Inner Asia, 26 (Bloomington, IN: Indiana University
     Press, 1994) refers to these debates.

14   Paul, *The State and the Military*, 5.

15   See my book entitled *Mystics, Monarch and Messiahs: Cultural Land-
     scapes of Early Modern Iran* (Cambridge MA: Harvard Middle Eastern
     Monographs, 2003).

16   Martin Dickson, *Shah Tahmasb and the Uzbeks*, PhD dissertation (Princeton:
     Princeton University, 1958).

17   Ibid., 7.

18   Ibid., 8.

19   Ismail had married his sister to Abdi Bek Shamlu. For a detailed study of
     Safavid–Qizilbash marriage alliances see Maria Szuppe, 'La participation
     des femmes de la famille royale à l'exercise du pouvoir en Iran Safavide

au XVI siècle,' part I and II in *Studia Iranica*, 23.2 (1994) and 24.1 (1995): 61–122.

20   For a notable study of the first sixteen years of the reign of Shah Tahmasb see Martin Dickson, *Shah Tahmasb and the Uzbeks*, PhD dissertation (Princeton: Princeton University, 1958).

21   Hasan Bek Rumlu, *Ahsan al-tavarikh* (Tehran: Intisharat-i Babak, 1978): 543–47.

22   On the Qurchis see Masashi Haneda, *Le Chah et les Qizilbash: Le système militaire Safavide* (Berlin: Karl Schwarz, 1987).

23   This could easily be expected from the Takkalu in particular, since except for Herat, this *oymaq* had been driven from all major posts and appanages in the course of the Grand Sedition (1534) of the early Tahmasb period.

24   See Martin Dickson's notes on Ibrahim Mirza and the Khusaran Administration 1556–76, Notebook no 140, Regenstein Library, University of Chicago. Dickson seems to be quoting from Khuzani's *Afzal al-tavarikh*.

25   Ibid.

26   Iskandar Bek Munshi, *Tarikh-i alam ara-yi Abbasi*, ed. Iraj Afshar, 2 vols (Tehran: Intisharat-i Amir Kabir, 1350/1971): 875.

27   Bidlisi, Amir Sharaf Khan, *Sharafnama*, Muhammad Abbasi (ed.) (Tehran, 1964): 577.

28   Martin Dickson and Stuart Cary Welch, *The Houghton Shahnamah* (Harvard University Press, 1981): 242a, n. 30. I have added some of my own translations here.

29   Hasan Bek Rumlu, *Ahsan al-tavarikh*, 34, recorded under the year 1532–33. Even Safavid courtiers like Mirza Shah Husayn, an architect responsible for early buildings in Isfahan under Ismail, owned slaves. Rumlu refers to the slaves of (*ghulaman-i*) Mirza Shah Husayn. This architect/builder was made vizier of Isfahan and was patronized by a Qizilbash tutor of Tahmasb, Durmish Khan Shamlu, 233.

30   Ibid., 209, 215 and 472. Hasan Bek Rumlu was born in 1531–32 and completed his history in 1578.

31   Nizam al-Mulk, 106.

32   Ibid., 107.

33   Nasir al-din Tusi, *Akhlaq-i Nasiri*, 154.

34   For a detailed account of this massacre see Kathryn Babayan, *The Waning of the Qizilbash*, PhD dissertation (Princeton University, 1993); and *Mystics, Monarch and Messiahs: Cultural Landscapes of Early Modern Iran* (Cambridge MA: Harvard Middle Eastern Monographs, 2003). This segment of the chapter draws on these two aforementioned studies.

35   See Leslie Peirce, *The Imperial Harem*, op. cit., for an Ottoman parallel.

36 Iskandar Bek Munshi, *Tarikh*, vol. 2, 1088. Twenty-one *ghulams* held such positions at the death of Abbas I.

37 Mulla Salih Qazvini, *Muhazirat al-udaba va muhavirat al-shu'ara' wa al-bulaqa'*. Cited in Rasul Jafaryan, *Safaviyya dar 'arsa-yi din, farhang va siyasat* (Qum: Pajuhishkada-i Hawza va Danishgah, 1379) vol. 2, 790.

38 Abd al-Hayy Razavi Kashani, *Hadiqat al-shi'a*, f 41, as cited by Rasul Ja'faryan, 'Intiqad az vazi'at-i Jami'i-yi dini-yi asr-i safavi', *Kayhan-i Andisha*, 37, 159.

39 See Iskandar Bek Munshi's list of *ghulams* at the end of Abbas I's reign; the *ghulams* were assigned to gubernatorial posts that also entailed leadership of tribes and clans (*oymaq va il*). *Tarikh-i alam ara-yi Abbasi*, vol. 2, 1088.

40 One of Abbas I's sons, Sam Mirza, had been married to the daughter of the ruler of Gilan, Khan Ahmad Khan, continuing the policy of marriage with regional rulers, until Abbas I finally incorporated Gilan into Safavid *khassa*. Sam Mirza had also been given a Georgian concubine who was the mother of Shah Safi. In another marriage that reveals a shift in Safavid dynastic policy, Abbas I married his son to a Safavid princess, a cousin, the daughter of Ismail II and the Georgian royal princess, Fakhr-i Jihan Begum. Those Safavid princesses who were not married to Persian notables and Imami *ulama* were kept in the family.

41 This practice was terminated with the killing of Safi Quli Mirza, in 1614. Safi Quli Mirza, Shah Abbas I's talented son, had been killed by order of his father on charges that along with some Circassian *ghulams* who were related to his mother, he was fomenting a revolt against Abbas I. According to Röhrborn, the last time that a prince was sent out to the provinces was in 1591–92. Iskandar Bek Munshi, *Tarikh*, vol. 1, 444.

42 See Appendix for the shifting power of various slave factions at the court of Shah Safi and Shah Abbas II. Though the *ghulams* do not dominate the majority of administrative posts they do possess the most important military and administrative offices under the vizierate of Mirza Talib Khan (1632–34), Saru Taqi (1634–42) and Muhammad Bek (1654–61). The reigns of Shah Sulayman (r. 1642–66) and Shah Sultan Husayn (r. 1666–1722) remain to be studied.

43 The Gharib Shah rebellion in June 1630 represented another manifestation of centrifugal opposition. This local dynastic revolt started in Gilan with the blessing of Pir Shams-i Gulgiluva'i, the spiritual guide of Gharib Shah, and spread to Lahijan and Mazandaran. It was led by descendents of local Mazandarani and Gilani dynasties who were reclaiming their hereditary rights to ancestral lands that had been annexed by the Safavids under Abbas I. The number killed reached eight thousand, according

to the chroniclers. Abd al-Fattah Fumani, *Tarikh-i Gilan* (Tehran: Intisharat-i Bunyad-i Farhang-i Iran, 1970): 222–28; Muhammad Khwajagi Isfahani, *Khulasat al-siyar* (Tehran: Intisharat-i Ilmi, 1989), 49–53; Mir Taymur Mar'ashi, *Tarikh-i khandan-i Mar'ashi-yi Mazandaran* (written in 1664) (Tehran, 1977), 312–16. Externally too, Iran experienced unrest. Khusraw Pasha made his sortie from Diyar Bakr and headed for Baghdad in 1629. The Uzbeks attacked the Safavid eastern frontier in May–June 1629.

44 A philological study of the chroniclers' use of the terms '*qizilbash*' and '*sufi*' remains to be done. For the time being, see, for example, Vali Quli Shamlu, *Qisas al-khaqani*. Hasan Sadat Nasiri (ed.). 2 vols (Tehran: Vizarat-i Irshad-i Islami, 1371/1992): f 179a, 'The qizilbash sword of the general, Safi Quli Bek...'

45 Muhammad Khwajagi Isfahani, *Khulasat al-siyar*, 83. Another important event occurred during this period when the harem was cut off from its normal access to the Shah. Najaf Quli Bek, the son of Imam Quli Mirza, was blinded and sent to Alamut (14 June 1630). This blinding put an end to any lingering aspirations held by the Imam Quli Mirza cabalists to attain power. With the maiming of their healthy five-year-old Safavid princeling, the conspirators of this cabal had no legitimate candidate around whom to voice their opposition.

46 Muhammad Khwajagi Isfahani, *Khulasat al-siyar*, 94. Zaynal Khan was a pro-Safi cabalist of the Shamlu tribe. He held a few sensitive posts at court. He was the *ishik aqasi* of the divan (master of ceremonies) and had been named the commander-in-chief of the Iranian armies, as well as vice regent (*vakil*) in the beginning of Safi's reign. The *Khuld-i barin* (f 29b) states, 'he was sent to the wind of destruction by the lightning of the eunuchs' (*khwaja sarayan*) thorn.' In addition, Abul Qasim Bek, *ishik aqasi* of the harem was fired, given that he had apparently informed Zaynal Khan of this assassination plot. See Appendix for details on changes in government posts.

47 Ali Quli Khan Shamlu was the grandson of the famous tutor of Shah Tahmasb, Durmish Khan Shamlu. Zaynal Khan had been made *vakil* during the Nowruz celebrations (20–21 March 1629) – ten days after Zaynal Begum was brought back to the Ali Qapu (*dawlatkhana*) as *banu* of the harem. Naming Zaynal Khan Shamlu as *vakil* may have been one of the conditions she placed on her return to the harem.

48 See Giorgio Rota, 'Three Lesser Known Persian Sources of the Seventeenth Century,' PhD dissertation (Naples, 1995). I would like to thank the author for providing me with a copy of his dissertation as well as his unpublished paper entitled 'The Shah's Janissaries: Safavid *Ghulams* (1587–1722)' presented at MESA 1997. Rota has identified Rustam Khan as belonging to the Saak'aje family.

49 Rustam Bek was made *divan begi* in 1628, a year before the death of Abbas I. Bijan, *Tarikh-i Safavi Khan* (British Library, Add. 7655, f10a). The post of *divan begi* would be held by a *ghulam* throughout the reign of Shah Safi. See Appendix on the cabinets of Shah Safi.

50 He received the title of *sipahsalar* in 1631 and the title of *tufangchi aqasi* (head of the infantry) on 15 July 1631. The *Tazkirat al-muluk* makes no mention of the *sipahsalar*. The *Dastur al-muluk*, 80, states, 'The *sipahsalar* is one of the important military [*jangi*] amirs, and his rank precedes that of the *qurchi bashi*. He can dismiss governors and other military-related personnel.' On the *tufangchi aqasi*, see the *Tazkirat al-muluk*, 48, 86, 118. The *tufangchi aqasi* is one of the four 'pillars' (*arkan*) of state who resides at court. He is the senior officer of the musketeers (*tufangchi*), the 'master of a thousand' (*min-bashi*), the 'master of a hundred' (*yuz-bashi*), the herald (*jarchi*), and the artillery department. On different renderings of the *sipahsalar* see Roger Savory, 'The Office of *Sipahsalar* (commander-in chief) in the Safavid State,' in Bert Fragner (ed.), *Proceedings of the Second European Conference of Iranian Studies* (Rome, 1995) 597–615; and Willem Floor, *Safavid Government Institutions* (Costa Mesa CA: Mazda Publishers, 2001): 17–18. One of Floor's disagreements with Savory is that the *sipahsalar* did not command Qizilbash troops as well as 'other' (I assume he means *qurchi* and *tufangchi*) troops nor was he superior in status to the *qurchi bashi* in the seventeenth century. Both the case of Rustam Bek and Qarachaqay Khan as well as the *Dastur al-muluk's* delineation of the role of *sipahsalar* contradicts Floor's assertion.

51 Qarachaqay Khan is referred to by the title of *sipahsalar* in 1619.

52 Iskandar Bek, *Tarikh*, vol. 2, 1039–40. A genre of manumission declarations (*azadname*) ought to be studied to determine the contours of freedom and enslavement in respect to the ownership of body and property in Safavid contexts.

53 Ibid.

54 Vladmir Minorsky, *Tazkirat al-muluk*, 117. Minorsky states that in earlier times the *amir al-umara* was also the *qurchi bashi*; however, according to Martin Dickson this is not the case. Minorsky argues that by the days of Abbas I the prerogative of the *amir al-umara* was curtailed through the creation of new troops. The *Tazkirat al-muluk* calls him the senior officer [*rish safid*] of all the tribes of Iran, but not of the armed forces.' By the time of Abbas I's death, 21 *ghulams* had been given the titles of *amir*, *khan*, or *sultan* in their capacity as *beglarbegis*, *hakims* in the provinces. Along with these posts in the provinces came their novel function as *mir* (short for *amir*) of a tribe (*il*), *oymaq* (clan), and troops of an *oymaq* (e.g., Farukh Sultan was named *beglarbegi* of

Shirvan and the *mir* of the Bayat and Rumlu *ghazis*; *Tarikh-i alam ara-yi Abbasi*, vol. 2, 1088. From this author's research it can be concluded that by the time of Safi and Abbas II, the title of *amir al-umara* had been deflated so that it was bestowed upon governors of provinces and had come to be used synonymously with the title *beglarbegi*. For example, Rustam Khan *sipahsalar* was given the post of *beglarbegi* of Azerbaijan along with the title of *amir al-umara* in 1635. In 1635–36 Kalb Ali Khan was given the title of *amir al-umara* of Erevan. During Saru Taqi's administration, there were the *amir al-umara* of Qandahar, Shirvan, Herat, Azerbaijan, Erevan, Qarabagh, Astarabad, Kuh Giluya, Marv, Qalamru, and Ali Shikar (11 out of the 13 provinces; the governors of Kirman and Mashhad were still referred to as *beglarbegi* only); see Appendix. Here again I disagree with W. Floor (*Safavid Government Institutions*, 17), who equates the function of *sipahsalar* with that of *amir al-umara* and states that the latter title was more commonly used in the sixteenth century. In general, my qualms with Floor emanate from his ahistorical analysis of the Safavid past that tends, in this case, to look at functions and titles as static nomenclature, which do not shift in meaning and role during different phases of Safavid rule.

55 See Appendix.

56 See the *Tazkirat al-muluk*, the *Dastur al-muluk*, and Klaus Michael Röhrborn, *Provinzen und Zentralgewalt Persiens im 16 und 17 Jahrhundert* (Berlin: De Gruyter, 1966), on the *darugha*.

57 This Rustam Khan/Khusraw Mirza of Bagrati royal Georgian blood should not be confused with the *divan begi*, Rustam Bek, the ambitious architect of the pro-Safi slave faction. It is possible that due to the similarity of the names of these two prominent slaves, Bijan, the author of Rustam Bek's (*divan begi*) biography (*Tarikh-i Safavi Khan*, written in 1692) claimed noble descent for his patron's family alluding to Rustam Khan/Khusraw Mirza's Georgian royal lineage. Rustam Bek, however, was a Saak'aje with no trace of royalty. See Rota 'The Shah's Jannissaries', for a discussion on the false claim of Bijan. Rota, however, does not address the possibility of an intentional lumping together of Rustam Bek with Rustam Khan/Khusraw Mirza Bagrati.

58 Although Rudi Matthee, 'Georgians in the Safavid Administration', *Encyclopaedia Iranica*, and Savory (1995) classify Allah Virdi Khan as an Armenian from Georgia, Giorgio Rota using Georgian sources has identified Allah Virdi Khan and his son Imam Quli Khan's family as that of the Georgian Undilajes.

59 This uprising in Georgia needs to be examined in the context of both Georgian dynastic politics and Safavid politics. The *Zayl-i tarikh-i alam*

ara-yi Abbasi, Iskandar Beg Munshi and Muhammad Yusuf Muvarrikh, *Zayl-i alam ara-yi Abbasi*, ed. Suhayli-Khwansari (Tehran: Islamiyya, 1317/1938): 114–15, talks about a fourth cabal that formed around the son of Imam Quli Khan, who, it is said, was actually the son of Abbas I. Davud Khan, another son of Imam Quli Khan, had apparently cajoled Tahmuras Khan into revolting against Shah Safi. He had claimed that one of his brothers was the son of Shah Abbas I and that he had already captured all of Fars, Bahrain, Lar, Hurmuz, Khuzistan, Arabistan and Huwayza. He informed Tahmurs Khan that his brother had thirty thousand troops fighting for him and that the *khutba* and coins had been read and minted in the name of that prince in Fars.

60   Khusraw Mirza was related to Shah Safi through one of Abbas I's marriages (Fakhr-i Jahan Begum). Safi's father (who had been executed on Shah Abbas I's orders in 1615) was the product of Shah Abbas I's marriage to Fakhr-i Jahan Begam, the daughter of Bikrat Khan VI, the *vali* of Gurgistan-i Kartil (1615–19) and the niece of Khusraw Miza. On the valiships of tributary states, see the *Dastur al-muluk*, 70–72. According to the *Dastur al-muluk*, there were five *valis* in Safavid Iran: of Arabistan, Luristan, Gurgistan (Kartil and Kakheti), Kurdistan and the Bakhtiyaris. Each *vali* payed a tribute to the court, both in kind and in cash. He provided troops for campaigns fought in the vicinity of his *vilayat*. Either his son or brother served at court – as a hostage – among the eunuchs (*aqayan*).

61   Muhibb Ali Bek's involvement with the slave faction of Rustam Khan was divulged later, when a corruption charge implicated him with this faction. The way in which Saru Taqi discredited the former Tajik grand vizier (Mirza Talib Khan) and acquired his post reveals the network of alliances that entwined the Tajik bureaucrats with Rustam Bek's *ghulam* faction. In addition, the case of Saru Taqi and his *ghulam* patron at court demonstrates one channel through which an individual could advance in the Isfahani phase (post-1590) of Safavid administrative history.

62   See this author's article on eunuchs in *Encyclopaedia Iranica* from which this information is derived. The *Dastur al-muluk* speaks of two tutors, one for the court (*ghulaman-i khassa-yi sharifa*) and the other referred to as *anbari*. The latter may have been a reserve of trained *ghulams* not yet employed for court service (306). See Chardin's description of Isfahan when he mentions the 'Anbar of ghoulaman' adjacent to the bazaar of Lalé Bek (Muhibb Ali Bek), *Voyages*, vol. 7, 326.

63   For the different forms of castration in Islamic societies see David Ayalon, *Eunuchs, Caliphs and Sultans*, Appendix E.

64   Chardin, *Voyages*, vol. 5, 42.

65   *Tazkirat al-muluk*, 56.

66   A second subgroup of *muqarrabs* introduced by the *Dastur al-muluk* are the *yuzbashi* (centurions), one to command the white *ghulams* and the other to command the black eunuchs. Once again these were posts introduced by Abbas I to expand the power of the eunuchs and by extension of the Safavid household.

67   Halil Inalcik, *The Ottoman Empire: The Classical Age 1300–1600*, trans. N. Itzkowitz and C. Imber (London: Weidenfeld and Nicolson, 1973): 86. See also H. Uzunçarsili, *Osmanli Devletinin Saray Teskilati* (Ankara, Turk Tarih Kurumu Basimevi, 1945). More is known about the Ottoman palace system in which eunuchs seemed to have enjoyed similar functions as in the Safavid court.

68   In the *Dastur al-muluk* three sub-groups (*maqala*) appear under the rubric of *muqarrab al-khaqan*. The *Tazkirat al-muluk* enumerates only two subgroups, for it does not include the *yuzbashis* in a separate division, 56. Two of the three subgroups of *muqarrabs* delineated by the *Dastur al-muluk* consist of eunuchs: white and black eunuchs (*khwaja sarayan-i safid va siyah*) and a separate group of white eunuchs (*khwaja sarayan-i safid*).

69   *Dastur al-muluk*, 302; *Tazkirat al-muluk*, 56.

70   Chardin, *Voyages*, vol. 6, 22.

71   The *Dastur al-muluk* notes that this post was split in two: one *rish safid* who went off on campaigns (*rish safid-i jilu*) and the *rish safid* of the harem in Isfahan who inherited all the prerogatives of the Shah in his absence. *Dastur al-muluk*, 302.

72   *Dastur al-muluk*, 302.

73   *Tazkirat al-muluk*, 56.

74   *Dastur al-muluk*, 303.

75   The posts of master of the wardrobe and the tutor of the *ghulams* could be held either by white or black eunuchs.

76   Ibid., 306.

77   Eunuchs between the ages of eight and sixteen would cost 1000–2000 French francs. Chardin, *Voyages*, vol. 6, 24 and 40–42.

78   See Floor (2001), 175, for a range of salaries received by slaves (from 6 tumâns to 180 tumâns), demonstrating both a multiplicity of posts and a hierarchy of slaves.

79   For more on Muhibb Ali Bek, see Robert McChesney, 'Four Sources on Shah Abbas I's Building of Isfahan', *Muqarnas* 5 (1988), 122–23; and 'Waqf and Public Policy: The Waqfs of Shah Abbas 1011–1023/1602–14', *Asian and African Studies* 15 (1981), 179.

80   On the *malik al-tujjar*, the *Tazkirat al-muluk* remains silent, but Minorsky speculates that he was probably elected by the merchants themselves. Chardin refers to the post as the 'prévôts des marchands' and states that

each town had one. The fact that in this period the *malik al-tujjar* was on the court payroll shows that he was appointed by the court as an official. The *malik al-tujjar* appears in the *Dastur al-muluk* (430), according to which he was the head of the tailoring and cutting department (*qaychachi khana and khayyat khana*). The profiteers of this pro-Safi alliance represented a marriage between Tajik bureaucrats, functionaries of the harem, and the representative at court of the merchants of Isfahan (*malik al-tujjar*). At the head of the civil administration stood the grand vizier (Mirza Talib Khan), without whose permission the *mustawfi-yi khassa* (Hashim Bek Tihrani) and the *nazir-i daftarkhana-yi humayun* and the *mustawfi-yi baqaya* (Mirza Ma'sum) could not have increased the sums due to the *lala* of the *ghulams* and the income of the *malik al-tujjar*.

81   On the Mar'ashi's in Isfahan see R.D. McChesney, 'Four Sources on Shah Abbas I's Building of Isfahan', *Muqarnas*, 5 (1988), 118.

82   Ibid. The Mar'ashi, Mir Qutb al-din Mahmud, together with the Chief Alid dignitary of Isfahan (*naqib al-nuqaba*), Mirza Muhammad Amin, were against Abbas I's building project in the old city quarter.

83   The posts of *qullar aqasi, tufangchi aqasi, sipahsalar, divan begi* and *ishik aqasi* of the harem were appropriated by Rustam Bek's faction of slaves, who had supported Safi's candidacy. Once the *qullar aqasi*, Rustam Khan was sent to Tiflis in 1632 as the *vali* of Georgia (Kartil), Siyavush Bek, another *ghulam*, was appointed to the post of *qullar aqasi*.

84   Sultan al-Ulama and the Mirza Rafi al-din Sadr were Persian religious notables. The Qizilbash were represented by the Shaykhavand *qurchi bashi* Isa Khan, Takhta Khan Ustajlu and the Yasavul Suhbat (aide-de-camp), who was a trusted advisor of the Shah. For more on the *yasavul suhbat*, see the *Tazkirat al-muluk*, 133.

85   The four royal sons of Hasan Khan Ustajlu were blinded. He had married the daughter of Sultan Haydar Mirza (d. 1576), the son of Shah Tahmasb (r. 1524–76).

86   On a similar phenomenon of nameless concubines see Leslie Peirce, *The Imperial Harem*.

87   On the eunuchization of Saru Taqi, see Chardin, *Voyages*, 7, 303; and Nasrullah Falsafi, 'Sarguzasht-i Saru Taqi', in *Chand maqalah-yi tarikhi va adabi*, 290. Saru Taqi had not entered the ranks of the court eunuchs in the traditional fashion, for he had not been castrated at an early age. Saru Taqi had entered the military, where he made the acquaintance of boys whom he sodomized. Two years later an official hired him as a secretary. According to Chardin, while working in this capacity, he kidnapped a young boy, whose parents found him in Saru Taqi's quarters. The parents complained to Shah Abbas I, who punished him by ordering his castration.

Technically then, Saru Taqi can be categorized as a eunuch, for his predicament allowed him access into the harem and therefore to the queen-mother.

88 For a recent article on Saru Taqi see W. Floor, 'The Rise and Fall of Mirza Taqi, the Eunuch Grand Vizier (1043–55/1633–45)'. '*Makhdum al-Omara va Khadem al-Foqara*', *Studia Iranica*, 26, II (1997), 237–66.

89 See Charles Melville's forthcoming article on his recent discovery of the third volume of the *Afzal al-tavarikh* by Fazli Bek Khuzani, Cambridge, Christ's College Ms. Dd.5.6, f 359b. I would like to thank Melville for generously sharing this article.

90 On the position of vizier of the royal provinces, see Röhrborn, 172–204.

91 Iskandar Bek Munshi, *Zayl-i tarikh-i alam ara-yi Abbasi*, 260. The *Tarikh-i alam ara-yi Abbasi*, vol. 2, 1093 states that Saru Taqi was the grandson of Khwaja Inayat, who was the vizier of Hasan Bek Yuzbashi under Tahmasb. Iskandar Bek Munshi notes that Saru Taqi's uncle (Khwaja Qasim Ali) had been the governor of Azerbaijan under Shah Tahmasb (1524–76). Khwaja Qasim Ali was the ex-vizier of Hasan Bek Yuzbashi-i Ustajlu, who was the vizier of Azerbaijan. He remained at Tahmasb's court, however, until the death of Tahmasb. He was originally from Tabriz and had relatives in Isfahan. Khwaja Inayat Turka was his (Khwaja Qasim Ali's) brother, and took his brother's position as the vizier of Hasan Bek, the son of Husayn Bek. He was an important vizier in those times. Iskandar Bek Munshi, *Tarikh*, vol. 1, 165. According to the *Tarikh-i alam ara-yi Abbasi* (vol. 2, 1093), in 1616 Saru Taqi was the vizier of the Beglarbegi of Qarabagh, and a year later he was made vizier of Tabaristan (Mazandaran and Rustamdar). The vizierate of Gilan was added later.

92 When Saru Taqi asked his father why he had been refused a job, his father replied, 'Perhaps when your uncle Khwaja Qasim Ali was governor of Azerbaijan, he may have offended Hatim Bek's father (Bahram Khan), the Malik of Urdubad.' The prestige of the Urdubadis, who were from Urdubad in the Aras valley, goes back to the Mongol invasion of Qarabaq. Bahram had the title *malik* and received a land grant from Ismail I, who named him *kalantar* (civil administrator) of Urdubad. His son Hatim succeeded his father in this post and was given the title Bek. Hatim Bek was grand vizier for nineteen years, until his death in 1610–11, at which time his son Mirza Talib Khan inherited his post. Iskandar Bek Munshi, *Tarikh*, vol. 2, 723, 877, 1091.

93 The sources speak of a drinking party at Mirza Talib Khan's house that provoked his execution. Ughurlu Khan Shamlu (*ishik aqasi bashi*) and Hasan Bek (*yasavul suhbat* and son-in-law of Mirza Talib Khan) had been drinking at Mirza Talib Khan's house before their guard (*kishik*) duty at court. Once they arrived at the sleeping quarters (*khwabgah*) of the Shah

– located in the *dawlatkhana* in the harem – they instigated a fight with the Ustajlu guard. The Shah was awakened, and the next day Mirza Talib Khan was executed, for it is said that he had provided the accoutrements for the drinking party. On the drinking party at Mirza Talib Khan's house (7 August 1633) see the *Zayl*, 141–48; *Khuld-i barin*, ff. 87a–89a.

94 See Chardin on Hatim Bek's palace (vol. 7, 302). Chardin speaks of a large palace in the district of Hasanabad where the old palace of Uzun Hasan stood. Its construction was begun by Hatim Bek Urdubadi and finished by his son, Mirza Talib Khan. Saru Taqi took over the house and remodelled it so that it was one of the most beautiful buildings in Iran.

95 Concerning the alleged embezzlement the chroniclers state that Muhibb Ali Bek and Mulayim Bek had appropriated sums totalling 500,000 tumâns, which had been entered into the registers as a deficit. See *Khuld-i barin*: f 76a.

96 The sources vary on the precise date of Abbas II's birth: *Khuld-i barin*: Saturday night, 4 Rajab 1042 in Qazvin; *Zayl-i tarikh-i alam ara-yi Abbasi*: Pichi 1041–42; *Zubdat al-tavarikh*: Friday night, 18 Jamadi al-akhar 1043; *Tarikh-i Safavi Khan*: Pichi 1041–42. The date provided by the *Zubdat al-tavarikh* must be correct since at Abbas II's accession on 16 Safar 1052, the *Qisas al-khaqani*, *Khuld-i barin* and *Tarikh-i Safavi Khan* say that Abbas II was 9 years, 8 months and 28 days old. The year, however, must be 1042 (1632), since it is at Safi's *qishlaq* in Qazvin in the year that Abbas II was born (Friday night, 18 Jamadi al-akhar 1042/ December 31, 1632).

97 *Khuld-i barin*, f 75a.

98 Ibid.

99 For the role of the wife who bears the first son (*Hasseki sultana*) of the Ottoman sultans see H.A.R. Gibb and H. Bowen, *Islamic Society and the West*, vol. 1, 73; on the *hasseki/has odalik* that H. Inalcik defines as those women chosen for the Sultan's bed see his *The Ottoman Empire: The Classical Age 1300–1600*, 86; also see Leslie Peirce's *The Imperial Harem* for the changing role of the Ottoman harem in the period of Ottoman sedentarization.

100 We know from an endowment deed (*waqfname*) dated September–October 1643 that Shah Safi's mother survived her son and endowed a Quran for Safi's mausoleum located in the Sitti Fatima mosque in Qum. Sayyid Husayn Mudarrisi Tabataba'i, *Turbat-i pakan* (Qum: Chapkhana Mihr, 1355/1976): vol. 1, 152.

101 Anna Khanum was Circassian according to Falsafi, *Chand maqalah-yi tarikhi va adabi*, 301. See the article on Saru Taqi by Willem Floor (1997), who questions my analysis of Saru Taqi and court politics during the

reigns of Safi and Abbas II detailed in my dissertation (1993). One of the main objections he raises is that Abbas II's mother could not have collaborated with Saru Taqi because she was dead. He cites Falsafi's article to support his point but has misread the Persian, which in fact confirms that she was alive during the early reign of her son Abbas II. Most of my analysis is based on information from the Persian court chroniclers, in this case Kamal ibn Jalal Munajjim, *Zubdat al-tavarikh* (Royal Asiatic Society: MS Morley 43, 1677), f. 102b; where the author records the death of Anna Khanum (*khanum-i validah va hakimah*) on the 9 September 1647.

102 Chardin, *Les Voyages*, vol. 7, 306–7, and 314. Chardin states this in his discussion of Saru Taqi's assassination by the *qurchi bashi* (Jani Khan Shamlu) three years after Abbas II ascends the Safavid throne (1645).

103 Ibid., vol. 5, 237.

104 For details on the *qurchi bashi* Jani Khan Shamlu's cabal see my dissertation (1993), 123–29.

105 See Appendix for the administrations of the three subsequent grand viziers.

106 The next phases of *ghulam* hegemony need to be explored during the vizierate of Muhammad Bek (1654–61) as well as the reigns of Shah Sulayman and Sultan Husayn.

107 Ibid., 315.

108 See Ina Baghdiantz McCabe, *The Shah's Silk for Europe's Silver: The Eurasian Trade of the Julfa Armenians in Safavid Iran and India (1530–1750)*, University of Pennsylvania, Armenian series 15 (Atlanta: Scholar's Press, 1999).

109 On Saru Taqi and his building projects see Sussan Babaie, 'Building for the Shah: The Role of Mirza Muhammad Taqi (Saru Taqi) in Safavid Royal Patronage of Architecture', *Safavid Art and Architecture*, Sheila Canby (ed.) (The British Museum, 2002): 15–21. These holy Shi'i shrines in Mesopotamia had just been recaptured from the Ottomans, who held them in 1587–1623.

110 For a detailed narrative on the Nuqtavis see Kathryn Babayan, *Mystics, Monarch and Messiahs: Cultural Landscapes of Early Modern Iran* (Cambridge, MA: Harvard Middle Eastern Monographs, 2003).

111 For *hadith* on the Mahdi's emergence in Isfahan see Majlisi Jr., *Mahdi-yi Maw'ud* (Qum, n.d.).

112 Iskandar Bek Munshi, *Zayl-i tarikh-i alam ara-yi Abbasi* (Tehran, Islamiyya, 1938–39), 87.

113 Mir Muhammad Baqir Damad, better know as Mir-i Damad. His maternal grandfather was the famous Shaykh Ali Karaki. His father, Shams al-din Muhammad, was from Astarabad.

114 Iskandar Bek Munshi, *Tarikh*, vol. 2, 632. Shah Safi's first accession was on 28 January 1629. Mir-i Damad read the sermon (*khutba*) in Safi's name four days after his accession, on Friday the 1 February 1629. According to the *Khulasat al-siyar*, however, the *khutba* was read one day after his accession, Tuesday 29 January 1629. *Sikkes* were coined in the name of Safi five days after his accession, on Saturday 2 February 1629. The *urdu* arrived in Isfahan nineteen days after Shah Safi's accession, on 17 February 1629, when a second coronation was held.

Chapter 3

1 The commercial aspects of Abbas I's urban planning have been pointed out by Robert McChesney, 'Waqf and Public Policy: The *Waqfs* of Shah Abbas, 1011–1023/1602–1614', *Asian and African Studies* 15 (1981): 165–190 and 'Four Sources on Shah Abbas' Buildings of Isfahan', *Muqarnas*, 5 (1988): 103–34, see also Maxime Sirioux, 'Les caravansarails routiers safavides,' *Iranian Studies*, 7 (1974): 348–79.

2 Jean Chardin, *Voyages du Chevalier Chardin, en Perse, et autres lieux de l'Orient. Enrichis de Figures en Taille-douce, qui représentent les Antiquités et les choses remarquables du Païs. Nouvelle Edition, augmentée du Couronnement de Soliman III. & d'un grand nombre de Passages tirés du Manuscrit de l'Auteur qui ne se trouvent point dans les Editions precedents, 4 vols. Aux dépens de la Compagnie* (Amsterdam, 1735), vol. 2, 116.

3 Rudolph Matthee, 'Merchants in Safavid Iran: Participants and Perceptions', *Journal of Early Modern History*, 4, 3–4 (2000): 233–68.

4 Stephen Frederic Dale, *Indian Merchants and Eurasian Trade*, 1600–1750 (Cambridge: Cambridge University Press, 1994) and Scott Levi, 'The Indian Merchant Diaspora in Early Modern Central Asia and Iran', *Iranian Studies*, 32, 4 (1999): 483–513, Tabrizi merchants remain to be studied.

5 Ina Baghdiantz McCabe, *The Shah's Silk for Europe's Silver: The Eurasian Silk Trade of the Julfan Armenians* (1530–1750). University of Pennsylvania, Armenian series 15 (Atlanta GA: Scholar's Press, 1999): chapter 5.

6 See chapter on the Julfans by S. Faroqhi, *An Economic and Social History of the Ottoman Empire*, vol. 2 (Cambridge: Cambridge University Press, 1997): 503.

7 See Edmund Herzig, 'The Volume of Iranian Raw Silk Exports in the Safavid Period', *Iranian Studies*, 25 (1992): 61–81 for numbers.

8 H. Inalcik, 'Bursa and the Silk Trade', in *An Economic and Social History of the Ottoman Empire* (Cambridge: Cambridge University Press, 1997), 1, 218–55.

9   For the Dutch in Iran see Willem Floor, 'The Dutch in the Persian Silk Trade', in Charles Melville (ed.) (London: I. B. Tauris, 1996), 323–68, Rudolph Matthee (1999), 105–18 and 183–92. Also M.A.P. Meilink-Roelofsz, 'The Earliest Relations Between Persia and the Netherlands', *Persica. Jaarboek van het Genootschap Netherland-Iran. Stchting voor Culturele Betrekkingen*, 4 (1972–74), 1–51.

10 For this view see Rudolph Matthee, 'Merchants in Safavid Iran', 260–61 and 234, Willem Floor, *Safavid Government Institutions* (Costa Mesa CA: Mazda, 2001).

11 McCabe, *The Shah's Silk*, chapter 4.

12 Appendix B in McCabe, *The Shah's Silk*, 367–69.

13 That the Julfans were a service bourgeoisie is first argued in: Vladimir Minorsky, *Tazkirat al-mulak, a Manual of Safavid Administration* (henceforth *TM*), Gibb Memorial Series, vol. 16 (London, 1943).

14 See the reproduced royal edicts spelling out the inclusion of the Julfans in the Royal Household in the Annexes of McCabe, *The Shah's Silk* and chapters 5 and 6 in the same work.

15 This is argued in McCabe, *The Shah's Silk*, chapters 3 through 6.

16 Recent studies have brought this role to light: E. Herzig, 'The Armenian Merchants of New Julfa: A Study in Premodern Asian Trade' (unpublished diss., Oxford University, 1991), K. Babayan, 'The Waning of the Qizilbash: The Spiritual and the Temporal in Seventeenth Century Iran' (PhD dissertation, Princeton University, 1993), McCabe, *The Shah's Silk*.

17 Bernard Lewis, *The Middle East: A Brief History of the Last 2000 Years* (New York: Scribner, 1995), 330.

18 For a fuller discussion of Iran's silk trade before the seventeenth century see McCabe, *The Shah's Silk*, chapter 1.

19 H. Inalcik, 'Bursa and the Silk Trade', in *An Economic and Social History of the Ottoman Empire* (Cambridge: Cambridge University Press, 1997): 1, 218–55.

20 Inalcik, 'Bursa and the Silk Trade', 227.

21 Bruce Masters, 'Merchant Diasporas and Trading "Nation"', chapter 3 in *The Origins of Western Economic Dominance in the Middle East* (New York: New York University Press, 1988).

22 E. Herzig, 'The Rise of the Julfa Merchants', 304–19.

23 For details see McCabe, *The Shah's Silk*, chapter 2.

24 See McCabe, *The Shah's Silk*, 35. *Mann* is a measurement used for many goods including silk. See chapter 3, note 62.

25 For this unusual interpretation of events see McCabe, *The Shah's Silk*, 48–66. Also see Edmund Herzig 'The Deportations of the Armenians in 1604–5 and Europe's Myth of Shah Abbas I', in *History and Literature in*

Iran: Persian and Islamic studies in honour of P.W. Avery, Charles Melville (ed.) (London; New York: British Academic Press, 1998 and 1990), first edition (1990): 59–71.

26 Herman Vahramian, *Documenti di Architettura Armena. Nor Djulfa.*, no 21 (Milano: OEMME Edizioni, 1992), 102.

27 Rudolph Matthee, 'Merchants in Safavid Iran', 260–61, and his conclusion for arguments for the vulnerable subordination of the merchants to the state.

28 For a full account of New Julfa see McCabe, *The Shah's Silk*, chapter 3. For an example of the use of this calendar see Levon Khachikian, 'Le registre d'un marchand arménien en Perse, en Inde et au Tibet (1682–1693)', *Annales-économies-Société-Civilizations* 22, 2 (March–April 1967): 231–78.

29 *A Chronicle of the Carmelites* (London, Eyre & Spottiswoode, 1939), 100. Henceforth cited as CHOC.

30 W. Barthold in *An Historical Geography of Iran*, C.E. Bosworth (ed.) (Princeton: Princeton University Press, 1984): 177, 222.

31 Both quotations are from *CHOC*, 100.

32 A Dutch letter, Stick, Isfahan to Visnich, Gamroni, 3 February 1630, describes this greeting at Safi's accession cited in Rudolph P. Matthee, *The Politics of Trade in Safavid Iran: Silk for Silver, 1600–1730*. Cambridge Studies in Islamic Civilization (Cambridge: Cambridge University Press, 1999): 121, n. 12.

33 Floor, *Safavid Government*, 31–33.

34 McCabe, *The Shah's Silk*, chapter 3 for a full account of New Julfa.

35 McCabe, *The Shah's Silk*, chapter 7.

36 McCabe, *The Shah's Silk*, 372.

37 Jean Baptiste Tavernier, *Les Six Voyages en Turquie et en Perse* (Paris: La Découverte, 1981), 2, 94.

38 For an analysis of this see McCabe, *The Shah's Silk*, chapter 11.

39 For parallels to France see McCabe, *The Shah's Silk*, 254–56, and for a different view, especially of the role of the Armenians in Iran's mercantilist policy see Matthee, *The Politics of Trade*, 70–72.

40 For the difficult beginnings of the EIC in the silk trade in Iran and India see Niels Steensgaard, *Carracks, Caravans and Companies: The Structural Crisis in the European–Asian Trade of the Early Seventeenth Century* (Chicago: University of Chicago Press, 1973).

41 Sanjay Subrahmanyam, 'Iranians Abroad: Intra Asian Elite Migration and Early Modern State Formation', *The Journal of Asian Studies*, 51, 2 (1992): 340–63.

42 McCabe, *The Shah's Silk*, chapter 10.

43 McCabe, *The Shah's Silk*, chapter 3.

44   See further the passage quoted from *TM*, introduction and 61.

45   Matthee, *The Politics of Trade*, 74–76.

46   For governorships of the provinces see Klaus Michael Röhrborn, *Provinzen und Zentralgewalt Persiens im 16 und 17 Jahrhundert* (Berlin: De Gruyter, 1966), 172–204.

47   This step was first noticed by Linda Steinmann, 'Shah Abbas and the Royal Silk Trade' (PhD dissertation, New York University, 1986), especially chapter 3 on the change to *ghulam* rulers.

48   Pietro Della Valle, *il Pellegrino...La Persia...*, part 2/vol. 2 (Rome, 1658), letter 14. Also see *The Pilgrim* (1990), 147.

49   Chardin (1724; reprint, 1927), 132.

50   Paul Ricault (Rycault), *The Present State of the Armenian Church: Containing the Tenets, Form and Manner of Divine Worship in That Church, 1678* (London: John Starkey, 1679), 388.

51   The letter from Farahabad is accessible in its English translation in *The Pilgrim: The Travels of Pietro Della Valle*, abridged and introduced by George Bull (London: Hutchinson, 1990): see 141–76.

52   Matthee, *The Politics of Trade*, 74–76.

53   London, 16 October 1619, Isfahan to London E. I. Co 16/10/19; cited in full in *Armenian Merchants of the Seventeenth and Eighteenth Centuries: English East India Company Records*, Vahe Baladouni and Margaret Makepeace (eds) (Philadelphia: American Philosophical Society, 1998): 16–18.

54   For the correspondence of these English factors see Baladouni and Makepeace (1998), 16–24.

55   Cited in Matthee, *The Politics of Trade*, 103.

56   Jean Aubin, 'La propriété foncière en Azerbaijan', *Le Monde Iranien et L'Islam: Sociétés et Cultures (1967–77)*, 78–133.

57   Cited by John Carswell, *New Julfa: The Armenian Churches and Buildings* (Oxford, 1968). See Steensgaard (1973), 332–35 for a full description of the auction.

58   Persian text of this royal edict for the land grant in Ismail Raiin, *Iranian-i Armani* (Armenian Iranians) (Tehran, 1970), 114.

59   The third volume of the *Afzal al-tavarikh* cites a royal decree and ascertains the date of 1028/1619 for the monopoly. This volume was discovered by Charles Melville, 'A Lost Source for the Reign of Shah Abbas: The *Afzal al-tawarikh* of Fazli Khuzani Isfahani', *Iranian Studies* 31, no 2 (1998): 263–65. See Matthee (1999), 101–2.

60   *Sarkar-i khassa-yi sharifa* is given as 'royal workshops' in Rudolph Matthee's translation.

61   A *mann-i-shahi*, the measure used for silk, was 5.8 kg; a *mann-i Tabriz* was half of that and weighed 2.9 kg. A *kharvar* was an assload, from the

word *khar* meaning donkey, and it weighed 100 *tabrizi mann*, or 290 kg, or 600 lbs.

62 Khuzani Isfahani, *Afzal al-tavarikh*, vol. 3, folios 405b–6a, Christ College ms. Dd. 5.6. The officials named are Miza Isfahani and Aslan Beg, viziers of Gilan; Husayn Beg, vizier of Shirvan; Malik Sharif *kalantar* and Sharif Beg, viziers of Ganja and Qarabagh; Malik Safar *kalantar* and the *hakims* of Tabriz and Ardabils. Cited by Matthee, *The Politics of Trade*, 102.

63 See McCabe, *The Shah's Silk*, chapter 7 for a detailed analysis.

64 Ibid.

65 Della Valle, cited by Steinman (1986), 94.

66 *TM* (1980), 61. Quoted earlier in this chapter.

67 Yet despite the edict Rudolph Matthee finds the term 'monopoly' itself misleading because it implies matching intent with implementation. Matthee, *The Politics of Trade*, 104.

68 The real consequence of the 1622 war would be the creation of Bandar Abbas, not, as Steensgaard maintains, a crisis in Asian trade. See Matthee (1999), 106.

69 Steinman, 103.

70 Matthee, *The Politics of Trade*, 110.

71 The best source for both production numbers and export is: Edmund Herzig, 'The Volume of Iranian Raw Silk Exports in the Safavid Period', *Iranian Studies* 25 (1992): 61–81.

72 See McCabe, *The Shah's Silk*, chapter 5. The important role played by the Armenians in breaking the silk monopoly and the privilege of the provost of Julfa is mentioned in a Dutch letter dated 3 February 1630, and cited in note 12 in Matthee, *The Politics of Trade*, 121.

73 Steinmann, 'Shah Abbas and the Royal Silk Trade', 94–97 and 84–113.

74 Babayan, 'The Waning of the Qizilbash', 114–18.

75 India Office Record, letter from Isfahan to London, 26 September 1631.

76 Abd al-Fattah Fumani, *Tarikh-i Gilan*. Tehran: Intisharat-i Bunyad-i Farhang-i Iran, 1970, 261.

77 Matthee (2001), 243. The important role of several Jewish merchants in the silk trade, although it is slowly emerging, still remains to be studied.

78 See this edict in Persian in McCabe, *The Shah's Silk*, 365–67.

79 Vahe Baladouni and Margaret Makepeace (eds) (1998), 35, original spelling of the letter.

80 Ibid., 24.

81 Sevket Pamuk, *A Monetary History of the Ottoman Empire* (Cambridge: Cambridge University Press, 1999), 137.

82 Tavernier, *Les Six Voyages*, 1, 191 and the *TM* quoted further in this chapter also states this.

83   Tavernier, *Les Six Voyages*, vol. 2, 92–96.

84   See the two maps in Rudolph Matthee, 'Mint Consolidation and the Worsening of the late Safavid Coinage: the Mint at Huwayza', *Journal of Economic and Social History of the Orient* 4, 44 (2001).

85   Matthee, 'Mint Consolidation', states it may be due to the 'lingering of the local nature of monetary politics'.

86   *TM* (1980), 66.

87   Linda Steinmann (1986), especially chapter 3.

88   Chardin (1735), vol. III, 321.

89   For this, see chapter 5 in McCabe, *The Shah's Silk*, and also Ina Baghdiantz McCabe 'Silk and Silver: The Trade and Organization of New Julfa at the End of the Seventeenth Century', *Revue des Etudes Arméniennes*, n.s. 25 (1994–95): 245–72.

90   The word *qurush* refers to a specific Ottoman coin, used erroneously by the author of the manual to describe all the silver and gold coming into Iran from the Ottoman markets.

91   *TM* (1980), 61. Some of the Persian terms are omitted here to facilitate reading.

92   *TM* (1980), 130 and 58. The *TM* examines the Shah's revenue from the mint in four different periods, including the later reigns when the coinage was debased.

93   Matthee, 'Mint Consolidation'.

94   Ibid.

95   Ibid.

96   For this diary look under Library of Congress transliteration in card catalog: Zacharia Akouletsi, *Diary* (Armenian Academy: Erevan, 1938).

97   Ibid., 81.

98   Pietro Della Valle, *il Pellegrino...La Persia...*, part 2/vol. 2 (Rome, 1658): letter 14.

99   For the Julfans a financiers McCabe, *The Shah's Silk*, for the Genoese F. Braudel, *La Méditerranée et le monde mediterranéen à l'époque de Philippe II* (Paris: Armand Colin, 1949) is still one of the best sources for this.

100 *CHOC*, vol. 1, 157.

101 Tavernier, *Les Six Voyages*, 2, 190.

102 Pietro Della Valle cited by Carswell, 6.

103 *TM* (1980), 85.

104 Rudolph Matthee 'The Career of Mohammad Beg, Grand Vizier of Shah Abbas II (r.1642–1666)', *Iranian Studies*, 24 (1991): 17–36. The master of the hunt should not be confused with his namesake, a general under Abbas I.

105 Matthee, *The Politics of Trade*, 120, based on Dutch documents.

106 Roemer, H. R. 'The Safavid Period', in *The Cambridge History of Iran: The Timurid and Safavid Periods*, Peter J. Jackson and Laurence Lockhart (eds) (Cambridge: Cambridge University Press, 1986) vol. 6, 189–347, see 189–235; and 291–96.

107 Matthee, *The Politics of Trade*, 164.

108 Roemer, 'The Safavid Period', 294.

109 For details of this balance of power see Babayan, 'The Waning of the Qizilbash'.

110 McCabe, *The Shah's Silk*, chapter 6 gives all the political reasons of this decline.

111 Pamuk, *A Monetary History of the Ottoman Empire*, 134.

112 McCabe, *The Shah's Silk*, 155–158, Pamuk, *A Monetary History of the Ottoman Empire*, 149–51.

113 Pamuk, *A Monetary History of the Ottoman Empire*, 149–158.

114 McCabe, *The Shah's Silk*, 157–70.

115 I. Baghdiantz, 'The Merchants of New Julfa: Some Aspects of their International Trade at the End of the Seventeenth Century' (PhD dissertation, Columbia University, 1993).

116 Willem Floor, *A Fiscal History of Iran in the Safavid and Qajar Period* (New York: Bibliotheca Persica Press, 1999), and Floor, *Safavid Government*.

117 These two branches of Safavid administrations have been studied by many scholars, such as K.S. Lambton, 'Quis Custodiet Custodes: Some Reflections on the Persian Theory of Government', *Studia Islamica* 6 (1956): 125–27 and R.M. Savory, 'The Principal Offices of the Safavid State' (Shah Isma'il) *Bulletin of the School of Oriental and African Studies* 22 (1960): 91–105. (Shah Tahmasb) *Bulletin of the School of Oriental and African Studies* 24 (1961): 65–85.

118 They are cited in Floor, *A Fiscal History of Iran*, 73.

119 *TM*, 116.

120 Floor, *Safavid Government*, cites several European sources for this on page 27.

121 Floor, *A Fiscal History of Iran*, 73–74.

122 *TM*, 45, 123. For a complete description and a partial list of the *mustawfi-yi khassa* see Floor (2001), 43–46. The names of these officials are missing from 1602–29 and 1642–84.

123 Chardin (1735), vol. 3, 358.

124 Chardin (1735), vol. 3, 359.

125 According to documents published in Puturidze's work see them organized in Table 3.5 Variation in Pay Scale of *Ghulams*, in Floor, *Safavid Government*, 175.

126 Chardin says a cavalryman is paid 400 *livres* on 321 and 400 *francs* on 322, indiscriminately equating *francs* and *livres*. If a tumân is this sum divided by 4.5, the pay of a cavalryman was well under 10 tumâns and that of the infantry more than 5. Chardin himself is very imprecise; for example, he says a horse costs 60 tumâns, or 250 *livres*, while if he were to apply his own accounting, he would get 270. The French *livre* fluctuated widely, as much as 60% during Chardin's lifetime, nor was the tumân stable, so these conversions are not accurate.

127 Floor, *Safavid Government*, 175.

128 Chardin (1735), vol. 3, 320–22.

129 *TM*, 58.

130 See chart in Babayan, 'The Waning of the Qizilbash', 320.

131 *TM*, 48–49.

132 *TM*, 66.

133 Matthee, *The Politics of Trade*, 45.

134 Chardin (1735), vol. 2, 375 and 319.

135 Willem Floor, *A Fiscal History of Iran in the Safavid and Qajar Period* (Bibliotheca Persica Press, 1999) has a short passage on the *khassa*, which has been studied by Herbert Busse, *Unterzuchungen zum islamschen Kanzleiwesen* (Cairo, 1959). Jean Chardin and the *Tazkirat al-muluk* remain the two most important sources for the *khassa*.

136 Chardin (1735), vol. 3, 357.

137 Chardin (1735), vol. 2, 358.

138 Floor, *Safavid Government*, 79.

139 Subrahmanyam, Sanjay, *The Political Economy of Commerce: Southern India, 1500–1650* (Cambridge; New York: Cambridge University Press, 1990) 299–300, and Sanjay Subrahmanyam and C.A. Bayly, 'Portfolio Capitalists and the Political Economy of Early Modern India', in *Merchants, Markets and the State in Early Modern India*, Sanjay Subrahmanyam (ed.) (Delhi; Oxford: Oxford University Press, 1990) 242–65.

140 That this model is the same for Iran is argued in McCabe, *The Shah's Silk*, 250–59. Also see Ina Baghdiantz McCabe, 'Trading Diaspora, State Building and the Idea of National Interest', in *Views from the Edge: Essays in Honor of Richard W. Bulliet* (Columbia Middle-East Institute, Columbia University Press, 2003): 18–37.

141 Jean Aubin, 78–133.

142 For the decline of New Julfa see chapter 6 in McCabe, *The Shah's Silk*.

143 For these see Ina Baghdiantz McCabe, 'The Socio-Economic Conditions in New Julfa post 1650: The Impact of Conversions to Islam on International Trade', *Revue des études arméniennes*, 26 (1996–97): 367–97.

144 See Anahid Perikhanian, *Materialy k etimologicheskomu slovariu drev-nearmianskogo iazyka* (Erevan: Izd-vo NAN Respubliki Armeniia, 1993).

145 Ter Hovaneants, Harutiwn, *Patmutiwn Nor Jughayi* (*History of New Julfa* [Isfahan]), in Armenian (New Julfa: New Julfa All Savior's Museum, 1980): 1, 55; first ed., 1880.

146 Matthee, *The Politics of Trade*, 72.

Chapter 4

1   On Baghdad and Samarra, see, for example, J. Lassner, *The Topography of Baghdad in the Early Middle Ages* (Detroit: Wayne State University, 1970); ibid., *The Shaping of Abbasid Rule* (Princeton: Princeton University Press, 1980); J.M. Rogers, 'Samarra: A Study in Medieval Town-Planning', in *The Islamic City: A Colloquium*, Albert Hourani and S.M. Stern (eds) (Philadelphia: University of Pennsylvania Press, 1970): 119–55; Alastair Northedge, 'An Interpretation of the Palace of the Caliph at Samarra', *Ars Orientalis* 23 (1993): 143–70.

2   Many structural and conceptual characteristics of Abbasid Samarra may be found in other periods of Muslim history. Both Mamluk and Ottoman slave systems matured at their respective capitals of Cairo and Istanbul, but in both cases the new centring embedded itself into the preexisting and symbolically important metropolises. Fatehpur Sikri (sixteenth century) and Shahjahanabad (seventeenth century) too visualize this conception of centring, but neither the Mughal capitals nor the foundation of the Mughal Empire depended on military slavery.

3   Mahmud ibn Hidayat-Allah Afushta Natanzi, *Nuqavat al-asar fi zikr al-akhyar*, Ihsan Ishraqi (ed.) (Tehran: Bongah-i tarjuma va nashr-i kitab, 1350/1971): 376; Mulla Muhammad Jalal al-Din Yazdi Munajjim, *Tarikh-i Abbasi ya ruznama-yi Mulla Jalal*, S. Vahidniya (ed.) (Tehran: Intisharat-i Vahid, 1366/1987): 113.

4   See, for example, Iskandar Beg Munshi, *Tarikh-i alam ara-yi Abbasi,* Iraj Afshar (ed.) 2 vols (Tehran: Intisharat-i Amir Kabir, 1350/1971): 544–45; Mirza Beg ibn Hasan Junabadi, *Rawzat al-Safaviyya*, Ghulamriza Majd Tabatabai (ed.) (Tehran: Bunyad-i Mawqufat-i Duktur Mahmud Afshar, 1378/1999): 758–62.

5   The Allah Virdi Khan Bridge remains to be studied. For a preliminary note, see M. Ferrante, 'Quelques Précisions Graphiques au Sujet des Ponts Séfévides d'Isfahan', in *Travaux de Restauration de Monuments Historiques en Iran*, Giuseppe Zander (ed.) (Rome: IsMEO, 1968): 441–50. See also Robert D. McChesney, 'Four Sources on Shah Abbas's Building of Isfahan',

Muqarnas V (1988): 124, and Lutf-Allah Hunarfar, *Ganjina-yi asar-i tarikhi-yi Isfahan* (Isfahan, 1344/1965–66): 48. For the new quarters see footnote 10 below. For the palaces, see Sussan Babaie, 'Safavid Palaces at Isfahan: Continuity and Change (1590–1666)' (PhD dissertation, New York University, 1994) and the author's forthcoming monograph, *Feasting in the City of Paradise: Isfahan and its Palaces*. For a recent discussion of many aspects of the urban scheme in Isfahan see, Stephen Blake, *Half the World: The Social Architecture of Safavid Isfahan, 1590–1722* (Costa Mesa, CA: Mazda Publishers, 1999). Blake's book, however, presents some fundamental errors in documentation and analysis; see a review by Sussan Babaie in *Iranian Studies* 33/3–4 (2000): 478–82.

6   On the local resistance and diverted plans of Abbas I, see Robert D. McChesney, 'Four Sources', 117–18. Blake counters this view in *Half the World*, 15–23.

7   Ibid. Safavid sources identify two powerful figures in this face-off. One, Mirza Muhammad Amin, was the *naqib* (the head of the *siyyids*) of Isfahan, a position he had inherited from his father, who was the chief *naqib* and *sadr* under Shah Tahmasb. The other, Mir Qutb al-Din Mahmud, was from a prominent Mazandarani family that had settled in Isfahan and had developed marital ties with Abbas I as well. Both families' wealth and commercial interests are highlighted in these sources.

8   Some insight into Tabriz can be gained from the memoirs of the Italian traveller Michele Membré in *Mission to the Lord Sophy of Persia*, translated and introduced and notes by A.H. Morton (London: SOAS, 1993): especially 29–33. For Qazvin's royal precinct and its links to the urban centre, see Maria Szuppe, 'Palais et jardin: le complexe royal des premiers Safavides á Qazvin, milieu XVI siècle', *Res Orientales* VIII (1996): 143–78.

9   Szuppe, 'Palais et jardin', 171.

10   The new quarters and the seventeenth-century houses of Isfahan were the subject of a paper presented by the author at the Third Safavid Round Table convened in August 1998 in Edinburgh. For an important study of the building activities of various social classes in Safavid Isfahan see Masashi Haneda, 'The Character of the Urbanization of Isfahan in the Later Safavid Period', in Charles Melville (ed.) *Safavid Persia. The History and Politics of an Islamic Society* (London and New York: I.B.Tauris, 1996): 369–87. Haneda's findings will be discussed later in this chapter.

11   A list of the gardens along the Chahar Bagh, some identified by name, others by the profession of the owner, appears in Mirza Hasan Khan Jabiri Ansari, *Tarikh-i Isfahan*, Jamshid Mazahiri (ed.) (Tehran: Chapp-i Amir, 1378/1999): 165–67. Gardens belonging to *ishik aqasi* (master of ceremonies), *qurchi bashi* (head of the guards), *khwaja* (eunuch), *tofangchi*

aqasi (head of the musketeers), *qushchiyan* (falconeers) and *ghulaman-i matbakh* (kitchen attendants) clearly indicate a high concentration of *ghulams* in this elite residential neighbourhood.

12 Hunarfar, *Ganjina*, 506–8, and Nasr-Allah Falsafi, *Zindigani-yi Shah Abbas-i avval*, 3 vols (Tehran: Intisharat-i Ilmi, 1369/1990): 3, 1129–30. The *farman* is at the City Museum in Naples.

13 The Edjmiazin stones are currently housed in a building adjacent to the Church of Surb Gevorg (St. George). The transfer of stones and other sacred objects is more fully recorded in Arak'el's history. There is some confusion, however, about whether the existing Edjmiazin stones were the ones intended for the church Abbas I had ordered or were origi-nally installed in Surb Gevorg, financed and built by Khoja Nazar, the Armenian provost of New Julfa, in 1610/11. For Arak'el's account and Surb Gevorg Church, see John Carswell, *New Julfa: The Armenian Churches and Other Buildings* (Oxford: Clarendon Press, 1968): 7 and 37–40.

14 The Persian text is worth transliterating for, as shall be discussed, its terminology reveals the role of the *ghulams*. The relevant section, at the end of the *farman* reads: 'be ittifaq-i yekdigar mi'maran-i khassa-yi sharifa ra hamrah barand va dar pusht-i Bagh-i Zirishk dar zamini ki bi jahat-i kilisa qarar dada budim kilisa-yi 'ali tarh namayand ki kishishan va padrian qarar dahand va tarh-i anra dar takhta va kaghaz kishida bi khidmat-i ashraf firistada ki mulahaza nama'im va ba'd az mulahaza amr farma'im ki ustadan shuru' dar kar karda bi itmam risanand'.

15 Either this church was never built or has vanished alongside the buildings and gardens west of the Chahar Bagh and behind the famed Bagh-i Zirishk. Much of this area was destroyed in the late nineteenth century. Rudolph Matthee has suggested that this was the Vank Cathedral; *The Politics of Trade in Safavid Iran; Silk for Silver 1600–1730* (Cambridge: Cambridge University Press, 1999): 86.

16 Armenian architectural idiom and its stone material are fundamentally different from central Iranian building traditions. The fact that the churches and houses of the Armenians of New Julfa closely approximate the local Isfahani style and materials has puzzled many a student of this field of inquiry. A document such as this decree may in fact be taken as further evidence of the layered intermingling of the life and culture of this minority community with its new home and its cultural fabric. For the churches of New Julfa, see Carswell, op. cit., and Nor/Djulfa. *Documents of Armenian Architecture* 21 (Venice: Faculty of Architecture of the Milan Polytechnic Academy of Sciences of Armenia, 1991).

17 Munshi, *Tarikh-i alam ara*, 949–50.

18   Ibid. and Munajjim, *Tarikh-i Abbasi*, 413.

19   Vali Quli Shamlu credits Muhibb Ali Beg Lala with road construction in Mazandaran as well; *Qisas al-khaqani*, 2 vols, Hasan Sadat Nasiri (ed.) (Tehran: Vizarat-i Irshad-i Islami, 1371/1992): 198. See also Charles Melville, 'Shah Abbas and the Pilgrimage to Mashhad', in Charles Melville (ed.), *Safavid Persia. The History and Politics of an Islamic Society* (London and New York: I. B. Tauris, 1996): 213.

20   Munshi, *Tarikh-i alam ara*, 950. For Imam Quli Khan we also have the record of his mansion in Isfahan, which Chardin considered among the most excellent in the city. At the time of Chardin, the mansion was occupied by the grand vizier and his brother, the Shaykh al-Islam.

21   Lala Beg's caravanserai is recorded in the list of caravanserai of Isfahan in MS Sloane 4094 (lines 15–21) and by Chardin; see Gaube and Wirth, *Der Bazar von Isfahan* (Wiesbaden: Ludwig Reichert Verlag, 1978): 168–70 and 264–65.

22   Hunarfar, *Ganjina*, 429; McChesney, 'Four Sources', 122.

23   McChesney, op. cit., and see his discussion of Alpan Beg and the palace for Hajim Khan.

24   Ibid. The reference to Lala's palace appears in a map, drawn by Wilber, approximating Chardin's description of the city. My own research on the seventeenth-century houses of Isfahan has yet to confirm Wilber's conjecture; Donald Wilber, 'Aspects of the Safavid Ensemble', *Iranian Studies* 7/1–2 (1974): 412.

25   This was by Alpan Beg; for his role in the construction, see McChesney, 'Four Sources', 119–20 and 122.

26   Munajjim, *Tarikh-i Abbasi* calls Badi' al-Zaman-i Tuni *ustad* (master) and *mi'mar* (architect) in connection with the mosque's early stages of building. Yet his name does not appear on the foundation inscription. The inscription refers to the other architect, Ali Akbar-i Isfahani, as the 'unique of the age', McChesney, 'Four Sources', 123.

27   The book donations were divided between the shrine of Imam Riza in Mashhad and the Ardabil shrine. For details see chapter 5 in this book.

28   McChesney, 'Four Sources', 113 and 125.

29   The bridge has been dated to 1602 but, according to a recently discovered source by the historian Fazli Khuzani, its completion dates to 1607. I (Babaie) am grateful to Charles Melville for sharing a draft of his article and this new information; see his article 'New Light on the Reign of Shah 'Abbas: Volume III of the Afdal al-Tawarikh', in Andrew J. Newman (ed.), *Society and Culture in the Early Modern Middle East. Studies on Iran in the Safavid Period* (Leiden: Brill, 2003): 63–96.

30   Allah Virdi Khan pleaded with Abbas I for the Sarab dam, arguing that its construction could significantly alleviate the water shortages in Shiraz; Munajjim, *Tarikh-i Abbasi*, 211.

31   None of these buildings have survived or are identifiable. For the dam, dated 1600, see McChesney, 'Four Sources', note 91 and Munajjim, *Tarikh-i Abbasi*, 211; for the fortification, Munajjim, *Tarikh-i Abbasi*, 151; for the *madrasa* in Shiraz, also enthusiastically described by Figuera, and the bazaars in Lar, see Don Garcia de Silva y Figuera, *L'Ambassade de D. Garcias de Silva y Figueroa en Perse*, trans. by De Wicqfort (Paris, 1667); for the house, dated 1020/1611, see Munajjim, *Tarikh-i Abbasi*, 420.

32   Ali Sami, *Shiraz, shahr-i javidan* (Tehran, 1363/1984): 586–88.

33   For a brief discussion of the architectural merits of the *madrasa*, see Hillenbrand, 'Safavid Architecture', in *The Cambridge History of Iran: The Timurid and Safavid Periods*, Peter J. Jackson and Laurence Lockhart (eds) (Cambridge: Cambridge University Press, 1986): 795.

34   Imam Quli Khan's son was appointed the superintendent of the holy city of Qum, another indication of the significant posts this *ghulam* family held; this issue is further discussed by Farhad in the next chapter.

35   Munshi, *Tarikh-i alam ara*, 871. I (Babaie) thank May Farhat for her help in locating images of this tomb and for directing me to the inscriptions, all of which are devoted to the genealogy of the Twelve Imams. Her dissertation on the shrine in Mashhad, 'Islamic Piety and Dynastic Legitimacy: The Case of the Shrine of Ali b. Musa al-Rida in Mashhad (10th–17th Century)' (PhD dissertation, Harvard University, 2002) sheds much-needed light on Safavid patronage at this sacred site.

36   The other one, known as Hatam Khani, is of uncertain date and patronage but by legend is believed to have been built for Hatam Beg Urdubadi (d. 1610), a Tajik vizier of Abbas I; Mihdi Siyyidi, *Tarikh-i shahr-i Mashhad* (Tehran, 1378/1999): 175.

37   Muhammad Ibrahim Bastani-Parizi has devoted much of his copious publications (in Persian) to Ganj Ali Khan and Kirman; see especially his *Ganjalikhan* (n.p.: Asatir Publications, 1368/1989). For his architectural patronage, see Hillenbrand, 'Safavid Architecture', 793–95. A study of Ganj Ali Khan's complex in Kirman, by Babaie, will form part of a larger study, led by Lisa Golombek, on the urban development of Kirman, its ceramic production and trade from the Saljuq through the Safavid periods.

38   The most detailed discussion of the Zu'lqadar opposition can be found in Sholeh A. Quinn, *Historical Writing during the Reign of Shah Abbas; Ideology, Imitation, and Legitimacy in Safavid Chronicles* (Salt Lake City: The University of Utah Press, 2000): 95–124.

39 After the death of Ganj Ali Khan, and as an expression of the honour and trust he held in Abbas's mind, the Shah granted the governorship of both Kirman and Qandahar to his son, Ali Mardan Khan. But this son proved unreliable as he betrayed his position and defected to the Mughal side, resulting in the loss of Qandahar in 1638. It is interesting to note here that where Ganj Ali Khan's personal bonds with Abbas I remained intact throughout their lives, the son was under no such familial obligation to Safi I and refused to accede to the Shah's demands. See H.R. Roemer, 'The Safavid Period', in *The Cambridge History of Iran: The Timurid and Safavid Periods*, Peter J. Jackson and Laurence Lockhart (eds) (Cambridge: Cambridge University Press, 1986): vol. 6, 282–83.

40 The pavilion is illustrated and identified by the early eighteenth-century Dutch traveller Cornelius le Bruyn; see Roger Stevens, 'European Visitors to the Safavid Court', *Iranian Studies* 7 (1974): 456, Fig. 5.

41 Whether this building is a caravanserai or a *madrasa* is still debated. Recently uncovered Quranic inscriptions inside the building have led the Iranian restoration team to suspect a religious function for the building. My (Babaie) own research, however, points to a commercial function for the structure, with the very intriguing addition of royal/ceremonial features that have thus far escaped scholarly notice. This aspect of the building will be the focus of my projected publication on Ganj Ali Khan's complex in Kirman.

42 In my view, the decorative and architectural details of this porch and the adjoining spaces leave no doubt about their royal function.

43 There are two *waqf* documents regarding the *maydan* ensemble of Ganj Ali Khan; one is dated 1605, the other 1615. Bastani-Parizi has published both in *Ganjalikhan*, but he is not clear about the relationship of these documents to the ensemble and its building history. Dr. Nozhat Ahmadi and I (Babaie) will address this problem in our joint project on Kirman.

44 The following discussion on the patronage of Saru Taqi incorporates research from my article, 'Building for the Shah: The Role of Mirza Muhammad Taqi (Saru Taqi) in Safavid Royal Patronage of Architecture', in Sheila Canby (ed.) *Safavid Art and Architecture* (London: British Museum, 2003): 20–26, where most details of Saru Taqi's building works can be found. Here, however, the emphasis is on Saru Taqi as a *ghulam* patron.

45 See Munshi, *Tarikh-i alam ara*, 849–51, for Farahabad and 855–56 for Ashraf.

46 Opening such roads posed a challenge, for they had to be dug through the formidable Alburz mountain range. The Savadkuh causeway is credited to Saru Taqi, but the Siyahkuh, the other major road, was evidently built under the supervision of Muhammad Beg Lala, the tutor of the *ghulams*;

see Shamlu, *Qisas*, 198 and Melville, 'Shah Abbas and the Pilgrimage to Mashhad', 212–13.

47 In locating the genesis of the *talar* in Isfahan palaces to Mazandaran, I (Babaie) diverge from earlier scholarly opinion that has been fixated on the Achaemenid Apadana or on vaguely described Timurid prototypes. This aspect of the Mazandaran vernacular and its impact on the palatine architecture of Isfahan is the subject of a chapter in my forthcoming manuscript, *Feasting in the City of Paradise*.

48 For a preliminary discussion of the architectural linkages through the *talar* between Mazandaran and Isfahan, see Babaie, 'Building for the Shah', 19.

49 Roemer, 'The Safavid Period', 267 and Munshi, *Tarikh-i alam ara*, 820–25.

50 The Mashhad campaign is described in Munshi, *Tarikh-i alam ara*, 854–55. May Farhat has located and analysed much of the Safavid and earlier works in the holy city; 'Islamic Piety and Dynastic Legitimacy: The Case of the Shrine of Ali b. Musa al-Rida in Mashhad (10th–17th Century)' (PhD dissertation, Harvard University, 2002) sorts out much of the Safavid and earlier works in the holy city.

51 Traditionally, the semi-autonomous shrine authorities (the Razavis) have administered the affairs of the shrine in Mashhad while constructions in and around the shrine were under the charge of city and provincial authorities.

52 Iskandar Beg Munshi and Muhammad Yusuf Muvarrikh, *Zayl-i alam ara-yi Abbasi*, Suhayli-Khwansari (ed.) (Tehran: Islamiyya, 1317/1938): 94–95 and 264. The Najaf project is also recorded in Muhammad Masum ibn Khwajigi Isfahani, *Khulasat al-siyyar*, Iraj Afshar (ed.) (Tehran: Intisharat-i Ilmi, 1368/1989): 130–31.

53 Munshi, *Tarikh-i alam ara*, 831 and McChesney, 'Four Sources', 122.

54 Saru Taqi's report is noted in Khwajigi Isfahani, *Khulasat al-siyyar*, 149.

55 *Divan-i Sa'ib-i Tabrizi*, Muhammad Qahraman (ed.) (Tehran: Intisharat-i ilmi va farhangi, 1370/1991): vol. 6, 3543–45 and esp. 3545; translation is mine.

56 Jean Chardin, *Les Voyages du Chevalier Chardin en Perse*, L. Langlès (ed.) (Paris, 1811): vol. VII, 302, notes that the mansion was begun by Hatim Beg Urdubadi and completed by his son, Mirza Talib Khan.

57 The mansion must have been quite sumptuous for even after Saru Taqi's death it was used to house Nadr Muhammad Khan, the deposed Uzbek ruler. There is also a reference to Shah Safi visiting Saru Taqi at his mansion and inviting the Mughal ambassador to join him there.

58 Adam Olearius, *The Voyages and Travels of the Ambassadors Sent by Frederick Duke of Holstein, to the Great Duke of Muscovy, and the King of Persia*, trans. John Davis (London, 1669): 212. Amy Landau's dissertation project (University of Oxford) on the reception and impact of

European painting in seventeenth-century Safavid Iran shall enhance our understanding of the significance of such patronage.

59 Chardin, *Voyages*, vol. VII, 302 ff.

60 On the meaning of the term *khadim* as eunuch in Mamluk context, see David Ayalon, *Eunuchs, Caliphs and Sultans: A Study of Power Relationships* (Jerusalem: The Magnes Press, the Hebrew University, 1999): 207–84.

61 Heinz Gaube and Eugene Wirth, *Der Bazar von Isfahan* (Weisbaden: Ludwig Reichert Verlag, 1978): 143–45.

62 British Library MS Sloane 4094; the text is reproduced in its original Persian, with German translation, in Gaube and Wirth, *Der Bazar von Isfahan*, 263 ff.; for the Jadda Caravanserai and Saru Taqi, see 277, especially line 112.

63 Chardin, *Voyages*, vol. VII, 366–67.

64 Muhammad Ali Gulriz, *Minudar ya bab al-jannat-i Qazvin* (Tehran: Intisharat-i danishgah-i Tehran, 1337/1958): 563–64. I (Babaie) thank Professor Ihsan Ishraqi for his help in locating this inscription.

65 On the cistern, see Siyyid Husayn Muddarisi Tabatabai, *Turbat-i pakan*, 2 vols (Qum: Chapkhana Mihr, 1355/1976): 140–41.

66 Suru Taqi also dedicated a sumptuous copy of the Quran to the memory of Shah Safi by making it *waqf* to the tomb of Safi at the shrine in Qum; Muhammad Mahriyar, 'Mu'arrefi majmu'a-yi tarikhi-yi Masjid-i Saru Taqi va madrasa-yi Saqat al-Islam va roqabat-i an', *Vaqf miras-i javidan* 19/20 (1376/1998): 77, note 13.

67 For a discussion of the thematic particularities of Safavid epigraphy, see Sussan Babaie, 'Epigraphy. iv, Safavid and Later Inscriptions', *Encyclopaedia Iranica* VIII (1998): 498–504.

68 The building history and functions of the Ali Qapu are discussed in Babaie, 'Safavid Palaces at Isfahan', 99–135.

69 Shamlu, *Qisas*, 280.

70 In my forthcoming monograph, *Feasting in the City of Paradise*, I (Babaie) argue that the appearance of the *talar* as an architectural unit in the palaces of Isfahan manifests a culturally specific Persian/Safavid construct of kingship in which the etiquette of royal feasting forms a pivotal conceptual link.

71 A preliminary version of this argument appears in Babaie, 'Safavid Palaces at Isfahan', 253–60.

72 Dates and titulars for these buildings are found in Sheila Blair, *The Monumental Inscriptions from Early Islamic Iran and Transoxiana* (Leiden: Brill, 1992): 160–63. Oleg Grabar, *The Great Mosque of Isfahan* (New York: New York University Press, 1990) provides an analysis of these domed chambers and the mosque in general.

73   Taj al-Din Ali Shah's other buildings included a cloth bazaar in Sultaniyya, the new capital of the Ilkhanid Sultan Uljaytu. For Ilkhanid buildings and their patrons, see Donald Wiber, *The Architecture of Islamic Iran: The Il Khanid Period* (Princeton: Princeton University Press, 1955) and Sheila Blair, *The Ilkhanid Shrine Complex at Natanz*, Iran (Cambridge: Harvard Middle East Papers, 1986).

74   Bernard O'Kane, *Timurid Architecture in Khurasan* (Costa Mesa, CA: Mazda Publishers, 1987): 86–87; Lisa Golombek and Donald Wilber, *The Timurid Architecture of Iran and Turan*, 2 vols (Princeton: Princeton University Press, 1988): 63–65.

75   O'Kane, *Timurid Architecture*, 179–87.

76   Op. cit, 211–14.

77   Hunarfar, *Ganjina*, 360–79. Despite scattered construction, and additions to established buildings, the largest concentration of architectural activity in the sixteenth century was at the Safavid ancestral shrine in Ardabil (see note 79 below) and the palace precinct at Qazvin (destroyed but for a single pavilion and a gateway). For sixteenth-century Safavid architecture see Hillenbrand, 'Safavid Architecture', 759–74 and Sussan Babaie, 'Building on the Past: The Shaping of Safavid Architecture, 1501–76', in Jon Thompson and Sheila Canby (eds), *Hunt for Paradise: Court Arts of Safavid Iran, 1501–1576* (New York and Milan: Asia Society, Museo Poldi Pezzoli and Skira Editore, 2003): 27–47.

78   The poetic inscription above the doorway of the shrine reads: '*Bi iqbal-i khan Durmish-i kamkar; bemanad az Husayn in bana yadgar*', claiming responsibility for the khan and a lasting memory for the architect; see Babaie, 'Building on the Past', 33–35.

79   Kishwar Rizvi's 'Transformations in Early Safavid Architecture: The Shrine of Shaykh Safi al-din Ishaq Ardabili in Iran (1501–1629)' (PhD dissertation, Massachusetts Institute of Technology, 2000) is the most complete study thus far of this principal early Safavid monument.

80   Op.cit. and see Kishwar Rizvi, 'Gendered Patronage: Women and Benevolence during the Early Safavid Empire', in D. Fairchild Ruggles (ed.), *Women, Patronage, and Self-Representation in Islamic Societies* (New York: State University of New York Press, 2000): 123–54.

81   Qazi Ahmad Qumi, *Khulasat al-tavarikh*, Ihsan Ishraqi (ed.), 2 vols (Tehran: Intasharat-I danishgah-I Tehran, 1359/1980): 79.

82   The dearth of and disarray in sixteenth-century architectural patronage may also be considered as a consequence of continuous wars, shortage of funds and natural or willful destructions.

83   This neglected aspect of Ottoman architectural patronage is the subject of a forthcoming study by Gülru Necipoğlu.

84   Much has been written on Sinan; see especially Gülru Necipoğlu, 'Challenging the Past: Sinan and the Competitive Discourse of Early-Modern Islamic Architecture', *Muqarnas* 10 (1993): 169–80.

85   Haneda notes a sharp difference in patronage between Timurid Herat and Safavid Isfahan; 'The Character of the Urbanization of Isfahan in the Later Safavid Period', 369–88, esp. 377.

Chapter 5

1   For a recent analysis of Qizilbash patronage, see Barbara Schmitz, 'Miniature Painting in Harat, 1570–1640', 2 vols, PhD dissertation (New York: New York University, Institute of Fine Art, 1981); see also, Roger M. Savory, 'The Qizilbash, Education, and the Arts', *Turcica* 6 (1975): 188–96.

2   For a recent discussion, see Abolala Soudavar, 'Between the Safavids and the Mughals: Art and Artists in Transition', *Iran* 37 (1999): 51–54.

3   Although Ismail II briefly re-established the royal atelier in Qazvin and even commissioned a luxurious copy of the *Shahnama*, he was murdered the following year and the manuscript was never completed; see Anthony Welch, *Artists for the Shah: Late Sixteenth Century Painting at the Imperial Court of Iran* (New Haven and London: Yale University Press, 1976): 21–28, 77–85; 212–14.

4   According to Lâle Uluç, 'Selling to the Court: Late-Sixteenth-Century Manuscript Production in Shiraz', *Muqarnas* 17 (2000): 73–96, many of these manuscripts were acquired by Ottoman noblemen, who were avid collectors of Persian illustrated texts. For a discussion of Persian manuscripts in Ottoman collections, see Filiz Çağman and Zeren Tanındı, 'Remarks on Some Persian Manuscripts from the Topkapi Palace Treasury in the Context of Safavid-Ottoman Relations', *Muqarnas* 13 (1996): 132–48.

5   Welch, *Artists for the Shah*, 174; the historian Qazi Ahmad even dedicated his famous *Gulistan-i Hunar*, a treatise on calligraphy and painting, in part to Farhad Khan.

6   For the patronage of Ali Quli Shamlu and his descendants, see Schmitz, 'Miniature Painting', passim. Apart from Herat, Mashhad had also developed into a major centre for manuscript production during the governorship of Shah Tahmasb's nephew and son-in-law, Sultan Ibrahim Mirza in the 1550s and 1560s; see Marianna Shreve Simpson with contributions by Massumeh Farhad, *Sultan Ibrahim Mirza's Haft Awrang: A Princely Manuscript from Sixteenth-Century Iran* (Washington, DC, New

Haven and London: Freer Gallery of Art, Smithsonian Institution and Yale University Press, 1997).

7 A *Divan* by Hafiz (1581–89), completed for Sultan Sulayman, the Turkoman governor of Tun and Tabas, is clearly inspired by the style associated with Sultan Ibrahim Mirza's *kitabkhana* in Mashhad, while the elaborate lacquered bindings of numerous Shirazi manuscripts emulate those associated with Shah Tahmasb's patronage, see Lâle Uluç, 'Selling to the Court', 75–78; figs. 2–8.

8 For an examination of Habibullah's career, see Marie L. Swietochowski, 'Habibullah', in *Persian Painting: From the Mongols to the Qajars. Studies in Honour of Basil W. Robinson*, Robert Hillenbrand (ed.) (London: I.B. Tauris Publications, 2000): 283–301. Ali Riza Abbasi's rivalry and subsequent murder of Mir Imad is discussed in Nasrullah Falsafi, *Zindigani-yi Shah Abbas-i avval*, 5 vols (Tehran: Intisharat-i ilmi, 1364/1985): vol. 2, 373–90.

9 Several of the single-page compositions in Abbas I's possession bear his seal, ranging in date from the year of his accession in 1586–87 to 1601–02; see, Adel T. Adamova, 'On the Attribution of Persian Paintings and Drawings of the Time of Shah Abbas I: Seals and Attributory Inscriptions', in *Persian Painting from the Mongol to the Qajar Period*, Robert Hillenbrand (ed.) (London, I.B. Tauris, 2000): 19–39. The *Shahnama* folios are now dispersed among Western public and private collections; see Welch, *Artists for the Shah*, 106–25.

10 Engelbert Kaempfer, *Am Hofe des Persischen Grosskönigs (1684–85). Das erste Buch des Amoenitas Exoticae; Eingeleitet und in Deutscher Bearbeitung herausgegeben von Walther Heinz* (Leipzig: K.F. Koeher Verlag, 1940): 121–22. Jean Chardin, *Voyage de Chevalier Chardin en Perse et autres lieux de l'Orient*, 10 vols (Paris: Nouvelle Edition par L. Langlès, 1811): vol. 7, 737. By the later seventeenth century, the *kitabkhana* or the repository for manuscripts, was distinguished from the *naqqaskhana* (painting studio), where texts were illustrated and illuminated. Even if the production and storage of manuscripts now occupied different physical spaces, they still represented part of the same continuum of manuscript production; see *Tadkhirat al-muluk: A Manual of Safavid Administration (ca. 1177/1725)*, translated and explained by V. Minorsky, reprint (Cambridge and London: Trustees of the E.G. Gibb Memorial, 1980), 100.

11 Welch, *Artists for the Shah*, 69; Sadiqi Beg fell out of favour with the Shah because of his difficult personality and his theft of a Timurid painting in the royal collection (ibid., 68–69); Abbas I's album is mentioned in Mulla Jallal al-din Munajjim, *Tarikh-i Abbasi ya Ruznama-yi Mulla Jallal*, Sayf Allah Vahidniya (ed.) (Tehran: Vahid Publications, 1366/1987): 170.

12   New York, Metropolitan Museum of Art, 63.210.11; see M. Lukens and E. Grube, 'The Language of the Birds', *Bulletin of the Metropolitan Museum of Art* (May 1967); A. Welch, *Artists for the Shah*, 184. According to Welch, the illustrations of a 1593 *Divan* of Hafiz, now in the Bodleian Library, Oxford (MS Elliott 163), also exhibits certain Timurid stylistic characteristics (ibid., 182–83). Furthermore, Riza Abbasi completed several drawings based on the work of the legendary Timurid painter, Bihzad; see Sheila R. Canby, *The Rebellious Reformer: The Drawings and Paintings of Riza-yi Abbasi of Isfahan* (London: Azimuth Press, 1996), chapter 8.

13   Sholeh A. Quinn, *Historical Writing During the Reign of Shah 'Abbas: Ideology, Imitation, and Legitimacy in Safavid Chronicles* (Salt Lake City: The University of Utah Press, 2000): 44–45. Until the suppression of the Nuqtavi movement in 1593, Sufi doctrine, like Firdawsi's epic, served as an important idiom of sovereignty in Safavid Iran.

14   J.M. Rogers, *Islamic Art and Design 1500–1700* (London: British Museum Publications, 1983): 50–51. The significance of the 'Crusader' Bible, now in the Pierpont Morgan Library, London was first examined by Sussan Babaie and Vera Moreen in a paper presented at the annual MESA meeting (New York, 22 November 1999), entitled, 'The Adventures of a French Illuminated Manuscript in Safavid Iran'. For a recent discussion see, Marianna Shreve Simpson, 'Shah Abbas and His Picture Bible', in *The Book of Kings. Art, War and the Morgan Library's Medieval Picture Bible*, William Noel and Daniel Weiss (eds) (Baltimore: The Trustees of the Walters Art Gallery, 2002): 120–44.

15   Gauvin A. Bailey, 'In the Manner of the Frankish Masters: A Safavid Drawing and its Flemish Inspiration', *Oriental Art* 40, no 4 (1995): 29–34; Robert Skelton, 'Giyath al-Din Naqshband and an Episode in the Life of Sadiqi Beg', in *Persian Painting*, 250–63; Gauvin A. Bailey, 'Supplement: The Sins of Sadiqi's Old Age', in ibid., 264–65.

16   Iskandar Beg Turkoman, *Alam aray-i Abbasi*, 2 vols, Iradj Afshar (ed.) (Tehran: Amir Kabir Publication, 1350/1971): vol. 1, 175; Eskandar Monshi, *History of Shah Abbas the Great*, Roger M. Savory (ed.), 2 vols (Boulder CO: Westview Press, 1978): vol. 1, 267.

17   For works inscribed to patrons other than the Shah, see Esin Atil, *The Brush of the Masters: Drawings from Iran and India.* (Washington DC: Freer Gallery of Art, Smithsonian Institution, 1978): nos 27, 29, 34–37, 41.

18   Welch, *Artists for the Shah*, 69.

19   Robert Skelton, 'Abbāsī, Šayk', *Encyclopaedia Iranica* (1985) 1:86. Although it is generally assumed that Riza Abbasi's son Shafi inherited the title 'Abbasi' from his father, he could have also received it from his royal patron, Abbas II.

20 Amir Sharaf Khan Bitlisi, *Sharafnama. Tarikh mufasal-i Kurdistan*, intro. and Muhammad Abbasi (ed.) (Tehran: n.p., 1343/1964): 576–77.

21 Iskandar Beg, *Alam ara*, 1: 176. Eskandar Monshi, *Shah Abbas*, 1: 272–73; A discussion of Siyavush's career appears in Welch, *Artists for the Shah*, 17–41.

22 Qazi Ahmad Qumi, *Gulistan-i Hunar*, Ahmad Suhayli Khunsari (ed.) (Tehran: Manuchihri Publications, n.d.): 148; *Calligraphers and Painters: A Treatise by Qadi Ahmad, son of Mir Munshi* (circa A.H. 1015/1606), trans. and V. Minorsky (ed.) (Washington DC: Freer Gallery of Art Occasional Papers, 1959): 191.

23 For a detailed analysis of this event in contemporary chronicles, see Quinn, *Historical Writings*, part 3.

24 Lâle Uluç ('Manuscript production', 89–91) argues that the appointment of Allah Virdi Khan to Fars marked the demise of manuscripts production in that province. She proposes that unlike the Zu'lqadar governors, the Georgian *ghulam* was more preoccupied with his architectural projects in Isfahan. While the number of manuscripts may have decreased under Allah Virdi Khan's governorship, Shiraz still produced several significant works in the early seventeenth century. These include a copy of the *Shahnama*, dated 1601 in the Bodleian Library, Oxford, MS. Ousely 344; see B.W. Robinson, *A Catalogue of the Persian Paintings in the Bodleian Library* (Oxford: Oxford University Press, 1958), 115–18; another *Shahnama* dated to *ca.* 1600, India Office Library, London, Ethé 2992; see B.W. Robinson, *Persian Paintings in the India Office Library* (London: Philip Wilson Publishers, 1976): 376–434; a copy of the *Rawzat al-Safa* (1601–1605), Bibliothèque Nationale, Paris, Mss. Or. Suppl. Persan 151; see Francis Richard, *Splendeurs persanes: Manuscrits du XIIe au XVIIe siècle* (Paris: Bibliothèque Nationale, 1997): no 145.

25 Richard, *Splendeur*, no 144; Chahryar Adle, 'Recherche sur le module et le tracé correcteur dans la miniature orientale, I. La mise en évidence à partir d'un example', *Le Monde Iranien et l'Islam* 3 (1975): 81–105.

26 Zabih-allah Safa, *Tarikh-i Adabiyat Iran* (Tehran: Intisharat-i Firdawsi, 1363/1984): part 1: 581; Falsafi, *Zindigani*, 4, 1544.

27 Ibid. For a summary of Imam Quli Khan's career, see Roger M. Savory, 'Emamqoli Khan', *Encyclopaedia Iranica* (1998) 8:394; for the *Jarunnama* (London, British Library, Add. 7801), see Norah M. Titley, *Persian Miniature Painting and Its Influence on the Art of Turkey and India* (London: British Library, 1983): 126 and Fig. 46; Idem, *Miniatures from Persian Manuscripts: A Catalogue and Subject Index of Paintings from Persia, India and Turkey in the British Library and the British Museum* (London: British Museum Publications Ltd, 1977): no 226.

28   Muhammad Mahriyar, 'Muarrefi majmu'a-yi tarikhi-yi Masjid-i Saru
     Taqi va madrasa-yi saqat al-Islam va ruqabat-i an', *Vaqf miras-i javidan*
     19/20 (1376/1998): 77, note 13.

29   *Tazkira-yi Nasrabadi*, Vahid Dastgiridi (ed.) (Tehran: Furuqi Bookshop,
     n.d), 414. The word *musavvir* literally means 'painter' and was often used
     as part of an artist's signature. Without a personal name, the identity of
     this particular painter is difficult to determine, but several seventeenth-
     century artists systematically used the term *musavvir*. Apart from the
     celebrated Mu'in Musavvir, another of Riza Abbasi's close followers
     consistently signed himself Riza Musavvir; for a discussion of his work,
     see Ivan Stchoukine, *Les peintures des manuscrits de Shah 'Abbas Ier à la
     fin des Safavis* (Paris: Librairie Orientaliste Paul Geuthner, 1964): 75–76.

30   For Hassan Khan Shamlu's patronage, see Schmitz, 'Harat', chapter 4.

31   Iskandar Beg, *Alam-ara* 2:1039–40; Eskandar Monshi, *Shah Abbas* 2:
     1260–61.

32   Robert D. McChesney, '*Waqf* and Public Policy: The *Waqfs* of Shah Abbas,
     1011–1023/1602–1614', *Asian and African Studies* 15 (1981), 165–90.
     An inventory list of the religious manuscripts donated to Mashhad is
     included in Muhammad Hassan Khan, Itimad al-saltana, *Matla' Shams*, 3
     vols (Tehran, 1302/1884): vol. 2, 469–500. The endowment to Ardabil
     originally included the celebrated *Haft awrang* ('Seven Thrones') by Jami,
     completed for Sultan Ibrahim Mirza between 1556 and 1566 and the
     1486 *Mantiq al-tayr* ('Conference of the Birds'), mentioned earlier (Fig. 13).
     In 1827, the Russians sacked Ardabil and took much of the manuscript
     collection to St. Petersburg. According to a recent source, some 120 texts
     from Ardabil are now housed at the Museum of Islamic Art in Tehran; see
     Ardabil (Qum: Dafatar-i kungira, 1375/1996): 363.

33   Kishwar Rizvi, 'Transformation in Early Safavid Architecture: The Shrine
     of Shaykh Safi al-Din Ardabili in Iran', PhD dissertation, Harvard
     University, Cambridge MA, 2000, chapter 4, n.p. I consulted a final copy
     of Dr. Rizwi's dissertation, dated 18 March 2000, before its submission.

34   Mehdi Sayyidi, *Tarikh-i shahr-i Mashhad* (Tehran: Intisharat-i Jami,
     1378/1999): 117.

35   J.A. Pope, *Chinese Porcelains from the Ardabil Shrine* (Washington DC:
     Freer Gallery of Art, Smithsonian Institution, 1956): 49; this publication
     remains the only study and partial survey of this remarkable collection.
     M. Medley, 'Ardabil Collection of Chinese Porcelain', *Encyclopaedia Iranica*
     (1987): vol. 2, 364–65. See also Pedro Moura Carvalho, 'Porcelains for
     the Shah, Ardabil and the Chinese Ceramics Trade in the Persian Gulf',
     The Oriental Ceramic Society (2003): 47–56. Presently, the majority of
     the extant collection is housed in the Museum of Islamic Art in Tehran; a

small number is on display in the Ardabil shrine complex and at the Tabriz National Museum. The exact number of vessels gifted to the shrine, however, is unclear. Mulla Jallal, Abbas I's court historian and astrologer, who was an eyewitness to the official dedication of the collection to the shrine in 1610–11, maintains that the endowment included 1221 pieces, but lists only 1162; see *Tarikh-i Abbasi*, 424. When Pope surveyed the collection for his 1956 publication, he mentions some 900 pieces (*Ardabil Shrine*, 160). I would like to thank Mr. Muhammad Reza Kargar, director of the National Museum, Tehran, Mrs. Zahra Jafar-Muhammadi, chief curator, and Mrs. Zohreh Ruhfar, curator of the Islamic collection, for kindly allowing me to see the collection in September 2000.

36   Adam Olearius, *Moskowitische und Persische Reise* (Berlin: Rütten & Loening, 1959): 301. A.H. Morton, 'The Ardabil Shrine in the Reign of Shah Tahmasp', *Iran* XII (1974): 56. According to Morton, although Olearius' description of the space leaves little doubt that it is the *chini-khana*, the term 'Tsenetsera' is closer to *jannat-serai*, an entirely different space altogether. For in-depth discussion of Ardabil, see Rizwi, 'Ardabil'.

37   Munajjim, *Tarikh-i Abbasi*, 424; Pope, *Ardabil Shrine*, 8–10; Medley, 'Chinese Porcelain', 364. The angular configuration and wording of Shah Abbas I's inscription here recalls his seal impression on some of the album pages; for examples, see Adamova, 'On the Attribution', 20–21 and Fig. 13.

38   Interestingly, the terms 'Bihbud', and 'Naringi' also appear on several Chinese porcelain wares in the Topkapi Palace collection, Istanbul. Nurdan Erbahar has proposed that the term 'Naringi' may have been coined because of the reddish colour of the clay. Alternatively, it may suggest the use of the vessel for different kinds of citrus fruits; see, 'Non-Chinese Marks and Inscriptions,' in *Chinese Ceramics in the Topkapi Saray Museum, Istanbul: A Complete Catalogue I. Yuan and Ming Dynasty Celadon Wares*, Regina Krahl, Nurdan Erbahar and John Ayers (eds) (London: Sotheby's Publication in association with the Directorate of the Topkapi Saray Museum, 1986): 125–26. Pope has suggested that 'Bihbud' may refer to the keeper of the treasury under Sultan Husayn Bayqara, the Timurid ruler (1470–1506), but the name also appears on some Timurid coins not necessarily associated with the mint in Herat. Another candidate is the Safavid nobleman Bihbud Beg, who was charged by Abbas I to murder his son Prince Safi Mirza, after Qarachaqay Khan refused to carry out the deed. Pope, *Ardabil Shrine*, 53–55.

39   Pope, *Ardabil Shrine*, 160.

40   For illustrations see ibid., pls 25 (29.412) and 53 (29.471).

41   Ali Akbar, *Khataynama*, Iradj Afshar (ed.) (Tehran: Markaz-i asnad-i farhang-i asia, 1372/1994): 116–17; Julian Raby and Ünsel Yücel, 'Chinese

Porcelain at the Ottoman Court', in *Chinese Ceramics in the Topkapi Seray Museum*, Istanbul, 46–47.

42   Among the *ghulams*, Imam Quli Khan was reputed for his lavish gifts that even surpassed those presented by foreign ambassadors and envoys, see Falsafi, *Zindigani*, 3: 1216–17. In the Ottoman Empire, where Chinese porcelain was an equally coveted luxury item, collections were commonly confiscated and appropriated by the court. According to Raby and Yücel, when a government official died, the sultan would declare the deceased official a slave, which would allow him to assume automatic possession of the person's belongings and legally justify his act; see Raby and Yüsul, 'Chinese Porcelain at the Ottoman Court', 33.

43   For a description of Ulugh Beg's celebrated *chini-khana* that housed his porcelains in Samarqand, see Zahiruddin Muhammad Babur, *Baburnama*, trans. Annette Susannah Beveridge (London: Luzac & Co., 1971), 80; *Baburnama*, translated, edited and annotated by Wheeler M. Thackston (Washington DC: Freer Gallery of Art and Oxford: Oxford University Press, 1996): 86; see also Tom W. Lentz and Glenn D. Lowry, *Timur and the Princely Vision: Persian Art and Culture in Fifteenth-Century Iran* (Los Angeles: Los Angeles County Museum of Art and Washington DC: Arthur M. Sackler Gallery, 1989): 229.

44   Raby and Yücel, 'Chinese Porcelain at the Ottoman Court', 32, 30. One of the largest gifts consisted of 63 pieces of porcelain, sent by Shah Safi to Murad IV in 1637.

45   Ibid., 31 and 36; Pope, *Ardabil Shrine*, 54.

46   For the drilled and incised name of Qarachaqay Khan, see Pope, *Ardabil Shrine*, Plate 6, Fig. F and G; Plate 53, Fig. H (29.471) show his name together with that of Bihbud.

47   Raby and Yücel 'Chinese Porcelain at the Ottoman Court', 33.

48   Baltimore, Walters Art Museum, no 10.691. For a discussion of this painting and the particular turban worn by Qarachaqay Khan, see Barbara Schmitz, 'On a Special Hat Introduced during the Reign of Shah Abbas the Great', *Iran* 22 (1984): 103–13; Schmitz proposes (110) that the turban was reserved for governors but as is evident from this and other paintings, the taj-like headgear was most probably intended for members of the Safavid elite in general. Basil Robinson has suggested that the portrait represents Qarachaqay Khan's grandson and name-sake, whose patronage will be discussed below; see B.W. Robinson, 'Two Manuscripts of the *Shahnama* in the Royal Library, Windsor Castle-II: MS Holmes 151 (A/6),' *Burlington Magazine*, 110 (1968), 133. On the basis of the painting's style and the identity of some of the other noblemen, the figure probably represents the first Qarachaqay Khan.

49 Charles Melville, 'Shah 'Abbas and the Pilgrimage to Mashhad', in *Safavid Persia: The History and Politics of an Islamic Society*, Charles Melville (ed.), *Pembroke Persian Papers* 4 (1996): 215.

50 McChesney, '*Waqf*', 181; Melville, 'Pilgrimage', 217.

51 Lisa Golombek, Robert Mason and Patty Proctor, '"Safavid Potters" Marks and the Question of Provenance', *Iran* 39 (2001): 207–8 and note 12. See also Yolande Crowe, *Persia and China: Safavid Blue and White Ceramics in the Victoria and Albert Museum 1501–1738* (London: Victoria and Albert Museum, 2002).

52 Manuchihr Khan had been serving in that capacity since 1621; the post of *sipahsalar* went to Isa Khan. According to the *Tadhkhirat*, 36, the term *yüzbashi* implied 'master of a hundred'.

53 Interestingly, his name, 'Manuchihr', which is Persian in origin, is another indication of the adoption and integration of the *ghulams* within the Safavid cultural system.

54 Mudarrisi Tabataba'i, *Turbat-i Pakan*, 2 vols (Qum: Chapkhana-i Mihr, 1335/1976): vol. 2, 236–41. According to Iskandar Beg Munshi, Ali Quli Khan replaced Mirza Muhammad Qumi as royal head librarian; Iskandar Munshi and Muhammad Yusuf Muvarrikh, *Zayl alam ara-yi Abbasi*, Suhayli Khunsari (ed.) (Tehran: Islamiyya, 1317/1938): 247.

55 New York, Public Library, Spencer, Pers. Ms. 6; see Barbara Schmitz with contributions by Latif Khayyat, Svat Soucek, and Massoud Pourfarrokh, *Islamic Manuscripts in the New York Public Library* (New York and Oxford: Oxford University Press and the New York Public Library, 1992), no II.18; see also Massumeh Farhad, 'The Art of Mu'in Musavvir: The Art of his Times', in *Persian Masters: Five Centuries of Persian Painting*, Sheila R. Canby (ed.) (Bombay: Marg Publications, 1990): 114, where Manuchihr Khan was first identified as the patron of the manuscript; Anthony Welch, *Shah Abbas and the Arts of Isfahan* (New York: Asia House Society, 1973): no 52; because of the manuscript's high quality, Welch originally suggested that it was commissioned at the court of Shah Safi.

56 New York, Public Library, Spencer, Pers. Ms. 6, ff. 2–3v, 16.

57 D. Pingree, 'History of Astronomy in Iran', *Encyclopaedia Iranica* (1987) 2: 860.

58 Emmy Wellesz, 'An Early Al-Sūfī Manuscript in the Bodleian Library in Oxford: A Study in Islamic Constellation Images', *Ars Orientalis* 3 (1959): 1–59.

59 Based on the modelling and shading of the al-Sufi compositions, Barbara Schmitz has argued that the illustrations must have been executed by Muhammad Ali, Malik Husayn's son and one of the main practitioners of the new style in the 1640s and 50s (*Islamic Manuscripts*, 123). Muhammad

Ali may have contributed to the pictorial cycle, but a stylistic comparison of the al-Sufi illustrations to the frontispiece of a *Shahnama*, completed in 1648 and signed by Malik Husayn, discussed below, suggests that there is little reason to doubt his authorship of the illustrations as stated in the manuscript's preface.

60   Ibid.

61   Munajjim, *Abbasnama*, 113; Isfahan's association with the sign of Sagittarius has also been proposed by Stephen P. Blake, *Half the World: The Social Architecture of Safavid Isfahan 1590–1722* (Costa Mesa CA: Mazda Publishers, 1999), 109 but without an explanation. As evidence, Blake refers to a tile panel above the entrance to the *qaysariyya* that depicts two archers. For illustration, see Eleanor Sims with contributions by Boris I. Marshak and Ernst J. Grube, *Peerless Images: Persian Figural Painting and Its Sources* (New Haven and London: Yale University Press, 2002), Fig.83. I am grateful to Professor Gernot Windfur for suggesting that Sagittarius may also denote Manuchihr Khan's birth sign.

62   For examples see, Lentz and Lowry, *Timur*, cat. no 146.

63   For a copy of Ulugh Beg's *Zij*, see Soudavar, *Persian Courts*, cat. no 25.

64   Schmitz, *Islamic Manuscripts*, 123; notes 4 and 6. For illustration of the Cairo copy, see D.A. King, *A Survey of the Scientific Manuscripts in the Egyptian National Library* (Cairo, 1365/1986), pl. 3; for the Tehran copy, see S.H. Nasr, *Islamic Science: An Illustrated Study* (London: World of Islam Festival, 1976): 100–3, pls 48, 50, 53, 56–57, figs. 36–38.

65   The only dated manuscripts associated with Shah Safi is an unillustrated copy of the *Gulistan* by Sa'di, dated 1633–34; Arberry, A. et al., *The Chester Beatty Library: A Catalogue of the Persian Manuscripts and Miniatures*, 3 vols (Dublin: Hodges & Figgis, 1959): vol. 3, MS 272.

66   Upon his accession to the throne in 1642, Abbas II ordered Qarachaqay Khan II and several other notables to kill Rustam Khan, who had plotted the murder of Saru Taqi; Tahir Vahid, *Abbasnama*, 48.

67   According to Iskandar Beg Munshi, Vahshi (d.1583) was one of the leading poets of the period and his *mathnavi* of *Farhad u Shirin* was considered one of the most popular texts of the Safavid period; Iskandar Beg, *Alam-ara*, 1, 181; Eskandar Monshi, *Shah Abbas*, 1, 276.

68   *Sotheby Catalogue* (London, 9 October 1979), lot 266 and ibid. (27 April 1981), lot 170. I am grateful to Marcus Fraser, former head of the Department of Islamic Manuscripts and Ancient Near Eastern Art at Sotheby's, London, for helping me locate the manuscript. A painting, depicting Khusraw and Shirin in a mountainous landscape, also in the distinct style of Muhammad Qasim, may have originally belonged to or been intended for the same manuscript; see *Persian and Mughal Art* (London: P.D. Colnaghi

& Co. Ltd, 1976), no 52; for a discussion of Muhammad Qasim's work, see Massumeh Farhad, 'Safavid Single Page Paintings 1642–1666', PhD dissertation, Harvard University, Cambridge MA, 1988, passim; Adamova, 'On the Attribution of Persian Paintings', 22–23.

69 Tehran, Gulistan Library Collection, Album no 1629; B. Atabay, *Fihrist-i muraqqaʻat kitab-khana-yi saltanati* (Tehran, 1353/1974), no 145.

70 For an example, see Sheila R. Canby, *Princes, Poets, and Palladins: Islamic and Indian Paintings from the Collection of Prince and Princess Sadruddin Aga Khan* (London: Trustees of the British Museum by the British Museum Press, 1998): cat. no 52.

71 Marianna Shreve Simpson, 'A Manuscript made for the Safavid Prince Bahram Mirza', *Burlington Magazine* 83 (June 1991): 397 and n. 20. For a recent discussion of these two portraits, see also Soudavar, 'Between the Safavids and the Mughals', 50–51, 53.

72 Tahir Vahid, *Abbasnama*, 62, 89; Shamlu, *Qasas al-Khaqani*, 1:283, 296. Vahid maintains that Nadr Muhammad Khan, the Vali of Turkistan, complained about Qarachaqay Khan II to the Shah.

73 The manuscript was first published and discussed by B.W. Robinson in 'Two Manuscripts', 133–38 and illustrations. A forthcoming monograph by Basil W. Robinson, Eleanor Sims, and Manijeh Bayani, entitled *The Persian Book of Kings: the Windsor Shahnama of 1648*, is devoted to this manuscript. I am deeply grateful to Basil Robinson for sharing with me an early draft of his chapter. Several illustrations from the Windsor *Shahnama* are also included in Sims, *Peerless Images*, nos 10, 18 and 87.

74 See Yuri A. Petrosyan et al. *Pages of Perfection: Islamic Paintings and Calligraphy from the Russian Academy of Sciences*, St. Petersburg (Lugano, ARCH Foundation, 1995): cat. no 51, f. 6r.

75 William L. Hanaway, Jr., 'Borzu-nama', *Encyclopaedia Iranica* (1990) 4: 380–81. For late sixteenth-century manuscripts that include post-*Shahnama* epics, see Karin Rührdanz, 'About a Group of Truncated *Shahnamas*: A Case Study in the Commercial Production of Illustrated Manuscripts in the Second Part of the Sixteenth Century', *Muqarnas* 14 (1997):118–35.

76 M. M. Ashrafi, *Persian Tajik Poetry in XVI-XVII Centuries Miniatures* (Dushanbe, Academy of Sciences, the Writers' Association of Tajik SSR, 1974), nos 96–100; V. Loukonine and A. Ivanov, *Lost Treasures of Persia: Persian Art in the Hermitage Museum* (Washington, DC: Mage Publications, 1996): nos 214 and 215. The manuscript is almost identical in size to the Windsor Castle one and includes 192 illustrations. These are the work of a different group of artists, including Afzal al-Husayni and Riza Musavvir, whose styles are closer to that of Riza Abbasi. The paintings of a third painter, Pir Muhammad Hafiz, bear a certain stylistic

similarity to Muhammad Yusuf's compositions; see Ashrafi, *Persian Tajik Poetry*, nos 97 and 99.

77   Muhammad Hassan Semsar, *Golestan Palace Library: Portfolio of Miniature Paintings and Calligraphy*, trans. karim Emami (Tehran: Zarin & Simin Books, 2000): 112–27.

78   Arthur M. Sackler Gallery, Smithsonian Institution, Washington DC, S1986.485; Lowry et. al, Checklist, no 159. The paintings post-date the completion of the manuscript.

79   For a discussion of other collaborative projects by Muhammad Yusuf, Muhammad Qasim and Muhammad Ali see Massumeh Farhad, "'Searching for the New': Later Safavid Painting and the Suz u Gawdaz (Burning and Melting) by Nau'i Khabushani', *The Journal of the Walters Art Museum* 59 (2001): 115–30.

80   See idem, 'Mu'in Musavvir', 113–28.

81   For examples of these artists' work, see Canby, *Golden Age*, figs. 123–26. See also Robert Skelton, 'Abbāsī, Šayk', *Encyclopaedia Iranica* (1985): vol. 1, 86–88.

82   Sussan Babaie, 'Shah Abbas II, the Conquest of Qandahar, the Chihil Sutun, and Its Wall Paintings', *Muqarnas* 11 (1994): 125–42; idem, 'Safavid Palaces in Isfahan: Continuity and Change (1599–1666)', PhD dissertation, New York University, New York, 1993, 190–91. Babaie has convincingly argued that the stylistically different wall paintings of the Chihil Sutun Palace were created during the reign of Shah Abbas II.

83   Tahir Vahid, *Abbasnama*, 330.

84   Tabataba'i, *Turbat*, 235.

85   Shamlu, *Qisas*, 2: 153–54. Muhammad Ali must have also been active in the late 1650s for a copy of Nau'i Khabushani's *Suz u Gawdaz* (Melting and Burning) was completed for him in the year 1658. In the colophon, he is identified as 'Muhammad Ali, the painter from Mashhad' (*naqash-i Mashhadi*); see Massumeh Farhad, 'Suz u Gawdaz', 120, Fig. 10.

86   For Ali Quli's earliest signed work, dated 1649, see A.T. Adamova, *Persian Painting and Drawing of the 15th–19th Centuries from the Hermitage Museum* (St. Petersburg: AO 'Slaviia', 1996): cat. no 24; for the association of the Safavid arsenal with the white eunuchs see *Tadhkhirat al-muluk*, 56.

87   Soudavar, *Persian Courts*, 369; P.P. Soucek, 'Alī-Qolī Jobba-dār', *Encyclopaedia Iranica* (1985) I: 872; for examples of Ali Quli's inscribed paintings, see *The St. Petersburg Muraqqa' Album of Indian and Persian Miniatures from the 16th to the 18th Century and Specimens of Persian Calligraphy by 'Imād al-Hasanī* (Lugano: ARCH Foundation, 1996): pls 184 and 191.

88   The paintings were first published by Eleanor Sims, 'Five Seventeenth Century Persian Oil Paintings' in *Persian and Mughal Art*, 223–41. Chahryar

Adle has suggested recently that the works are Georgian in origin, which seems a less likely hypothesis; see 'Note sur la peinture à l'huile profane en Géorgie à la veille de la période russe, école Géorgie-Persane (inscriptions déchifrées grâce de D. Gauthier-Eligoulachvili)', *Archéologie et arts du monde Iranien, de l'Inde musulmane et de Caucase d'après quelques recherches recentes de terrain*, 1984–95, M. Chahryar Adle (ed.) (Paris, 1996), 349–57. Amy Landau's PhD dissertation, which focuses on painting during the reign of Shah Sulayman, will discuss these oil paintings in detail.

89 Istanbul, Istanbul University Library, T. 6045. Other Ottoman historical manuscripts, such as the *Şahinşahnama*, dated 1592, includes an illustration of Farhad Paşa's conquest of Revan. See Esin Atil, 'The Art of the Book', in *Turkish Art*, Esin Atil (ed.) (Washington DC: Smithsonian Institution Press and New York: Harry Abrams, 1980): pls 28 and 26 and 236, n. 70. I am grateful to Professor Gülru Necipoğlu for drawing my attention to these Ottoman manuscripts.

90 Paul E. Losensky, *Welcoming Fighānī. Imitation and Poetic Individuality in the Safavid-Mughal Ghazal* (Costa Mesa CA: Mazda Publishers, 1998).

Bibliography

A Chronicle of the Carmelites in Persia and the Papal Mission of the XVIIth and XVIIIth Centuries. London: Eyre and Spottiswoode, 1939.

Abbas, Mohammed Jalal. 'Slavery Between Islam and Western Civilization – A Comparative Study of Attitudes'. *Majallat al-azhar* 43 ix (1971): 11–16.

Abd al-Nur, Jabbur. *Al-jawari*. Cairo: Dar al-Ma'arif, n.d.

Adamova, Adel T. *Persian Paintings and Drawings of the 15th–19th Centuries from the Hermitage Museum*. St. Petersburg: AO 'Slaviia', 1996.

— 'On the Attribution of Persian Paintings and Drawings of the Time of Shah Abbas I: Seals and Attributory Inscriptions'. In *Persian Painting: From the Mongols to the Qajars. Studies in Honour of Basil W. Robinson*. Robert Hillenbrand (ed.). London and New York: I. B. Tauris, in association with Centre of Middle Eastern Studies, University of Cambridge, 2000, 19–39.

Adle, Chahryar. 'Recherche sur le module et le tracé correcteur dans la miniature orientale, I. La mise en évidence à partir d'un example'. *Le Monde Iranien et l'Islam* 3 (1975): 81–105.

— 'Note sur la peinture à l'huile profane en Géorgie à la veille de la periode russe, école Géorgie-Persane (inscriptions déchifrées grâce de D. Gauthier-Eligoulachvili)'. In *Archéologie et arts du monde Iranien, de l'inde musulman et de Caucase d'après quelques recherches recents de terrain*, 1984–1995. M. Chahryar Adle (ed.). Paris: 1996, 249–57.

Ali Akbar. Khataynama. Iraqdj Afshar. (ed.) *Tehran: Markaz-i asnad-i farhang-i asia*, 1372/1993.

Amitai-Preiss, Reuven. *Mongols and Mamluks: the Mamluk-Ilkhanid War, 1260–1281*. Cambridge and New York: Cambridge University Press, 1995 and 2002.

al-Amri, Husayn ibn Abdallah. 'Slaves and Mamelukes in the History of Yemen'. *Yemen: 3000 years of art and civilisation in Arabia Felix*. W. Daum (ed.). Innsbruck: Pinguin-Verlag; Frankfurt: Umschau-Verlag, 1988, 140–57.

An Economic and Social History of the Ottoman Empire 1300–1914. Halil Inalcik and Donald Quartaert (eds). 2 vols. Cambridge: Cambridge University Press, 1994.

Arafat, W. 'The Attitude of Islam to Slavery'. *Islamic Quarterly* 10 (1966): 12–18.

Arberry, A.J. et al. *The Chester Beatty Library: A Catalogue of the Persian Manuscripts and Miniatures*. 3 vols. Dublin: Hodges & Figges, 1959–1962.

Ardabil. *Qum, Dafatar-i kungara*, 1375/1996.

Armenian Merchants of the Seventeenth and Eighteenth Centuries: English East Company Sources. Vahe Baladouni and Margaret Makepeace (eds). Philadelphia: American Philosophical Society, 1998.

Afshar, Iraj. 'Kitabdari dar kitabkhanaha-yi qadimi Iran'. *Bar-risiha-yi tarikhi* 2 (1353/1974): 153–73.

Ashrafi, M.M. *Persian Tajik Poetry in XVI–XVII Centuries Miniatures*. Dushanbe: Academy of Sciences, the Writers' Association of Tajik SSR, 1974.

Atabay, Badri. *Fihrist-i muraqqa'at kitab-khana-yi saltanati*. Tehran: Chapkhana-i Ziba, 1353/1974.

Atil, Esin. *The Brush of the Masters: Drawings from Iran and India*. Washington DC: Freer Gallery of Art, Smithsonian Institution, 1978.

— *Turkish Art*. Washington DC: Smithsonian Institution and New York: Harry Abrams, 1980.

Aubin, Jean. 'La propriété foncière en Azerbaydjan'. *Le Monde Iranien et L'Islam: Sociétés et Cultures*, 4 (1976–1977): 79–132.

Ayalon, David. *The Mamluk Military Society*. London: Variorum Reprints, 1979.

— 'On the Eunuchs in Islam'. *Jerusalem Studies in Arabic and Islam* 1 (1979): 67–124.

— 'The Mamluk Novice (on his Youthfulness and on his Original Religion)'. *Revue des Études Islamiques* 54 (1986): 1–8.

— 'Mamlukiyyat'. In *Outsiders in the Lands of Islam: Mamluks, Mongols and Eunuchs*. London: Variorum, 1971, 1988, 321–49.

— *Islam and the Abode of War: Military Slaves and Islamic Adversaries*. Aldershot, Great Britain; Brookfield, VT: Variorum, 1994.

— *Eunuchs, Caliphs and Sultans: A Study in Power Relationships*. Jerusalem: Magnes Press, 1999.

Babaie, Sussan. 'Building on the Past: The Shaping of Safavid Architecture, 1501–76', in Jon Thompson and Sheila Canby (eds), *Hunt for Paradise: Court Arts of Safavid Iran, 1501–1576* (New York and Milan: Asia Society, Museo Poldi Pezzoli and Skira Editore, 2003): 27–47.

— 'Safavid Palaces in Isfahan: Continuity and Change (1599–1666)'. PhD dissertation, New York University, 1994.

— 'Shah Abbas II, the Conquest of Qandahar, the Chihil Sutun, and its Wall Paintings'. *Muqarnas* 11 (1994): 125–42.

Babaie, Sussan and Vera Moreen. 'The Adventures of a French Illuminated Manuscript in Safavid Iran'. Paper presented at the annual meeting of the Middle Eastern Studies Association, Washington DC, November 1999.

— 'Building for the Shah: The Role of Mirza Muhammad Taqi (Saru Taqi) in Safavid Royal Patronage of Architecture'. In *Safavid Art and Architecture*. Sheila Canby (ed.). London: The British Museum, 2002, 20–26.

— 'Epigraphy. iv, Safavid and Later Inscriptions'. In *Encyclopaedia Iranica*. Ehsan Yarshater (ed.). London/Boston: Routledge and Kegan Paul, 1988, 5 (1998), 498–504.

— *Review of Half the World: The Social Architecture of Safavid Isfahan 1590–1722*, by Stephen Blake. Iranian Studies 33/3–4 (2000): 478–82.

Babayan, Kathryn. 'The Waning of the Qizilbash: The Spiritual and the Temporal in Seventeenth Century Iran'. PhD dissertation, Princeton University, 1993.

— 'Eunuchs under the Safavids'. In *Encyclopaedia Iranica*. Ehsan Yarshater (ed.). London/Boston: Routledge and Kegan Paul, 1985, vol. 9, 67–68.

— *Mystics, Monarch and Messiahs: Cultural Landscapes of Early Modern Iran*. Cambridge: Harvard Middle Eastern Monographs, 2003.

Babur, Zahiruddin Muhammad. *Baburnama*. Annette J. Beveridge (trans.). London: Luzac and Co., 1912.

— *Baburnama: The Memoirs of Babur, Prince and Emperor*. Wheeler Thackston. (trans.). Washington, DC/New York/Oxford: Freer Gallery of Art and Oxford University Press, 1996.

Bacharach, J.L. 'African Military Slaves in the Medieval Middle East: The Cases of Iraq (869–955) and Egypt (868–1171)'. *International J. Middle East Studies* 13 (1981): 471–95.

Baghdiantz McCabe, Ina. *The Shah's Silk for Europe's Silver: The Eurasian Trade of the Julfa Armenians in Safavid Iran and India (1530–1750)*. Atlanta, GA: Scholars Press, 1999.

— 'The Socio-Economic Conditions in New Julfa post 1650: The Impact of Conversions to Islam on International Trade'. *Revue des études arméniennes* 26 (1996–1997): 367–97.

— 'Trading Diaspora, State Building and the Idea of National Interest'. *Views from the Edge: Essays in Honor of Richard W. Bulliet*. New York: Columbia Middle-East Institute, Columbia University Press, 2003, 18–37.

— 'Silk and Silver: The Trade and Organization of New Julfa at the End of the Seventeenth Century'. *Revue des études arméniennes* 25 (1994–95): 389–415.

Bailey, Gauvin A. 'In the Manner of the Frankish Masters: A Safavid Drawing and Its Flemish Inspiration', *Oriental Art* 40, no 4 (1995): 29–34.

— 'Supplement: The Sins of Sadiqi's Old Age', in *Persian Painting: From the Mongols to the Qajars. Studies in Honor of Basil W. Robinson*. Robert Hillenbrand (ed.). London: I.B.Tauris Publications, in association with Centre of Middle Eastern Studies, University of Cambridge, 2000, 283–301.

Barkan, Ömer Lutfi. 'Le sérvage éxistait-il en Turquie?' *Annales ESC* 2 (1956): 54–60.

Barthold, W. *An Historical Geography of Iran*. C.E. Bosworth (ed.). Svat Soucek (trans.) Princeton: Princeton University Press, 1984.

Bastani-Parizi, Muhammad Ibrahim. *Ganjalikhan*. NP: Asatir Publications, 1368/1989.

Bennassar, B. 'Les chrétiens convertis à l'Islam dans les procedures inquis-itoriales'. In *Actes du IIe Congres International sur: Chrétiens et Musulmans a l'epoque de la Renaissance. A'mal al-mu'tamar al-'alami al-thani hawl al-Masihiyun wa-'l-Muslimun fi 'asr al-Nahda al-gharbiya*. Abdeljelil Temimi Zaghouan (ed.). Fondation Temimi pour la Recherche Scientifique et l'Information, 1997, 73–78.

Bijan. *Tarikh-i Safavi Khan*. British Library, MS Add. 7655.

Binger, Louis Gustave. *Esclavage, islamisme et christianisme*. Paris: Société d'éditions scientifiques, 1891.

Bitlisi, Amir Sharaf Khan. *Sharafnama. Tarikh mufasal-i Kurdistan*. Muhammad Abbasi (ed). Tehran, 1343/1964.

Blair, Sheila. *The Monumental Inscriptions from Early Islamic Iran and Transoxiana*. Leiden: E.J. Brill, 1992.

— *The Ilkhanid Shrine Complex at Natanz*, Iran. Cambridge, MA: Center for Middle Eastern Studies, Harvard University, 1986.

Blake, Stephen P. *Half the World: The Social Architecture of Safavid Isfahan 1590–1722*. Costa Mesa, CA: Mazda Publishers, 1999.

Braudel, Fernand. *La Méditerranée et le monde mediterranéen à l'époque de Philippe II*. Paris: Armand Colin, 1949.

Brockopp, Jonathan Eugene. 'Slavery in Islamic Law: An Examination of Early Maliki Jurisprudence (Abdallah b. Abd Al Hakam, Malik B. Anas)'. PhD dissertation, Yale University, 1995.

Brunschvig, R. 'Abd'. *Encyclopaedia of Islam*. 2nd edition. Leiden: E.J. Brill, 1954–, I, 24–40.

Busse, Heribert. *Unterzuchungen zum islamschen Kanzleiwesen an Hand turkmenischerf und safawidischer unkunden*. Cairo: Komissionsverlag Sirovic Bookshop, 1959.

Çağman, Filiz and Zeren Tanindi. 'Remarks on Some Manuscripts from the Topkapi Palace Treasury in the Context of Ottoman-Safavid Relations', *Muqarnas* 13 (1996): 132–48.

Canby, Sheila R. *The Rebellious Reformer: The Drawings and Paintings of Riza-yi Abbasi of Isfahan*. London: Azimuth Press, 1996.

— *Princes, Poets, Paladins: Islamic and Indian Paintings from the Collection of Prince and Princess Sadruddin Aga Khan*. London: The British Museum Press, 1998.

Carswell, John. *New Julfa: The Armenian Churches and Other Buildings*. Oxford: Clarendon Press, 1968.

Chardin, Jean. *Voyages du Chevalier Chardin, en Perse, et autres lieux de l'Orient. Enrichis de Figures en Taille-douce, qui représentent les Antiquités et les choses remarquables du Païs. Nouvelle Edition, augmentée du Couronnement de Soliman III. and d'un grand nombre de Passages tirés du Manuscrit de l'Auteur qui ne se trouvent point dans les Editions précédentes.* 4 vols. Aux dépens de la Compagnie. Amsterdam, 1735.

— *Voyages du Chevalier Chardin, en Perse, et autres lieux de l'Orient.* L. Langlès (ed.). Paris: Le Normant, 1811.

Chirichigno, Gregory T. *Debt-slavery in Israel and the Ancient Near East.* Sheffield: JSOT Press, 1993.

Cilardo, A. 'The Transmission of the Patronate in Islamic Law'. Miscellanea Arabica et Islamica: dissertationes in Academia Ultrajectina prolatae anno MCMXC. F. de Jong (ed.). *Orientalia Lovaniensia Analecta*, 52. Leuven: Peeters, 1993, 31–52.

Collins, R.O. 'Slavery in the Sudan in History'. *Slavery and Abolition* 20/3 (1999): 69–95.

Cooper, Frederick. *Plantation Slavery on the East Coast of Africa.* Portsmouth, NH: Heinemann, 1977 and 1997. New Haven: Yale University Press, 1977 and 1995.

Carvalho, Pedro Moura, 'Porcelain for the Shah: Ardabil and the Chinese Ceramic Trade in the Persian Gulf,' *The Oriental Ceramic Society* (2003): 47–56.

Crone, Patricia. *Slaves on Horses: The Evolution of the Islamic Polity.* Cambridge, MA: Cambridge University Press, 1980, 2002.

Crowe, Yolande. *Persia and China: Safavid Blue and White Ceramics in the Victoria and Albert Museum 1501–1738.* London: Victoria and Albert Museum, 2002.

Dale, Stephen Frederic. *Indian Merchants and Eurasian Trade, 1600–1750.* Cambridge and New York: Cambridge University Press, 1994.

Dandamayev, M.A., M. Macuch, C.E. Bosworth, W. Floor and H. Algar. 'Barda and Bardadârî'. In *Encyclopaedia Iranica.* Ehsan Yarshater (ed.). London/ Boston: Routledge and Kegan Paul, 1985, vol. 3, pt. 2, 762–79.

Davis, Dick. *Epic and Sedition: The Case of Ferdowsi's Shahname.* Washington, DC: Mage Press, 1992 and 1999. Fayetteville: University of Arkansas Press, 1992.

Dickson, Martin. 'Shah Tahmasb and the Uzbeks'. PhD dissertation, Princeton University, 1958.

Dickson, Martin and Stuart Cary Welch. *The Houghton Shahnamah.* Cambridge, MA: Harvard University Press, 1981.

Divan-i Sa'ib-i Tabrizi (ed.). *Muhammad Qahraman.* Tehran: Intisharat-i ilmi va farhangi, 1370/1991.

Ehrenkreutz, A. 'Strategic Implications of the Slave Trade Between Genoa and Mamluk Egypt in the Second Half of the Thirteenth Century'. *The Islamic Middle East, 700–1900: Studies in Economic and Social History.* A. I. Udovitch (ed.). Princeton, NJ: Darwin, 1981, 335–45.

Eiler, W. and C. Herrenschmidt. '*Banda*'. In *Encyclopaedia Iranica.* Ehsan Yarshater (ed.). London/Boston: Routledge and Kegan Paul, 1985–, III, pt. 2, 682–85.

Engin, Nihat. *Osmanli Devletinde kölelik.* Istanbul: Marmara Universitesi Ilahiyat Fakültesi Vakfi, 1998.

Erbahar, Nurhan and Regina Krahl. 'Non-Chinese Marks and Inscriptions'. In *Chinese Ceramics in the Topkapi Saray Museum*, Istanbul: A Complete Catalogue I. Yuan and Ming Dynasty Celadon Wares. J. Ayers (ed.). London: Sotheby's Publication in association with the Directorate of the Topkapi Saray Musuem, 1986, 125–38.

Erdem, Y. Hakan. *Slavery in the Ottoman Empire and its Demise, 1800–1909.* New York: St. Martin's Press, 1996.

Falsafi, Nasr-Allah. *Zindigani Shah Abbas avval.* 5 vols. Tehran: Intisharat-i ilmi, 1968–1974.

— *Zindigani-yi Shah Abbas-i avval.* 5 vols. Tehran: Intisharat-i Ilmi, 1369/ 1990.

Farhad, Massumeh. 'Safavid Single Page Paintings 1642–1666'. PhD dissertation, Harvard University, Cambridge, Mass., 1988.

— 'The Art of Mu'in Musavvir: A Mirror of his Times'. In *Persian Masters: Five Centuries of Persian Painting.* Sheila R. Canby (ed.). Bombay: Marg Publications, 1990, 113–28.

— '"Searching for the New": Later Safavid Painting and the Suz u Gawdaz (Burning and Melting) by Nau'i Khabushani'. *The Journal of the Walters Art Museum* 59 (2001): 115–30.

Farhat, May. 'Islamic Piety and Dynastic Legitimacy: The Case of the Shrine of Ali al-Rida in Mashhad (10th–17th Century)'. PhD dissertation, Harvard University, 2002.

Fay, Mary Ann. 'Women and *Waqf*: Toward a Reconsideration of Women's Place in the Mamluk Household'. *International J. Middle East Studies* 29/i (1997): 33–51.

Ferrante, M. 'Quelques Précisions Graphiques au Sujet des Ponts Séfévides d'Isfahan'. In *Travaux de Restauration de Monuments Historiques en Iran.* Giuseppe Zander (ed.). Rome: IsMEO, 1968, 441–50.

Ferdowsi, Abul Qasim. *Shahnama.* Dick Davis (trans.). Washington, DC: Mage Publishers, 2000.

Figuera, Don Garcia de Silva y. *L'Ambassade de Don Garcias de Silva y Figueroa en Perse.* De Wicqfort (trans.). Paris: 1667.

Floor, Willem. 'The Rise and Fall of Mirza Taqi, the Eunuch Grand Vizier (1043–1055/1633–1645)', *Studia Iranica* 26 (1997): 237–66.

— 'The Dutch in the Persian Silk Trade'. In *Safavid Persia: The History and Politics of an Islamic Society*. Charles Melville (ed.). Pembroke Persian Papers, 4. London: I.B.Tauris, in association with the Centre of Middle Eastern Studies, University of Cambridge, 1996, 323–68.

— *A Fiscal History of Iran in the Safavid and Qajar Period, 1500–1925*. New York: Bibliotheca Persica Press, 1999.

— *Safavid Government Institutions*. Costa Mesa, CA: Mazda Publishers, 2001.

Foltz, Richard. *Mughal India and Central Asia*. Karachi: Oxford University Press, 1998.

Forand, Paul Glidden. 'The Development of Military Slavery under the Abbasid Caliphs of the Ninth Century A.D. (Third Century A.H.) with Special Reference to the Reigns of Mutasim and Mutadid'. PhD dissertation, Princeton University, 1961.

— 'The Relation of the Slave and Client to the Master or Patron in Medieval Islam'. *International J. Middle East Studies* 2 (1979): 59–66.

Fremineau, G. 'Bellama, esclave, eunuque, Sultan de Zinder, et puis mendiant'. *Islam et Societes au Sud du Sahara* 4 (1990): 185–90.

Fumani, Abd al-Fattah. *Tarikh-i Gilan*. Tehran: Intisharat-i Bunyad-i Farhang-i Iran, 1970.

Ganjina-yi Shaykh Safi. Tabriz: Nashriya Kitabkhana-yi Melli, no 16, 1348/1969.

Gaube, Heinz and Eugene Wirth. *Der Bazar von Isfahan*. Weisbaden: Ludwig Reichert Verlag, 1978.

Ghoraba, Hammouda. 'Islam and Slavery'. *Islamic Quarterly* 2 (1955): 153–59.

Gilli-Elewy, Hend. 'Soziale Aspekte frühislamischer sklaverei'. *Der Islam* 77/1 (2000): 116–68.

Golombek, Lisa and Donald N. Wilber. *The Timurid Architecture of Iran and Turan*. 2 vols. Princeton: Princeton University Press, 1988.

Golombek, Lisa, Robert Mason and Patty Proctor. 'Safavid Potters' Marks and the Question of Provenance'. *Iran* 39 (2001): 207–37.

Gordon, Matthew. *The Breaking of a Thousand Swords: A History of the Turkish Military in Samarra (AH200–275/815–889CE)*. Albany: State University of New York Press, 2001.

Gordon, Murray. *Slavery in the Arab World*. New York: New Amsterdam, 1989, 1992.

Grabar, Oleg. *The Great Mosque of Isfahan*. New York: New York University Press, 1990.

Grewal, Inderpal. *Home and Harem: Nation, Gender, Empire, and the Cultures of Travel*. Durham, NC: Duke University Press, 1996.

Gulriz, Muhammad Ali. *Minudar ya bab al-jannat-i Qazvin*. Tehran: Intisharat-i danishgah-i Tehran, 1337/1958.

Haas, Samuel Sheridan. 'The Contributions of Slaves to and their Influence upon the Culture of Early Islam'. PhD dissertation, Princeton University, 1942.

Hanaway, Jr., William L. 'Borzu-nama'. In *Encyclopaedia Iranica*. Ehsan Yarshater (ed.). London/Boston: Routledge and Kegan Paul, 1985, vol. 4, 380–81.

Haneda, Masashi. 'The Character of the Urbanization of Isfahan in the Later Safavid Period'. In *Safavid Persia: The History and Politics of an Islamic Society*. Charles Melville (ed.). Pembroke Persian Papers, 4. London: I. B. Tauris, in association with the Centre of Middle Eastern Studies, University of Cambridge, 1996, 369–88.

— *Le Chah et les Qizilbash. Le systeme militaire Safavide*. Berlin, 1987.

al-Heitty, Abd al-Kareem. 'The Contrasting Spheres of Free Women and Jawari in the Literary Life of the Early Abbasid Caliphate'. *Al-Masaq* 3 (1991): 31–51.

Herzig, Edmund. 'The Volume of Iranian Raw Silk Exports in the Safavid Period.' *Iranian Studies* 25/2–3 (1992, 1993): 61–79.

— 'The Deportations of the Armenians in 1604–1605 and Europe's Myth of Shah Abbas I'. In *Persian and Islamic Studies in Honour of P. W. Avery*. Charles Melville (ed.). Cambridge: Cambridge University Press, 1990.

— 'The Rise of the Julfa Merchants in the Late Sixteenth Century'. In *Safavid Persia: The History and Politics of an Islamic Society*. Charles Melville (ed.). Pembroke Persian Papers, 4. London: I. B. Tauris, in association with the Centre of Middle Eastern Studies, University of Cambridge, 1996, 305–22.

Hillenbrand, Robert. 'Safavid Architecture'. In *The Cambridge History of Iran: The Timurid and Safavid Periods*. Peter J. Jackson and Laurence Lockhart (eds). Cambridge: Cambridge University Press, 1986, vol. 6, 759–842.

Hiskett, M. 'Enslavement, Slavery and Attitudes Towards the Legally Enslavable in Hausa Islamic Literature'. *Slaves and Slavery in Muslim Africa*. John Ralph Willis (ed.). London: Frank Cass, 1985, 106–24.

Hunarfar, Lutf-Allah. *Ganjina-yi asar tarikhi-yi Isfahan*. Isfahan: Kitabfurushi-i Saqafi, 1344/1965–1966.

Hunwick John and Eve Trott Powell. *The African Diaspora in the Mediterranean Lands of Islam*. Princeton, NJ: Marcus Winer Publishers, 2002.

Inalcik, Halil. *The Ottoman Empire: The Classical Age 1300–1600*. N. Itzkowitz and C. Imber (trans.). London: Weidenfeld and Nicolson, 1973. London: Phoenix Press, 2000.

— 'Bursa and the Silk Trade'. In *An Economic and Social History of the Ottoman Empire*. Halil Inalcik (ed.) with Donald Quataert. Cambridge: Cambridge University Press, 1994, 218–55.

Jabiri Ansari, Mirza Hasan Khan. *Tarikh-i Isfahan*. Jamshid Mazahiri (ed.). Tehran: Chapp-i Amir, 1378/1999.

Jackson, P. 'The Mamluk Institution in Early Muslim India'. *Journal of the Royal Asiatic Society* 2 (1990): 340–58.

Jafariyan, Rasul. *Safaviyya dar arsah-yi din, farhang, va siyasat*. 3 vols. Qum: Pajuhishkada-i Hawza va Danishga, 1379/2000.

Jumare, Ibrahim M. 'The Ideology of Slavery in the Context of Islam and the Sokoto Jihad'. *Islamic Quarterly* 40/1 (1996): 31–38.

Junabadi, Mirza Beg ibn Hasan. *Rawzat al-safaviyya*. Ghulam. Riza Majd Tabatabai (ed.). Tehran: Bunyad-i Mawqufat-i Duktur Mahmud Afshar, 1999.

— *Rawzat al-safaviyya*. British Library, London, Ms. OR 3388.

Kaempfer, Engelbert. *Am Hofe des Persischen Grosskönigs (1684–85)*. Das erste Buch des Amoenitas Exoticae; Eingeleitet und in Deutscher Bearbeitung herausgegeben von Walther Heinz. Leipzig: K.F. Koeher Verlag, 1940.

Kelly, K.G. 'Slave Trade in Africa'. *Encyclopaedia of Precolonial Africa: Archaeology, History, Languages, Cultures, and Environments*. J.O. Vogel (ed.). Walnut Creek: Alta Mira Press, 1997, 532–35.

Kevorkian, A.M. and J.P. Sicre. *Les jardins du désir: sept siècles de peintures persans*. Paris: Phoebus, 1983.

Khachikian, Levon. 'Le registre d'un marchand arménien en Perse, en Inde et au Tibet (1682–1693)'. *Annales-économies-Société-Civilizations* 22/2 (March–April 1967): 231–78.

Khuzani Isfahani, Fazli. *Afzal al-tavarikh*. Cambridge University, Christ College Ms. Dd. 5.6, vol. 3, folios 405b–6a.

Khwajigi Isfahani, Muhammad Masum ibn. *Khulasat al-siyyar*. Iraj Afshar (ed.). Tehran: Intisharat-i Ilmi, 1368/1989.

Kilpatrick, H. 'Women as poets and chattels: Abu l-Farag al-Isbahani's "Al-Ima" al-sawa'ir'. *Quaderni di Studi Arabi* 9 (1991): 161–76.

King, David A. *A Survey of the Scientific Manuscripts in the Egyptian National Library*. Cairo/Winona Lakes, IN: Eisenbrauns, 1986.

Kongira-yi muqadas-i Ardabil. Qum: Congress Office, 1375/1955.

Krikorian, Mesrob K. *Armenians in the Service of the Ottoman Empire, 1860–1908*. London/Boston: Routledge and Kegan Paul, 1977.

Lal, Kishori Saran. *Muslim Slave System in Medieval India*. New Delhi: Aditya Prakashan, 1994.

Lambton, A. K. 'Quis Custodiet Custodes: Some Reflections on the Persian Theory of Government'. *Studia Islamica* 6 (1956): 125–48.

Lamsa, George Mamishisho. *The Secret of the Near East: Slavery of Women, Social, Religious and Economic Life in the Near East*. Philadelphia: Ideal Press, 1923.

Lassner, Jacob. *The Topography of Baghdad in the Early Middle Ages*. Detroit: Wayne State University, 1970.

— *The Shaping of 'Abbasid Rule*. Princeton: Princeton University Press, 1980.

— *The Middle East Remembered: Forged Identities, Competing Narratives, Contested Spaces*. Ann Arbor: University of Michigan Press, 2000.

Lentz, Thomas W. and Glenn D. Lowry. *Timur and the Princely Vision: Persian Art and Culture in the 15th Century*. Los Angeles: Los Angeles County Museum of Art; Washington, DC: Arthur M. Sackler Gallery, 1989.

Levi, Scott. 'The Indian Merchant Diaspora in Early Modern Central Asia and Iran'. *Iranian Studies* 32/4 (1999): 483–513.

Lewis, Bernard. *Race and Slavery in the Middle East: An Historical Inquiry*. Rev. ed. New York: Oxford University Press, 1990, 1992.

— 'Women and Children, Slaves and Unbelievers'. *Rapports entre Juifs, Chrétiens et Musulmans: Eine Sammlung von Forschungsbeiträgen*. J. Irmscher (ed.). Amsterdam: Hakkert, 1995, 29–37.

— *The Middle East: A Brief History of the Last 2000 Years*. New York: Scribner, 1995.

Little, Donald P. *History and Historiography of the Mamluks*. London: Variorum Reprints, 1986.

— 'Six Fourteenth-Century Purchase Deeds for Slaves from al-Haram as Sharif'. *Zeitschrift der Deutschen Morgenlandischen Gesellschaft* 131 (1981): 297–337.

— 'Two Fourteenth-Century Court Records from Jerusalem Concerning the Disposition of Slaves by Minors'. *Arabica* 29 (1982): 16–49.

Losensky, Paul E. *Welcoming Fighānī: Imitation and Poetic Individuality in the Safavid-Mughal Ghazal*. Costa Mesa: Mazda Publishers, 1998.

Loukonine, V. and A. Ivanov. *Lost Treasures of Persia: Persian Art in the Hermitage Museum*. Washington, DC: Mage Publication, 1996.

Lowry, Glenn et. al. *An Annotated and Illustrated Checklist of the Vever Collection*. Washington, DC: Arthur M. Sackler Gallery, 1987.

Lukens, M. and E. Grube. 'The Language of the Birds'. *Bulletin of the Metropolitan Museum of Art* (May 1967).

Maeda, Hirotako. 'The *Ghulams* of Safavid Dynasty: The Case of Georgian Origin'. *Toyo Gakuho* 81 (1999): 1–32.

— 'Innovation of the Political System under the Safavid Dynasty: The Historical Role of the Gholams'. *Shigaku-Zasshi* 57 (1998): n.p.

Mahriyar, Muhammad. 'Mu'arrefi majmu'a-yi tarikhi-yi Masjid-i Saru Taqi va madrasa-yi Saqat al-Islam va roqabat-i an'. *Vaqf miras-i javidan* 19/20 (1376/1998): 77.

Majlisi, Muhammad Baqir. *Mahdi-yi maw'ud*. Qum, n.d.

Marashi, Mir Taymur. *Tarikh-i khandan-i Marashi-yi Mazandaran*. Tehran: Intisharat-i Bunyad-i Farhang-i Iran, 1977.

Marmon, Shaun Elizabeth. 'Mamluk *Waqf* Documents and the Study of Slavery: an Interim Report'. *American Research Center in Egypt Newsletter* 127 (1984): 15–17.

— *Eunuchs and Sacred Boundaries in Islamic Society*. New York: Oxford University Press, 1995.

Masters, Bruce. *The Origins of Western Economic Dominance in the Middle East*. New York: New York University Press, 1988.

Matthee, Rudolph P. *The Politics of Trade in Safavid Iran: Silk for Silver, 1600–1730*. Cambridge: Cambridge University Press, 1999.

— 'The Consolidation and Worsening of the Late Safavid Coinage: The Mint of Huwayza'. *Journal of Economic and Social History* 44/4 (2001): 505–39.

— 'Merchants in Safavid Iran: Participants and Perceptions'. *Journal of Early Modern History* 4/3–4 (2000): 233–68.

— 'The Career of Mohammad Beg, Grand Vizier of Shah Abbas II (r. 1642–1666)'. *Iranian Studies* 24 (1991): 17–36.

— 'Georgians in the Safavid Administration'. In *Encyclopaedia Iranica*. Ehsan Yarshater (ed.). London/Boston: Routledge and Kegan Paul, vol. 10, 2001, 493–96.

McChesney, Robert. '*Waqf* and Public Policy: The *Waqf* of Shah 'Abbas, 1011–1023/1602–1614'. *Asian and African Studies* 15 (1981): 165–90.

— 'Four Sources on Shah Abbas's Building of Isfahan'. *Muqarnas* 5 (1988): 103–34.

Medley, M. 'Ardabil Collection of Chinese Porcelain'. In *Encyclopaedia Iranica*. Ehsan Yarshater (ed). London/Boston: Routledge and Kegan Paul, 1985, vol. 2, 364–65.

Melville, Charles. 'Shah 'Abbas and the Pilgrimage to Mashhad'. In *Safavid Persia: The History and Politics of an Islamic Society*. Charles Melville (ed.). Pembroke Persian Papers, 4. London: I. B. Tauris, in association with the Centre of Middle Eastern Studies, University of Cambridge, 1996, 191–229.

— 'A Lost Source for the Reign of Shah Abbas: The Afzal al-tawarikh of Fazli Khuzani Isfahani'. *Iranian Studies* 31/2 (1998): 263–65.

— 'New Light on the Reign of Shah 'Abbas: Volume III of the Afzal al-Tawarikh' *Society and Culture in the Early Modern Middle East. Studies on Iran in the Safavid Period*. Andrew J. Newman (ed.). Leiden: E. J. Brill, 2003.

Membré, Michele. *Mission to the Lord Sophy of Persia*. A.H. Morton (trans., introduced, notes). London: School of Oriental and African Studies, University of London, 1993.

Mendelsohn, Isaac. *Slavery in the Ancient Near East: A Comparative Study of Slavery in Babylonia, Assyria, Syria, and Palestine from the Middle of the Third Millennium to the End of the First Millennium*. New York: Oxford University Press, 1949.

Metin, Kunt. *The Sultan's Servants: The Transformation of Ottoman Provincial Government, 1550–1650*. New York: Columbia University Press, 1983.

Miller, Joseph. 'Muslim Slavery and Slaving: A Bibliography'. In *The Human Commodity: Perspectives on the Trans-Saharan Slave Trade*. Elizabeth Savage (ed.). London: Cass, 1992, 249–71.

Mirza Rafia. *Dastur al-muluk*. Muhammad Taqi Danishpajuh (ed.). *Majallah-yi danishkada-yi adabiyat va ulum-i insani*. Tehran University 16 (nos 1–4).

Morton, A.H. 'The Ardabil Shrine in the Reign of Shah Tahmasp I'. *Iran* 12 (1974): 31–64; 13 (1975): 39–58.

Mudarrisi Tabatabai, Sayyid Husayn. *Turbat-i pakan: asar va banaha-yi qadim-i mahdudah-yi kununi-i dar al-mu'minin-i Qum*. 2 vols. Qum: Chapkhana-i Mihr, 1355/1976.

Muhammad Hasan Khan, Itimad a-Salatana. *Matla' Shams*. 3 vols. Tehran, 1302/1884.

Munajjim, Mulla Jallal al-din. *Tarikh Abbasi ya ruznama-yi Mulla Jallal*. Sayf-Allah Vahidniya (ed.). Tehran: Intisharat-i Vahid, 1366/1987.

Munajjim, Kamal ibn Jalal. *Zubdat al-tavarikh*. Royal Asiatic Society. MS Morley 43.

Munshi, Iskandar Beg. *Tarikh-i alam ara-yi Abbasi*. Iraj Afshar (ed.). 2 vols. Tehran: Intisharat-i Amir Kabir, 1350/1971.

— *The History of Shah 'Abbas the Great*. Roger M. Savory (trans.). 3 vols. Boulder: Westview Press, 1978–1986; New York: Bibliotheca Persica, 1986.

Munshi, Iskandar Beg and Muhammad Yusuf Muvarrikh. *Zayl-i alam ara-yi Abbasi*. Suhayli-Khwansari (ed.). Tehran: Islamiyya, 1317/1938.

Nasr, Sayyed Hossein. *Islamic Science: An Illustrated Study*. Istanbul: Insan Yayinleri, 1989. [s.l.]: World of Islam Festival Publishing Co., 1976.

Nast, H.J. 'Islam, Gender, and Slavery in West Africa circa 1500: A Spatial Archeology of the Kano Palace, Northern Nigeria'. *Annals of the Association of American Geographers* 86/1 (1996): 44–77.

Natanzi, Mahmud ibn Hidayat-Allah Afushta. *Nuqavat al-asar fi zikr al-akhyar*. Ihsan Ishraqi (ed.). Tehran: Bungah-i tarjuma va nashr-i kitab, 1350/1971.

Necipoğlu, Gülru. 'A Kânûn for the State, A Canon for the Arts: Conceptualizing the Classical Synthesis of Ottoman Art and Architecture'. In *Soliman le Magnifique et son Temps*. Paris: École des Louvre, 1992.

— 'Challenging the Past: Sinan and the Competitive Discourse of Early-Modern Islamic Architecture'. *Muqarnas* 10 (1993): 169–80.

Nizam al-Mulk. *The Book of Government*. Hubert Darke (trans.). London: Routledge and Kegan Paul, 1960. 3rd edition. Richmond Surrey: Curzon Press, 2002.

Nor/Djulfa. *Documents of Armenian Architecture*. Faculty of Architecture of the Milan Polytechnic Academy of Sciences of Armenia, 21, Venice, 1991.

Northedge, Alastair. 'An Interpretation of the Palace of the Caliph at Samarra'. *Ars Orientalis* 23 (1993): 143–70.

Obermark, Peter Raymond. 'Adoption in the Old Babylonian Period (Babylonia)'. PhD dissertation, Hebrew Union College–Jewish Institute of Religion (Ohio), 1992.

O'Kane, Bernard. *Timurid Architecture in Khurasan*. Costa Mesa, CA: Mazda Publishers, 1987.

Olearius, Adam. *The Voyages and Travels of the Ambassadors Sent by Frederick Duke of Holstein, to the Great Duke of Muscovy, and the King of Persia*. John Davis (trans.). 2nd edition. London: John Starkey and Thomas Basset, 1669.

Pamuk, Sevket. *A Monetary History of the Ottoman Empire*. Cambridge: Cambridge University Press, 2000.

Patterson, Orlando. *Slavery and Social Death*. Cambridge: Harvard University Press, 1982.

Paul, Jürgen. *The State and the Military: The Samanid Case*. Papers on Inner Asia, 26. Bloomington, IN: Indiana University, Research Institute for Inner Asian Studies, 1994.

Peirce, Leslie Penn. *The Imperial Harem: Women and Sovereignty in the Ottoman Empire*. New York and Oxford: Oxford University Press, 1993.

Petrosyan, Yuri, A. et. al. *Pages of Perfection: Islamic Paintings and Calligraphy from the Russian Academy of Sciences*. St. Petersburg. Lugano: ARCH Foundation, 1995.

Perikhanian, A.G. *Materialy k étimologicheskomu slovaryu drevnearmyanskogo yasyka*. Erevan: Izdatel'stvo Natsional'noi Akademii Nauk Respubliki Armeniia, 1993.

Petry, C.F. 'From Slaves to Benefactors: the Habashis of Mamluk Cairo'. *Sudanic Africa*. 5 (1994): 57–66.

Pingree, D. 'History of Astronomy in Iran'. In *Encyclopaedia Iranica*. Ehsan Yarshater (ed.). London/Boston: Routledge and Kegan Paul, 1985, vol. 2, 860.

Pipes, Daniel. 'The Strategic Rationale For Military Slavery'. *J. Strategic Studies* 2/1 (1979): 34–46.

— *Slave Soldiers and Islam: the Genesis of a Military System*. New Haven: Yale University Press, 1981.

— 'Mawlas: Freed Slaves and Converts in Early Islam'. *Slaves and Slavery in Muslim Africa*. John Ralph Willis (ed.). London : Frank Cass, 1985, 199–247.

Pope, John Alexander. *Plates to Chinese Porcelains from the Ardebil Shrine*. *Washington DC: Smithsonian Institution, 1956*. Republished as *Chinese Porcelains from the Ardebil Shrine*. London/Totowa, NJ: Sotheby Parke Bernet, 1981.

Popovic, Alexandre. *The Revolt of African Slaves in Iraq in the 3rd/9th Century*. Leon King (trans.). Princeton, NJ: Markus Wiener Publishers, 1999.

Quinn, Sholeh A. *Historical Writing During the Reign of Shah Abbas: Ideology, Imitation, and Legitimacy in Safavid Chronicles*. Salt Lake City: The University of Utah Press, 2000.

Qumi, Qazi Ahmad Ibrahimi Husayni. *Khulasat al-tavarikh*. Ihsan Ishraqi (ed). 2 vols. Tehran: Mu'assasa-i Intisharat va Chap-i Danishgah, 1359/ 1980.

— *Gulistan-i Hunar*. Ahmad Suhayli Khwansari (ed.). Tehran: Manuchhri Publications, n.d.

— *Calligraphers and Painters: A Treatise by Qadi Ahmad, son of Mir Munshi (circa A.H. 1015/1606)*. Vladimir Minorsky (ed.), (trans.). Freer Gallery of Art Occasional Papers, vol. 3, no 2. Washington DC: Smithsonian Institution, 1959.

Raby, Julian and Ünsel Yücel. 'Chinese Porcelain at the Ottoman Court'. In *Chinese Ceramics in the Topkapi Saray Museum, Istanbul: A Complete Catalogue*. By Regina Krahl. John Ayers (ed.). London/New York: Sotheby Publications, 1986, 27–54.

Raiin, Ismail. *Iranian-i Armani*. Tehran, 1970.

Richard, Francis. *Splendeurs persanes: Manuscrits du XIIe au XVIIe siècle*. Paris: Bibliothèque Nationale, 1997.

Ricault [Rycaut], Paul. *The Present State of the Armenian Church: Containing the Tenets, Form and Manner of Divine Worship in that Church, 1678*. London: John Starkey, 1679.

Rizvi, Kishwar. 'Transformations in Early Safavid Architecture: The Shrine of Shaykh Safi al-din Ishaq Ardabili in Iran (1501–1629)'. PhD dissertation, Massachusetts Institute of Technology, Cambridge, MA, 2000.

— 'Gendered Patronage: Women and Benevolence during the Early Safavid Empire'. In *Women, Patronage, and Self-Representation in Islamic Societies*. D. Fairchild Ruggles (ed.). New York: State University of New York Press, 2000, 123–54.

Robinson, B.W. *A Descriptive Catalogue of the Persian Paintings in the Bodleian Library*. Oxford: Clarendon Press, 1958.

— 'Two manuscripts of the *Shahnama* in the Royal Library, Windsor Castle— I: Holmes 150 (A/5), II: MS Holmes 151 (A/6)'. *Burlington Magazine* 110 (1968): 73–80, 133–40.

— *The Chester Beatty Library: A Catalogue of the Persian Manuscripts and Miniatures*, vol. 3. Dublin: Hodges & Figgis, 1959.

— *Persian and Mughal Art: Catalogue to the Exhibition held at Colnaghi's, London, from 7 April to 20 May 1976*. London: P.D. Colnaghi and Co. Ltd, 1976.

— *Persian Paintings in the India Office Library: A Descriptive Catalogue*. London: Sotheby Parke Bernet, 1976.

Roemer, H. R. 'The Safavid Period'. In *The Cambridge History of Iran: The Timurid and Safavid Periods*. Peter J. Jackson and Laurence Lockhart (eds). Cambridge: Cambridge University Press, 1986, vol. 6, 189–347.

Rogers, J. M. 'Samarra: A Study in Medieval Town-Planning'. In *The Islamic City: A Colloquium*. Albert Hourani and S. M. Stern (eds). Philadelphia: University of Pennsylvania Press, 1970, 119–55.

— *Islamic Art and Design 1500–1700*. London: British Museum Publications Ltd, 1983.

Röhrborn, Klaus Michael. *Provinzen und Zentralgewalt Persiens im 16 und 17 Jahrhundert*. Studien zur Sprache, Geschichte und Kultur des Islamischen Orients, n.F., Bd. 2. Berlin: De Gruyter, 1966.

— *Nizam-i ayalat dar dawrah-yi Safaviyya*. Kaykavus Jahandari (trans.). Tehran: Bungah-i Tarjumah va Nashr-i Kitab, 1978.

Rorlich, Azade-Ayse. *The Volga Tatars: A Profile in National Resistance*. Stanford: Hoover Institution Press, 1986.

Rota, Giorgio. 'Three Lesser Known Persian Sources of the Seventeenth Century'. PhD dissertation, University of Naples, 1995.

— 'The Shah's Janissaries: Safavid *Ghulams* (1587–1722)'. Unpublished paper presented at Middle Eastern Studies Association Annual Conference, 1997.

Rührdanz, Karin. 'About a Group of Truncated *Shahnamas*: A Case Study in the Commercial Production of Illustrated Manuscripts in the Second Part of the Sixteenth Century'. *Muqarnas* 14 (1997): 118–35.

Rumlu, Hasan Bek. *Ahsan al-tavarikh*. Tehran: Intisharat-i Babak, 1978.

Safa, Zabiullah. *Tarikh-i adabiyat-i Iran*. Tehran: Intisharat-i Firdawsi, 1363/ 1984.

Safarnama-yi manzum-i Hajj. Rasul Jaffariyan (ed.). N.P., 1995.

Sami, Ali. *Shiraz, shahr-i javidan*. Tehran: Intisharat Luks, 1363/1984.

Savory, R.M. 'The Principal Offices of the Safawid State during the reign of Isma'il I (907–30/1501–24)'. *Bulletin of the School of Oriental and African Studies* 23 (1960): 91–105.

— 'The Principal Offices of the Safavid State during the reign of Shah Tahmasp I (930–84/1524–76)'. *Bulletin of the School of Oriental and African Studies* 24(1961): 65–85

— 'The Qizilbash, Education, and the Arts', *Turcica* 6 (1975): 188–96.

— 'The Office of Sipahsalar (commander-in chief) in the Safavid State'. In *Proceedings of the Second European Conference of Iranian Studies*. Bert Fragner (ed.). Rome, 1995, 597–615.

— 'Emamqoli Khan'. In *Encyclopaedia Iranica*. Ehsan Yarshater (ed.). London/ Boston: Routledge and Kegan Paul, 1998, vol. 8, 394.

Sayyidi, Mahdi. *Tarikh-i shahr-i Mashhad: az aghaz ta mashruta*. Tehran: Shahrdari-i Mashhad, ba hamkari-i Intisharat-i Jami, 1378/1999.

Schmitz, Barbara. *Miniature Painting in Harat, 1570–1640*. 2 vols. PhD dissertation, New York University, 1981.

— 'On a Special Hat Introduced during the Reign of Shah "Abbas the Great"'. *Iran* 22 (1984): 103–13.

Schmitz, Barbara with contributions by Latif Khayyat, Svat Soucek, and Massoud Pourfarrokh. *Islamic Manuscripts in the New York Public Library*. New York and Oxford: Oxford University Press and the New York Public Library, 1992.

Scolz, Piotr O. *Eunuchs and Castrati: A Cultural History*. John A. Broadwin and Shelley Frisch (trans.). Princeton, NJ: Marcus Wiener Publishers, 2000.

Segal, Ronald. *Islam's Black Slaves: the Other Black Diaspora*. New York: Farrar, Straus, and Giroux, 2001.

Semsar, Muhammad Hassan. *Golestan Palace Library: Portfolio of Miniature Paintings and Calligraphy*. Karim Emami (trans). Tehran: Zarin and Simin Books, 2000.

Shamlu, Vali Quli. *Qisas al-khaqani*. Hasan Sadat Nasiri (ed.). 2 vols. Tehran: Vizarat-i Irshad-i Islami, 1371/1992.

Simpson, Mariana Shreve. 'The Making of Manuscripts and the Workings of the Kitab-khana in Safavid Iran'. In *The Artist's Workshop, Studies in the History of Art*. P. M. Lukehart (ed.). *Center for Advanced Study in the Visual Arts*, Symposium Papers 22. Washington, DC: National Gallery of Art, 1993, 105–21.

Simpson, Mariana Shreve with contributions by Massumeh Farhad. *Sultan Ibrahim Mirza's Haft Awrang: A Princely Manuscript from Sixteenth-Century Iran*. Washington, DC, New Haven and London: Freer Gallery of Art, Smithsonian Institution and Yale University Press, 1997.

— 'Shah Abbas and His Picture Bible'. In *The Book of Kings. Art, War and the Morgan Library's Medieval Picture Bible*. William Noel and Daniel Weiss (eds). Baltimore: The Trustees of the Walters Art Gallery, 2002, 120–44.

Sims, Eleanor. 'Five Seventeenth-Century Persian Oil Paintings'. In *Persian and Mughal Art*. London: P.D. Colnaghi and Co. Ltd, 1976, 223–41.

Sims, Eleanor, with contributions by Boris I. Marshak and Ernst J. Grube. *Peerless Images: Persian Figural Painting and Its Sources*. New Haven and London: Yale University Press, 2002.

Siroux, Maxime. 'Les caravanserai's routiers safavids'. *Iranian Studies* 7/3–4 (1974): 348–79.

Skelton, Robert. 'Abbāsī, Šayk'. In *Encyclopaedia Iranica*. Ehsan Yarshater (ed.). London/Boston: Routledge and Kegan Paul, 1985, vol. 1, 86–88.

— 'Giyath al-Din Naqshband and an Episode in the Life of Saqiqi Beg', in *Persian Painting: From the Mongols to the Qajars. Studies in Honor of Basil W. Robinson*. Robert Hillenbrand (ed.). London: I. B. Tauris Publications, in Association with Centre of Middle Eastern Studies, University of Cambridge, 2000, 250–63.

Slave Élites in the Middle East and Africa: A Comparative Study. Miura Toru and John Edward Philips (eds) New York: Kegan Paul International, 2000.

Slavery in the Islamic Middle East. Shaun E. Marmon (ed.). Princeton Papers, 7. Princeton, NJ: M. Wiener, 1999.

Slaves and Slavery in Muslim Africa. John Ralph Willis (ed.). London: Frank Cass, 1985.

Sotheby Catalogue (London, October 9, 1979).

Soucek, P.P. 'Alī Qolī Jobba-dā'. In *Encyclopaedia Iranica*. Ehsan Yarshater. (ed.). London/Boston: Routledge and Kegan Paul, 1985, vol. 1, 874–75.

Soudavar, Abolala with contributions by Milo Beach. *The Art of the Persian Court: Selections from the Art and History Trust*. New York, Rizzoli, 1992.

Soudavar, Abolala. 'Between the Safavids and the Mughals: Art and Artists in Transition'. *Iran* 37 (1999): 51–54.

Sourdel, D., C.E. Bosworth, P. Hardy and H. Inalcik. '*Ghulam*'. *Encyclopaedia of Islam*. 2nd edition. Leiden: E.J. Brill, 1954–, vol. 2, 1079–91.

Stchoukine, Ivan. *Les peintures des manuscrits de Shah 'Abbas Ier à la fin des Safavis*. Paris: Librarie Orientaliste Paul Geuthner, 1964.

Steinmann, Linda. 'Shah Abbas and the Royal Silk Trade'. PhD dissertation, New York University, 1986.

Steensgaard, Niels. *Carracks, Caravans and Companies: The Structural Crisis in the European-Asian Trade of the Early Seventeenth Century*. Chicago: University of Chicago Press, 1973.

Stevens, Roger. 'European Visitors to the Safavid Court'. *Iranian Studies* 7/3–4 (1974): 421–57.

Subrahmanyam, Sanjay. 'Iranians Abroad: Intra-Asian Elite Migration and Early Modern State Formation'. *The Journal of Asian Studies* 51 (1992): 340–63.

— *The Political Economy of Commerce: Southern India, 1500–1650*. Cambridge and New York: Cambridge University Press, 1990.

Subrahmanyam, Sanjay and Christopher A. Bayly. 'Portfolio Capitalists and the Political Economy of Early Modern India'. In *Merchants, Markets and the State in Early Modern India*. Sanjay Subrahmanyam (ed.). Delhi and Oxford: Oxford University Press, 1990, 242–65.

Swietochowski, Marie L. 'Habibullah'. In *Persian Painting: From the Mongols to the Qajars. Studies in Honor of Basil W. Robinson*. Robert Hillenbrand (ed.). London: I. B. Tauris Publications, 2000, 283–301.

Swietochowski, Tadeusz. *Russian Azerbaijan, 1905–1920: The Shaping of National Identity in a Muslim Community*. Cambridge: Cambridge University Press, 1985.

Szuppe, Maria. 'Palais et Jardin: le complexe royal des premiers safavides à Qazvin, milieu XVIe-début XVIIe siècles'. In *Sites et monuments disparus d'après les témoignages de voyageurs*. R. Gyselen (ed.). Res Orientales, 8. Bures-sur-Yvette: Groupe pour l'Étude de la Civilisation du Moyen-Orient, 1996, 143–77.

— 'La participation des femmes de la famille royale à l'exercise du pouvoir en Iran Safavide au XVI siècle'. *Studia Iranica* 23/2 (1994) and 24/1 (1995): 61–122.

Tazkirat al-muluk: A Manual of Safavid Administration. Trans. and explained by V. Minorsky. Reprint. London: Trustees of the E.G. Gibb Memorial, 1980.

Tavernier, Jean Baptiste. *Les Six Voyages en Turquie et en Perse*. 2 vols. Paris: G. Clouzier, 1981.

Tazkira-yi Nasrabadi Vahid Dastgiridi (ed.). Tehran: Furuqi Bookshop, n.d.

Ter Hovaneants, Harutwin. *Patmutiwn Nor Jughayi*. New Julfa: Ne Julfa All Savior's Museum, 1980.

The St. Petersburg Muraqqa': Album of Indian and Persian Miniatures from the 16th to the 18th Century and Specimens of Persian Calligraphy by 'Imad al-Hasanī. Lugano: ARCH Foundation, 1996.

Thévenot, Jean de. *The Travels of Monsieur Thévenot into the Levant*. Archibald Lovell (ed.). 3 vols. London: Henry Clark, 1687.

Titley, Norah M. *Persian Miniature Painting and Its Influence on the Art of Turkey and India*. London: British Library, 1083.

— *Miniatures from Persian Manuscripts: A Catalogue and Subject Index of Paintings from Persia, India, and Turkey in the British Library and the British Museum*. London: British Museum Publications Ltd, 1977.

Toledano, Ehud R. *The Ottoman Slave Trade and its Suppression, 1840–1890*. Princeton, NJ: Princeton University Press, 1982, 2000.

— 'The Imperial Eunuchs of Istanbul: from Africa to the Heart of Islam'. *Middle Eastern Studies* 20 (July 1984): 379–90.

— *Slavery and Abolition in the Ottoman Middle East*. Seattle: University of Washington Press, 1998.

Tusi, Nasir al-din Muhammad ibn Muhammad. *The Nasirean Ethics*. G.M. Wickens (trans.) London: George Allen and Unwin Ltd, 1964.

Uluç, Lâle. 'Selling to the Court: Late-Sixteenth-Century Manuscript Production in Shiraz'. *Muqarnas* 17 (2000): 73–96.

Uzunçarshili, I.H. *Osmanli Devletinin Saray Teskilati*. Ankara: Türk Tarih Kurumu Basimeri, 1945.

Valle, Pietro Della. *The Pilgrim: The Journeys of Pietro Della Valle*. George Bull (trans., abridged, introduced). London: The Folio Society, 1989.

Warren, J.F. 'Looking Back on "The Sulu zone": State Formation, Slave Raiding and Ethnic Diversity in Southeast Asia'. *Journal of the Malaysian Branch of the Royal Asiatic Society* 69 i/270 (1996): 21–33.

Welch, Anthony. *Shah Abbas and the Arts of Isfahan*. New York: Asia House Society, 1973.

— 'Painting and Patronage Under Shah Abbas I'. *Iranian Studies* 7/3–4 (1974): 458–507.

— *Artists for the Shah: Late Sixteenth Century Painting at the Imperial Court of Iran*. New Haven and London: Yale University Press, 1976.

Wellesz, Emmy. 'An Early Al-Sufi Manuscript in the Bodleian Library in Oxford: A Study in Islamic Constellation Images'. *Ars Orientalis* 3 (1959): 1–26.

White Slaves, African Masters: An Anthology of American Barbary Captivity Narratives. Paul Baepler (ed.). Chicago: University of Chicago Press, 1999.

Wilber, Donald Newton. *The Architecture of Islamic Iran: The Il Khanid Period*. Princeton and Oxford: Princeton University Press/Oxford University Press, 1955. Reprinted, New York: Greenwood Press, 1969.

— 'Aspects of the Safavid Ensemble'. *Iranian Studies* 7/3–4 (1974): 406–15.

Willis, John Ralph. 'The Ideology of Enslavement in Islam'. In *Slaves and Slavery in Muslim Africa. I: Islam and the Ideology of Enslavement*. John Ralph Willis (ed.). London: Frank Cass, 1985, 1–15.

— 'Jihad and the Ideology of Enslavement'. In *Slaves and Slavery in Muslim Africa. I: Islam and the Ideology of Enslavement*. John Ralph Willis (ed.) London: Frank Cass, 1985, 16–26.

Index

Abbas I, Shah 2, 6, 7, 8–10
  armed forces of 15
  cage system and 33
  capture of Georgian slaves 28
  Caspian Sea area 60, 61
  centralizing reforms 31–32, 36, 49, 51, 85–86, 126–27
  Chinese porcelain collection 122–23, 125
  Christmas Day gifts 69–70
  construction of Isfahan 82–84
  deportations 54–55, 56, 98–99
  endowments 92, 121–23, 124, 137, 138
  and Ganj Ali Khan 94
  interest in Western art 117–18
  and Khurasan 25
  massacre following death 30–31, 34
  mercantile controls 58
  military victory against the Uzbeks 120
  and Qarachaqay Khan 13, 35
  royal library 115–16
  royal silk monopoly 65, 66
Abbas II, Shah 2, 9, 11, 17, 55, 71, 103, 136
  administration 142–45
  armed forces of 74–75
  and assassination of Saru Taqi 45
  birth 44, 161n
  burial 105
  financing of *khassa* 71, 72
  Isfahan 83
  scarcity of silver 75
Abbas (Prophet's uncle) 5
Abbasabad district, Isfahan 16, 87
Abbasi, Ali Riza (calligrapher) 97, 115, 116–17
Abbasi, Riza (artist) 116, 118, 121
Abbasi, Shafi 134
Abbasi, Shaykh 118, 134, 136
Abbasids 4–5, 23, 81–82
absolutism 13, 15
Abul Qasim Bek 154n
Africans 21
Afshar tribe 28, 95
Afzal al-tavarikh 63
Ahmad, Qazi 117, 119
Akbar, Ali 123
Aleppo 54, 62
Ali, Imam 46, 98, 101
Ali, Muhammad 129, 132, 133, 187–88n, 190n
Ali Akbar *see* al-Isfahani, Ali Akbar
Ali Mardan Khan 176n
Ali Qapu palace 16, 46, 83, 85, 98, 103, 106–8
Ali Quli Jabbadar 136
Allah Virdi Khan 13, 64, 121, 126, 127, 156n
  building works 93, 175n
  command of united armed forces 15, 71
  descendents of 17
  as governor of Fars 28, 37, 95
  mansion of 88
  patronage 119, 137, 183n
  tomb 16, 93–94
Allah Virdi Khan Bridge 57, 83, 92–93
Alpan Beg 126
al-Ulama, Sultan 140, 143
Amin Bek 72

amir al-umara 36, 155–56n
Anatolia 7
anbar-i ghulaman (storehouse of the slaves) 150n
Anna Khanum, queen-mother 44–46, 102, 161–62n
appanage system 24, 25, 26, 28
Aqquyunlu dynasty 86
Aqa Kafur (black eunuch) 17
Aqa Kamal (black eunuch) 17, 18
Aqa Riza 116
Aqa Shahpur (chief eunuch) 39
Arak'el 78
archery 29, 30
architectural patronage 16, 80–113
Ardabil shrine 13, 92, 110, 122, 125, 137, 184–85n
Armenia 21, 68
Armenian *ghulams* 27, 71–72
Armenian merchants 8–9, 13, 15, 41, 49–53, 77–79
  Christmas Day celebrations 69–70
  and converted Armenian *ghulams* 71
  and economy 46
  and English East India Company 66
  as financiers 66–69, 77
  and silk trade 61–62, 63–64
  and silver 58–60, 72, 73, 75
army 15
  finance for 60
  maydan parades 86–87
  pay 52, 68, 74–75
  Qurchis corps 26
arsenals 23, 40, 136
artists 97, 128–29, 130–31, 133–34, 136
arts patronage 27, 114–38
Ashraf, city of 98, 99, 107
astronomy 127–30
Aubin, Jean 62, 77
Ayalon, David 5–6, 23
Azerbaijan 13, 36, 77, 121, 126, 151n

Badi al-Zaman Tuni 91, 174n
Baghdad 4, 5, 35, 82, 101, 154n
Bahrain, island of 15
Bahram, Prince 25
Bahram (assassin) 35
Balkans 53, 73
Bandar Abbas, port of 64–65
Basra 72, 73, 75
bath houses 96
Bayqara, Husayn 109
bazaars 10, 41, 42, 82–84, 90, 96, 103–4
beglarbegi 155–56n
Bengal, Gulf of 40
Bidlisi, Sharaf Khan 29
Biktash Khan, governor of Kirman 95
Bitlisi (historian) 118–19
black eunuchs 16, 17, 21, 38–39
blindings 25, 31, 42, 154n
Bloody Mab'as Massacre (1632) 37, 41, 102
booty 21, 125
Bursa 53–54
Burzunama 132
Buyids 5